PRAISE FOR *TOWARI*

"As a senior IMF official, John Odling-Smee was intimately involved in the reform of the countries of the former Soviet Union in the 1990s. In this fascinating book, he explains how macroeconomic stability was established, albeit with ups and downs along the way. But he also shows how deep political weaknesses—above all the pervasive corruption and cronyism—prevented the creation of thriving and competitive market economies in nearly all the successor states. This is ultimately a story of failures. We are living with the consequences of these failures today."

—**Martin Wolf,** Senior Economics Commentator, *Financial Times*

"This book provides a clear and persuasive documentation of the role of the International Monetary Fund in the transformation of planned economies. But it is much more than that: it constitutes an essential guide to the big debates of the 1990s, including the question of 'who lost Russia?'"

—**Harold James,** Claude and Lore Kelly Professor in European Studies at Princeton University and Professor of History and International Affairs at the Woodrow Wilson School

"In this engrossing book, John Odling-Smee offers fascinating reflections on his work across the post-Soviet states as they—and he—wrestled with the dilemmas of economic reform in the 1990s. It has never been more important to understand the IMF's role in Russia's transition from a planned to market economy, and this book offers a unique account from one of the Fund's leading officials at the time."

—**Fritz Bartel,** assistant professor of International Affairs, The Bush School at Texas A&M University

"John Odling-Smee headed the IMF Department for the former Soviet Union from 1992 to 2003. In this easy and pleasant memoir with many insights and astute judgment, he guides us through truly historical events. More than any other writer, he tells us what the IMF actually did and the limitations of what it could do in the transition of the former Soviet Union. Rather than defending the IMF or himself, Odling-Smee contemplatively discusses what could possibly have been done differently. On the way, he offers many pertinent observations about how terrible the initial situation was and how few early decision makers understood market economics or the outside world, but he also has a good eye for the heroes."

Towards Market Economies

The IMF and the Economic Transition in Russia and Other Former Soviet Countries

John Odling-Smee

HAMILTON BOOKS
AN IMPRINT OF
ROWMAN & LITTLEFIELD
Lanham • Boulder • New York • London

Published by Hamilton Books
An imprint of The Rowman & Littlefield Publishing Group, Inc.

4501 Forbes Boulevard, Suite 200, Lanham, Maryland 20706
www.rowman.com

86-90 Paul Street, London EC2A 4NE, United Kingdom

British Library Cataloguing in Publication Information Available

Library of Congress Cataloging-in-Publication Data

Names: Odling-Smee, J. C. (John C.), author.
Title: Towards market economies : the IMF and the economic transition in Russia and other former Soviet countries / John Odling-Smee.
Description: Lanham : Hamilton Books, [2022] | Includes bibliographical references. | Summary: "The book is a personal account of the changes in the economies, politics, and societies of former Soviet Union countries, and the role of the IMF in helping them make the transition from planned to market economies. From 1992 to 2003, the author was in charge of the IMF's work on the fifteen countries that emerged from the former Soviet"—Provided by publisher.
Identifiers: LCCN 2022029054 (print) | LCCN 2022029055 (ebook) | ISBN 9780761873624 (paperback ; alk. paper) | ISBN 9780761873631 (epub)
Subjects: LCSH: Russia (Federation)—Economic conditions—1991– | Former Soviet republics—Economic conditions. | Post-communism—Former Soviet republics. | International Monetary Fund—Europe, Eastern.
Classification: LCC HC340.12 .O3185 2022 (print) | LCC HC340.12 (ebook) | DDC 330.947—dc23/eng/20220722
LC record available at https://lccn.loc.gov/2022029054
LC ebook record available at https://lccn.loc.gov/2022029055

♾️™ The paper used in this publication meets the minimum requirements of American National Standard for Information Sciences—Permanence of Paper for Printed Library Materials, ANSI/NISO Z39.48-1992.

Contents

List of Illustrations

Preface

The disintegration of the Soviet Union at the end of 1991 was one of the major geopolitical events of the 20th century. It was much more than just the end of an empire and the emergence of fifteen new countries. Internationally it symbolized the end of the Cold War. In the domestic political arena, it brought the end of Communist Party rule and the beginning, more so in some of the fifteen new countries than in others, of multiparty democracies. And in the economic area it marked the end of central planning and the beginning, again with differences among countries, of the move towards market economies. Such enormous changes were to touch every part of social, political and economic life. Inevitably the transition, involving the construction of new institutions and changes in attitudes among whole populations, would be a long process stretching over more than one generation.

Economic reformers in Russia expressed the hope that Russia would one day be a "normal" country. This book is about the first decade or so of the economic transition towards normal countries in Russia and the fourteen other new countries. Within that, it is concerned primarily with the role of the International Monetary Fund (IMF) in that transition. It does not attempt to give a detailed picture of economic developments and policy issues. Even in the macroeconomic area, which was the IMF's focus, the discussion is selective in both the events and the policy issues it describes. The aim is to paint a picture of the key aspects of the IMF's involvement rather than a comprehensive account of the economic transition more generally.

I was closely involved in the IMF's work throughout the period. In the year leading up to the dissolution of the Soviet Union in December 1991, I was responsible under Massimo Russo, who was Director of the European Department, for the IMF's work on its economy. As the Soviet Union was not a member of the IMF, the work was initially not onerous. But it increased dramatically after July 1991 when Group of 7 (G7) leaders met in London and decided to respond to President Gorbachev's appeal for economic assistance by asking the IMF to become closely involved. Subsequently, there was a rapid build-up of IMF staff working on the Soviet Union. In December, the Managing Director of the IMF, Michel Camdessus, announced the creation of European II Department on 2 January 1992 to be responsible for work on the fifteen countries of the FSU, with me as its first director. I held this position for nearly twelve years, during which I witnessed dramatic changes in the economies, politics and societies of these countries. It was a most challenging and exceptional experience.

The main emphasis of the book is on the role of the IMF as an institution. I explain what the IMF was trying to do and why. I also record some of my own experiences and impressions. These elements of personal memoir add color and context to the main story about economic policies in the transition to market economies. While I seek to be as objective as possible about the work of the IMF, and many years have passed since the events described in the book, I remain generally supportive of what we were trying to do.

One risk of including a personal element in the story is that it may suggest that my role was more important than it was. I must therefore make clear that I was only one member of a large team in the IMF. Leading the team were the Managing Directors, Michel Camdessus (to 2000) and Horst Köhler (from 2000), and their main deputies, especially Stanley Fischer (1994–2001). I reported directly to them. My own staff, which numbered nearly 120 at its peak, fed me with information, analysis and interpretation without which I could not have done my job. I mention some of them by name in the book when they feature in stories that I am telling. But such references are not necessarily reflective of their importance in our collective work. Those not mentioned were also critical to the success of our work.

Outside my own department were many people in the IMF working on the former Soviet Union countries. The experts on monetary, fiscal and statistical systems who provided technical assistance to the countries in these areas made a major contribution to the creation of market economy institutions. The research and policy departments made valuable contributions to the analysis of economic developments and policies and to the internal debates about IMF policies. Special mention must be made of the translators and interpreters between Russian and English without whom we could not have operated.

Other books have been written by people with inside knowledge about the work of the IMF in the former Soviet Union. The most authoritative is the official history of the IMF written by Jim Boughton. He was able to draw on the records of the Executive Board of the IMF as well as other unpublished internal documents. Michel Camdessus' memoir covering his years as Managing Director of the IMF provides an insight into the thinking of the leadership, as well as accounts of his personal meetings with and impressions of the leaders of the countries. Martin Gilman, who was the head of the IMF's office in Moscow from 1997 to 2001, has written in detail about the interactions between IMF staff and management and the senior economic policymakers in the Central Bank and government of Russia.

My book goes further into the details of how the IMF staff worked with the former Soviet Union countries, with illustrations from my own activities. It explains our thinking about controversial aspects of the economics of the transition, such as the speed and sequencing of reforms, and the relative importance of macroeconomic stabilization and more fundamental reforms of the laws and institutions governing economic activity. It discusses these issues against the background of the evolution of the economies of the countries from the near collapse of the Soviet Union economy to the restoration of growth in the 2000s. I go into more detail about each of the fifteen countries than the other books (though, in the case of Russia, less detail than in Gilman's book).

There are no footnotes about sources that support the text. Instead, a list of books and articles for further reading to guide readers who wish to go more deeply into issues or examine alternative views is provided at the end. Full references to the books and articles explicitly mentioned in the text are included in the list, which is divided into works by IMF authors and works by others.

The first three chapters cover all fifteen countries of the former Soviet Union. Chapter 1 sets the scene with an account of the collapse of the Soviet economy, the beginnings of the IMF's involvement in the region and the dissolution of the Soviet Union. Chapter 2 covers the early stages of the IMF's work in the fifteen successor countries. It includes a discussion of two complicated problems arising from the creation of the new countries: whether and when to introduce national currencies, and the division of the external debts of the former Soviet Union. Chapter 3 addresses some of the controversial economic policy challenges facing countries making the transition from planned to market economies. These include: overall strategy, especially the sequencing and speed of reforms; the choice of macroeconomic stabilization policies; structural and institutional reforms; and the problems of vested interests, oligarchs and corruption.

The following four chapters are concerned with developments in individual countries. Russia and Ukraine each have their own chapters. Then there is one chapter on the three Baltic countries and another on the remaining ten Commonwealth of Independent States (CIS) countries.

The final chapter looks back at the experience of the first decade or so of transition from a more recent viewpoint. It notes that the IMF's contribution to macroeconomic policymaking was generally positive. But our efforts to persuade CIS countries to make the major structural and institutional reforms that were needed to create fully effective market economies were not very successful.

I am most grateful for helpful comments from Poul Thomsen and Thomas Wolf and for additions and corrections from Donal Donovan, Martin Gilman, Peter Hole, Peter Keller, Adalbert Knöbl, Piroska Nagy-Mohacsi, Tapio Saavalainen, and Siddharth Tiwari.

This book was written before Russia invaded Ukraine in February 2022. The consequences for the economies and societies of these two countries and others in the region and further afield will be considerable and long-lasting. At the time of writing, there is no need to change what I have written in the book about the history of the first decade or so of the economic transition or my take on it.

Abbreviations

ADB	Asian Development Bank
CBR	Central Bank of Russia
CIS	Commonwealth of Independent States
CMEA	Council of Mutual Economic Assistance
COMECON	Council of Mutual Economic Assistance
CSF	Currency Stabilization Fund
EBRD	European Bank for Reconstruction and Development
EFF	Extended Financing Facility
ESAF	Enhanced Structural Adjustment Facility
EU	European Union
FIMACO	Financial Management Company Ltd (A financial subsidiary of Eurobank, which was owned by the CBR)
GDP	Gross Domestic Product
Gosbank	State Bank of the Soviet Union
Gosplan	State Planning Committee of the Soviet Union
G7 and G8	Group of seven countries and group of eight countries
IBRD	International Bank for Reconstruction and Development (The World Bank)
IFI	International Financial Institution
IMF	International Monetary Fund
LTCM	Long-Term Capital Management
MEP	Memorandum of Economic Policies
OECD	Organisation for Economic Cooperation and Development
SBA	Stand-By Arrangement
STF	Systemic Transformation Facility
TA	Technical Assistance
UNDP	United Nations Development Program
UNESCO	United Nations Educational, Scientific and Cultural Organization

USSR	Union of Socialist Soviet Republics (Soviet Union)
VTB	Vneshtorgbank
WTO	World Trade Organization

Chapter 1

The Hammer and Sickle

On 22 December 1991, I looked out of my hotel window at the hammer and sickle on the USSR flag fluttering over the Kremlin. Next time I am in Moscow, I thought, that will not be there. I left Moscow later that day. When I returned in February 1992, the Russian white, red and blue flag, revived from Tsarist times, had taken the place of the hammer and sickle.

For most people, the decline and swift disintegration of the Soviet Union was a surprise. Just as unexpected for me personally, was that I was in Moscow at that moment. I had not been to the Soviet Union, or to any Soviet Bloc country, until my first visit to Moscow with a mission from the IMF in August 1991. How did I come to be there?

My career as a professional economist was in three parts. In the first part, I taught and engaged in research in economics at Cambridge and Oxford Universities and the London School of Economics. While I enjoyed the life of the university and teaching the students, I was not sufficiently interested in, or competent at, the kind of research that academic economists did to want to spend my life in academia. The aspect of economics I enjoyed most was the application of economic analysis to issues of public policy.

This led me to the second part of my career, namely as an economist working in government, briefly in Ghana and then for fifteen years in the UK, most of them in Her Majesty's Treasury. Here I learned that economic analysis can only be one input into the decisions that political leaders make. They also have to take account of the impact of their actions on different groups of the population, regions of the country and sectors of the economy, and on their broader political objectives. Thus I came to accept that distributional issues, and other political considerations, rather than "optimal" economic solutions, often determine the decisions made by leaders. As I became more senior in the Treasury, my job increasingly involved public appearances, mainly at conferences and other meetings of economists, but also at hearings of Parliamentary Committees. I was much less comfortable defending government policy in public than I was analyzing and explaining economic issues within the Treasury. I used to joke with friends that my job had two parts: telling the truth in the Treasury and telling lies outside. I did not really believe that I was telling lies, but the kind of spin that public presentation of policy often requires did not come easily to me.

The third part of my career began in November 1990 when I joined the staff of the IMF. I had spent two years on secondment to the IMF from the Treasury in the early 1980s and enjoyed the experience. The two aspects of its work that especially attracted me were the opportunity to work on economies other than the UK, and the lesser emphasis on political constraints when giving economic advice than in the Treasury. Apart from a year or so in Ghana, and the two earlier years in the IMF, all of my work had been focused on the UK economy. I knew that there was much to learn from other countries and wanted to broaden my knowledge.

IMF staff should (but do not always) understand the political constraints that bind policy makers in the countries where they are giving advice. They should, as far as possible, adjust their economic policy advice to fit within those constraints. There may, however, be little scope for this, especially when the economic situation is so dire that the necessary economic policy solution has to override any political aims of the government. In the end, the responsibility for reconciling economic and political objectives rests with the government, not the IMF. I preferred to work in such a situation rather than having to pay more active attention to non-economic considerations.

The IMF expanded in the 1980s with the entry of new members from Eastern Europe. The pace quickened after the fall of the Berlin Wall in 1989. Usually the IMF recruits senior staff internally, but the expansion this time was large enough that a few senior staff had to be recruited from outside. I was lucky enough to be among them, helped by my earlier experience in the IMF and my having met Massimo Russo, the Director of the European Department, in Europe when he was Director General for Economic and Financial Affairs at the European Commission. I therefore joined the European Department in November 1990.

In the first half of 1991, I led IMF missions to Yugoslavia, Spain and Israel. I was also responsible under Massimo for the IMF's work on the Soviet Union. Although the Soviet Union was not a member, there was a certain amount of work arising from the study of the Soviet economy that had been requested by the Group of 7 (G7) summit in Houston in July 1990. The summary and recommendations of the study were presented to the G7 in December 1990. The leader of one of the technical teams in the IMF, Thomas Wolf, assisted by one or two others, spent the first month or two of 1991 preparing the background papers for publication. Tom was one of the few experts on the Soviet Union in the IMF, having been recruited from a university job because he had done research on COMECON countries (the Soviet Union, Communist countries in Eastern Europe, Cuba, Mongolia and Vietnam), especially macroeconomic issues and their trade with the West. He was to become a central figure in our work on the Soviet Union and then Russia and other former Soviet Union countries, for over ten years. His knowledge of the countries, including the Russian language, his analytical skills and his guidance of more junior staff made him an invaluable member of our team.

Tom monitored developments in the Soviet Union in the first half of 1991, but there was very little contact with the authorities until the summer. Our work increased dramatically after July when G7 leaders met in London and decided to respond to President Gorbachev's appeal for economic assistance by asking the IMF to become more closely involved. Soon after that meeting, Massimo phoned me in London where I was on leave and told me that I had to go to Moscow before returning to IMF headquarters in Washington. That was the first of five visits to Moscow that year, the last one ending on 22 December when I saw the hammer and sickle for the last time.

We need to go back to earlier years to understand developments in the Soviet Union and the context in which its relationship with the IMF began.

The Soviet economy had been in trouble for many years. The underlying problem was that the model of industrialization created in the 1930s could not adapt to the needs of the more sophisticated economy and society that emerged during the post-World War II years. It relied on moving labor from agriculture into heavy industry and raw materials production, supported by big state investments. From the 1960s, there was less scope for such extensive development as the move from the countryside slowed down. Moreover, the growing complexity of the economy called for greater coordination than the central planning system could easily provide. To deal with this, enterprises were allowed more flexibility, but prices remained under central control and enterprises were not subject to hard budget constraints. They were motivated more to increase capacity and production than to improve efficiency or the quality of products. Labor and capital productivity were low by international standards.

Agriculture was a special problem. Managers and workers on state and collective farms did not have strong incentives to improve productivity, reduce costs or preserve capital and land. Despite considerable investments, and attempts to expand the area being farmed (such as in the ill-fated virgin lands scheme), food production was not able to keep up with demand. Increasing amounts of food, mainly grains, had to be imported. Having been the biggest grain exporter in the world at the beginning of the twentieth century, Russia/ the Soviet Union had now become the biggest grain importer in the world.

I was given a small insight into the inability of the central planning system to manage agriculture by Pyotr Aven, the Minister of Foreign Economic Relations in Russia in 1991–1992 and later a banker and businessman. He told a revealing story about his experience as a student when he was sent to work in a branch of Gosplan, the State Planning Committee, in a rural area in the late 1970s. The annual meeting between the planners and the farmers took place over two days. On the first day, they examined the outturn for the present year. The planners attacked the farmers for not meeting their production targets. The farmers counterattacked, blaming the planners for not ensuring that they got the inputs (for example, fertilizers and fuel) that were in the plan. They all got drunk together that evening. On the second day they set the targets for the next season. The planners said that production had to be above that in the present year. The farmers said that this was impossible. After much angry argument, a compromise was reached. The target for farm production would be raised above that for the present year, and was therefore even more above the outturn for the present year. In return, the plan would set targets for the provision of inputs that were also above what would be the planned levels for the present year. Both sides knew that none of the targets would be achieved, but they believed that they had done a good job.

While the details of the story may not be correct, it illustrates various features of the central planning system in the 1970s and 1980s. It could no longer be called either central or planning. The center was unable to coordinate the whole economy, and had to decentralize much of the work. The "planning" took the form of negotiations between the interested parties, thereby introducing non-economic considerations, such as the parties' relative bargaining power, political connections and corrupt practices.

The sanctions for not delivering the plan's targets had weakened. The fierce punishments of the Stalin era were history, and subsequent attempts to introduce flexibility into the economy further undermined sanctions. In the absence of free prices and hard budget constraints, the result was shortages, overproduction and waste, inefficient use of labor and capital, and weak incentives to innovate. At the macroeconomic level, this translated into low productivity (both the level and the growth of productivity).

The deterioration of the economy in the 1960s and 1970s was partly masked by the rapid increase in oil production and the sharp increase in the oil price in 1973–1974 and 1979–1981. Exports to hard currency areas provided the resources to import food, technologically advanced machinery and consumer goods.

The inefficiency of the economy was generally recognized. When Gorbachev became General Secretary of the Communist Party of the Soviet Union in 1985, the economy was one of his priorities. As he and his associates did not want to change the whole system, they hoped to make it work better by liberalizing in certain areas. Unfortunately, some of the major changes that were made worsened the situation. Together with factors that were outside the authorities' control, especially the fall in the oil price, they led eventually to the collapse of the economy.

Some modest reforms were made in 1985 and 1986 but they had little impact. Then, bigger reforms, embodied in the Law on Enterprises (1987) and the Law on Cooperatives (1988), together with some liberalization of foreign trade, were intended to free enterprise decision making, increase labor incentives, increase the role of profits, and switch from directive planning to state orders. However, hard budget constraints were not imposed on enterprises, and it was considered politically impossible to free consumer prices. The absence of hard budget constraints allowed the newly independent enterprises to increase wages, which quickly produced excess demand for consumer goods and shortages. It also imposed a heavy burden on the budget, which had to use subsidies to fill the gap between the wholesale and retail prices of consumer goods. An earlier policy mistake, the anti-alcohol campaign, had already hit the budget through the loss of duties on alcohol.

The Law on Cooperatives was beneficial in legalizing many small scale businesses, such as restaurants. However, it was abused by enterprise managers, many of whom set up cooperatives into which they were able to transfer the profits of their enterprises for their own use.

The crisis which was developing in foreign exchange, the consumer market and the budget grew rapidly during 1989–1991. Oil production fell, mainly because of geological factors, exacerbated by insufficient investment and imported equipment to overcome them. With export earnings down, and a reluctance to curtail imports of food or equipment for industry, foreign loans were sought. However, an inability to fully service suppliers' credits and bank loans reduced the availability of new commercial loans, and the government was forced to turn to Western Governments. While some credits were provided, especially by Germany, these governments were generally reluctant to offer large amounts, even when Gorbachev made a personal appeal to the G7 Heads of Government at the time of their meetings in 1990 and 1991. (He had already made clear that the Soviet Union would not stand in the way of regime change in Eastern Europe, and he had acquiesced in the reunification of Germany.)

Food shortages grew and many local governments introduced rationing. Black markets became more important. The miners in Kemerovo went on strike in 1990 to protest the shortage of meat. There was a breakdown of discipline in the agricultural sector. After the good grain harvest in 1990, producers hoarded grain or sold it directly rather than through state outlets at controlled prices. When at last retail prices were increased by 90 percent on average in April 1991, the impact was diluted by compensatory fiscal measures, increasing the budget deficit even more.

The combined deficit of the Union and republican budgets rose to 8.5 percent of GDP in 1990 and over twice that amount in 1991, representing a total loss of fiscal control. It was financed by the Gosbank, the State Bank of the USSR, using the deposits of the private sector in the banking system and some money creation. As these deposits mostly represented money that consumers were unable to spend because of shortages, there were strong pent-up inflationary pressures which would have to be managed later.

As the economic crisis evolved, there were intense discussions about what should be done. Most people recognized that a major move towards a market economy was required, involving price and trade liberalization, macroeconomic stabilization and privatization. A number of plans were prepared and discussed by the government. But conservative elements in the leadership were anxious about the social consequences of price liberalization, and more generally what they perceived as the loss of control over the economy. Gorbachev was not strong enough to go against them, and ruled against the plans. The future direction of economic policy was unclear, the smarter enterprise managers took matters (and, often, their enterprises' assets) into their own hands, and economic activity declined. GDP fell by 2 percent in 1990 and a huge 17 percent in 1991.

The economy may have been the most important of Gorbachev's problems, but it was not the only one. Foreign policy was always a critical issue for the Soviet Union. Gorbachev managed to make it less so by signing the INF and START agreements with the US and withdrawing from Eastern Europe and Afghanistan. His other major problem was the growth of nationalist pressures in the republics of the Soviet Union. The economic difficulties, which all parts of the Union experienced, were one source of nationalist dissatisfaction. The liberalization of politics and the media emboldened nationalists and enabled them to bring their grievances into the open.

The Baltic States (Estonia, Latvia and Lithuania) declared independence in early 1990, and some other republics did so later in the year. Conservative elements in the Soviet leadership were opposed to the drift towards the breakup of the Union. They supported the military intervention in Lithuania in January 1991 in which 14 people were killed. Gorbachev distanced himself from it, and agreed to create a much looser union. However, the conservatives engineered a coup on 19 August, the day before the new Union of Sovereign States agreement was to be signed, and when Gorbachev was at his holiday villa in Foros in Crimea. The refusal of the troops in the army, KGB and Interior Ministry to support the coup, together with Yeltsin's bold leadership, led to the banning of the Communist Party and, in due course, the disintegration of the Soviet Union.

There is a popular view in the West, especially the United States, that it was American policy, notably the firm stance of President Reagan, that brought the Cold War to an end. Without getting into the details of a complicated issue, I can say that I do not place much weight on this factor. It is true that the heavy burden of supporting the military-industrial complex held down living standards in the Soviet Union. But this did not increase during or after the Reagan years. Perhaps more important was the increasing dependence on credits from Western commercial sources and eventually governments. Chancellor Kohl and President Bush were able to use these as levers to encourage Gorbachev to disengage from Eastern Europe.

The desperate need for foreign credits takes us back to the failures of the economy, which were surely the single most important immediate cause of the end of the Cold War. These in turn have to be understood in the broader context of the increasing dysfunctionality of the Soviet political system. Communist ideology had been replaced by cynicism. Coercion by the state was not what it had been in Stalin's day. Finally, liberalization under Gorbachev (perestroika, meaning restructuring, and glasnost, meaning openness) led to increased criticism of the government (including on environmental issues, such as Chernobyl) and pressures for independence in the republics. The rivalry between Gorbachev and Yeltsin, the president of Russia, was another factor pushing towards the disintegration of the Union.

As Gorbachev ultimately discovered, the problems of the political and economic systems were too deep to overcome with the kind of reforms he introduced. Contrary to his intentions, the reform efforts hastened the collapse of the economy, the demise of the Soviet Union and the end of the Cold War.

The IMF came on the scene in the final stages of the collapse. The Soviet Union had never been a member of the IMF. Its delegation at the Bretton Woods conference, which led to the creation of the IMF, had signed the Articles of the IMF ad referendum, but Stalin subsequently decided not to join. He thought that the IMF was likely to be dominated by the US and its western allies, and too much would have to be revealed about the Soviet economy. The Soviet Union began to think about the IMF again, especially as a source of credits, in the late 1980s, and some informal contacts took place. Gorbachev's approach to the G7 ahead of their meeting in July 1990 led to a request from the G7 to the IMF to convene a task force drawn from the IMF, World Bank, OECD and EBRD to conduct the study of the Soviet economy already mentioned. Teams from the four institutions landed in Moscow in the succeeding months, and conducted the first detailed discussions with the Soviet government. The paralysis in the government in 1991 over both economic policy and the pressures for independence in the republics meant, however, that very little attention was paid in Moscow to the recommendations of the task force. Nevertheless, the work that had been done turned out to be useful preparation for the staff of the IMF and the other institutions for their major involvement in subsequent years.

John Major, as Prime Minister of the UK which held the rotating chair of the G7 in 1991, invited Gorbachev to the G7 Heads of Government meeting in London in July 1991. By then, Gorbachev had made clear that the Soviet Union wanted to join the IMF and the World Bank, to pursue market reforms and to continue opening the economy. The G7 were willing to help the Soviet Union integrate into the world economy, but were not enthusiastic about IMF membership. They proposed instead to create a kind of non-membership, to be called a Special Association, which would enable the Soviet Union to draw on technical assistance and policy advice from the IMF, but not to borrow. The IMF would prepare reports on the Soviet economy for the benefit of its members.

This is where I came in. The terms of the Special Association were agreed on my visits to Moscow in August and September. It was difficult to get Soviet officials to focus on the draft agreement. For one thing, they could not see its use as there was no immediate money in it. But, more importantly, the Union government was in such disarray after the coup in August that officials were reluctant to commit themselves to anything. Despite this, we reached an agreement by the end of September.

At the same time, the G7, especially the United States, were anxious for the IMF and World Bank to become engaged with the Soviet Union as quickly as possible. While I was in Moscow in September, I was summoned to a meeting with the US Treasury Secretary, Nicholas Brady, who was also there. With my colleague, Benedicte Christensen, I went to Brady's hotel where he was accompanied by David Mulford, the Under Secretary for International Affairs at the Treasury; Alan Greenspan, Chairman of the Federal Reserve Board; and others. Brady wanted us to know that the US expected us to complete our work quickly. He left the heavy work to Mulford who said: "Mr. Odling-Smee, how many people do you have in Moscow?" "Four," I replied. "Four? Only four? You should have forty. You should have four hundred. When I was in the private sector, I would immediately set up task forces to handle urgent tasks." This was my first experience of the kind of mild bullying that the US employs in international exchanges. As such, it was rather different from the less direct style of confrontation that I had been used to in Europe (other than once at a conference in Germany where blunt words had been used). At about the same time, Brady personally delivered the same message, no doubt in different language, to Camdessus, who was, of course, quite experienced at resisting US pressure. Michel Camdessus was Managing Director of the IMF from 1987 to 2000, having previously been Director of the French Treasury and Governor of the Banque de France. He and Richard Erb, the Deputy Managing Director from 1984 to 1994, were my bosses.

I accompanied Camdessus to Moscow in October when he and Gorbachev signed the Special Association agreement at a meeting in the Kremlin. In his meeting with us, Gorbachev spoke at length about the economic problems the Soviet Union faced. He wanted to move to a market economy, but it was a huge task and he was not yet ready to fully liberalize prices. Camdessus picked up on this point and insisted that price liberalization was an essential early step. Despite this disagreement, the meeting ended amicably. I was conscious of being in the presence of a superpower leader who had done so much to change his country and the world, not always with the outcome he desired. His opening speech was rambling and left me with the impression of a man with time on his hands, who knew that he no longer had the authority he once had, despite his title of President of the Soviet Union.

There were two minor incidents in the Kremlin that are worth recording. First, while we were waiting in an ante room, the Soviet interpreter for the meeting asked Camdessus whether there might be a job for him at the IMF. Such was the dismal outlook for Soviet government employees that a highly qualified professional such as this interpreter was on the lookout for opportunities to work abroad. Second, my colleague Jean Foglizzo found that a date in the document that Gorbachev and Camdessus had just signed was incorrect. The Kremlin official handling it promised to correct it in the next day or so, and we were to pick up the corrected version later. There followed an anxious day or two for me, but the corrected version appeared as promised and so the Special Association was properly documented.

Camdessus' party was accommodated in a government guest house near the Mosfilm studios in the Lenin Hills (later called Sparrow Hills) area. We were told that it was one of a group of villas built for high party officials during the Khrushchev era. Our counterparts held a dinner for us there after the meeting with Gorbachev. On our side were Camdessus, his wife Brigitte, Jean Foglizzo who was our first resident representative in Moscow, Murray Seeger from the IMF external relations department who had been Moscow bureau chief of the *LA Times* in the 1970s, and me. On their side were Viktor Gerashchenko, the chairman of Gosbank (the State Bank of the Soviet Union), and Ernest Obminsky and Andrei Bugrov of the Soviet Ministry of Foreign Affairs, among others. (Gerashchenko and Obminsky had been at the meeting in the Kremlin, as were Foglizzo, Seeger and me.)

It was the first of many official dinners that I was to attend in various parts of the former Soviet Union during the next twelve years. The usual convention on such occasions was to avoid talk about business, unless the dinner had been billed in advance as a business meeting. This one was clearly a social event, especially with Mrs. Camdessus being there. Despite Camdessus' efforts to gain some insights into what might happen in the Soviet Union, the Russians were naturally reluctant to say much of substance, given the fluidity of the situation. There was much smoking of cigarettes, and Gerashchenko filled in some of the time, as he often did, with somewhat tasteless stories.

Like all of us who had grown up in the West during the Cold War, Camdessus knew all the stories, both fact and fiction, about Soviet spying and intelligence gathering techniques. He liked to imagine that we were being spied upon in Moscow, and probably we were. When we walked in the garden of the villa to discuss tactics, we were careful to avoid any bushes, even small rose bushes, where microphones might be hidden. We could, of course, do nothing about the possibility that our conversations were being detected in other ways that we knew nothing about.

In addition to creating the Special Association between the IMF and the Soviet Union, our missions to Moscow in the three months or so from August 1991 attempted to collect information and discuss economic policies with the Soviet authorities. We were not very successful in this for various reasons. First and most important, the future of the Soviet Union itself was unclear to everyone. How would the relationship between the Union and the republics change? How would the huge budget deficits be reduced? How would the shortages of goods and foreign exchange be made up? The powerlessness of Gorbachev after the coup led to drift in the Soviet leadership, with no one able to authorize the drastic steps that the economic situation required. But without these, it was impossible to make projections or devise remedial policies. Second, the instincts of those who knew how rapidly the economy was collapsing, for example the depletion of the gold and foreign currency reserves, were to prevent foreign interlocutors from finding the truth. However, they gradually opened up, in keeping with the spirit of the Special Association.

Third, economists in centrally planned economies and economists in market economies focus on different things. The former are concerned with quantities—are enough goods being produced or imported? Are there shortages? The latter are more concerned with prices, for example the exchange rate or interest rates, that need to be such as to send the right signals to those in the private sector who produce the goods. The two sets of economists see the economy in such different ways that they almost talk past each other. I felt quite numb after my first meeting in Gosplan, the State Planning Committee, where I had received a long and confusing briefing full of numbers about the production of specific goods. In time, my colleagues and I learned how to translate Soviet economist-speak into terms we could readily understand.

The one senior Soviet official with whom we could have substantive discussions about economic policy was Grigory Yavlinsky. He had played a leading role in 1990, under the Commission on Economic Reform headed by Leonid Abalkin, a deputy prime minister, in preparing the reform plan known as the 500 days program. He had spent some time at Harvard earlier in the year, and was the joint author with Graham Allison of a proposal, popularly called the Grand Bargain, for the West to provide massive financial assistance to enable the Soviet Union to undertake major economic reforms. After the coup, Gorbachev appointed him Deputy Chairman of the Committee on the Management of the National Economy, in which position he was effectively in charge of economic policy. By then, the Soviet government was rapidly losing control over the levers of economic policy as the republics, especially Russia, took them into their own hands. Yavlinsky therefore tried to forge an agreement between the republics of the Soviet Union about the economic and monetary arrangements that would govern their relations. He argued, reasonably enough, that such an agreement was a prerequisite for economic policy-making in the Soviet Union. But it was too late. The centrifugal forces were too great, and there was no possibility that any such agreement would be implemented. We offered some suggestions about how to improve the draft agreement, while knowing that it had little chance of seeing the light of day.

We were also able to talk to people in the Gosbank. Gerashchenko himself had a good understanding of what was going on in the economy, especially the inflationary pressures that were building up through the monetary over-hang (the payment of excessive wage increases that the economy could not afford) and central bank financing of the large budget deficits. But, like many others, he was concerned to protect his reputation and future prospects in a very uncertain situation, and was not open with us. By contrast, the head of the unit in the Gosbank that monitored government finances, Tatiana Paramonova, was willing to stick her neck out and explain the situation to us. She had a strong personality, and later became a successful head of the Central Bank of Russia.

From Moscow, Camdessus and I went to Bangkok, where the IMF and the World Bank were holding their annual meetings. Every third year the meetings were held in a member country, those in the two intervening years being in Washington. 1991 was the year for Thailand. The Soviet Union was invited to send observers, for the first time ever, in recognition of its newly minted Special Association. Yavlinsky and Gerashchenko were the leaders of its delegation. There was great interest among the delegates of other countries, the private bankers who attend those meetings and the press in what was happening in the Soviet Union, both economically and politically. Yavlinsky and Gerashchenko were besieged with questions which they handled well. Both spoke excellent English, the language of the meetings. Yavlinsky was young, charming and open, and loved being the center of attention. Gerashchenko was also charming, but guarded and cautious, a traditional Soviet bureaucrat. Camdessus had asked me to help them navigate the meetings, but they did so quite well enough without me. They managed to give the impression that the Soviet Union had some sensible leaders on the economic side, but not to dispel the widespread expectation that the economy was close to final collapse and no one in the leadership was able to prevent it.

After the Special Association with the Soviet Union was established, my colleagues who gave technical assistance (TA) to member governments and central banks went to Moscow to make contacts and find out what help the Soviet authorities needed. Most of them came from the TA departments of the IMF, which at that time were the Central Banking Department, the Fiscal Affairs Department and the Statistics Department. The TA provided by teams from the IMF were to be very important over the following years as the countries that emerged from the collapse of the Soviet Union had to learn how to implement macroeconomic policies. My story does not cover their activities in any detail. But I must say here that this is because my work was mostly separate from theirs. It is not because I did not appreciate their contribution to the countries we were all working on, a contribution which was of great value.

As I have mentioned, my own staff, whose job it was to collect information about the economy and help the authorities devise appropriate macroeconomic policies, found it difficult to have useful discussions with them. This was also the experience of World Bank staff, with whom we had unnecessary competition in our separate attempts to make ourselves useful. Both the IMF and the World Bank were being pushed by the G7 to make rapid progress in helping the authorities improve the economic situation. Of course, the diplomatic missions of the G7 in Moscow understood that this was an impossible task given the disarray in the Soviet government as the Union was disintegrating. But the leaders of the G7 needed to indicate to the world that the IMF and the World Bank were their main instruments for helping the Soviet Union in part so that they could deflect attention from their own unwillingness to provide more financial support.

While the political and foreign policy implications of the rapid changes in the Soviet Union were of paramount importance to G7 governments, economic issues came a close second in their worry list. The G7 were especially concerned about the Soviet Union's debts to Western countries and companies. Who would service them if the Union disintegrated into fifteen republics? They came up with the idea of asking the representatives of the fifteen countries and the Soviet Union itself to sign a memorandum of understanding (MOU) stating that they were jointly and severally responsible for the debts. The heads of the international sides of their finance ministries, known as the G7 deputies, went to Moscow in October and November to negotiate the MOU and associated arrangements.

I was in Moscow and was invited to a meeting between the G7 deputies and the representatives of the republics. Accompanied by my colleague Benedicte Christensen, our specialist on external transactions and debts, we witnessed a scene in which the tensions between the republics were exposed in all their rawness. The representatives of many republics were suspicious that they would end up paying more than their fair share of the debt service. There was a widespread belief, often expressed bluntly, that the original credits had disproportionately benefited Russia, yet others were being expected to service them. At one point the prime minister of Ukraine, Vitold Fokin, walked out in disgust at what he called Russia's lies. The centrifugal forces tearing the Union apart were on open display at that meeting.

The G7 deputies were willing to offer some immediate relief from debt service obligations, recognizing the reality that arrears were already accumulating and there was limited ability to continue servicing debts. They met to agree among themselves which debts should be covered. This was not easy because they had different interests. In particular, the largest amount outstanding was due to Germany, while the US claims were comparatively small. One night after midnight, I was summoned from my hotel to the basement room in the British Embassy where the deputies were meeting. (As chair of the G7, the UK hosted the meeting.) I arrived in the middle of a heated argument between the shirt-sleeved German and American deputies, Horst Köhler and David Mulford. (The heat came not only from the argument itself, but also from the airless basement room which was lead-lined for security.) Germany wanted to minimize the debt relief, while the US could afford to be more generous. Jean-Claude Trichet (France) and Nigel Wicks (UK) tried unsuccessfully to find compromise solutions. Mario Draghi (Italy), who was new to the group, and Tadao Chino (Japan) said little. It was the Canadian, David Dodge, who came up with the formula that they could all agree to. In the excitement of the moment, they were not too interested in my answers to the questions they had brought me there to answer.

All of the deputies later moved on to higher things. Köhler became head of the EBRD and the IMF, and then President of Germany. Mulford became Chairman International of Credit Suisse First Boston and then US ambassador to India. Trichet and Draghi became president of the European Central Bank in turn and Draghi later became Prime Minister of Italy. Chino became head of the Asian Development Bank. Dodge became Governor of the Bank of Canada.

The outcome of the meetings between the G7 and the republics of the Soviet Union was an MOU saying that ten republics would be jointly and severally responsible for the debts of the Soviet Union. (Georgia and Ukraine did not sign the MOU until 1992. The three Baltic states, Azerbaijan and Uzbekistan never signed.) This gave the creditors some basis for their offer of deferrals of principal payments on medium and long term debt, and the maintenance of short term credit lines. However, the republics, which became independent countries after the Soviet Union disintegrated, did not implement the measures necessary to act "jointly and severally." To bring some order into the situation and enable negotiations about rescheduling the Soviet Union debt to proceed, Russia therefore proposed in 1992 that it would assume responsibility for the external liabilities of the Soviet Union if the other former Soviet Union republics would transfer their share of the external assets to Russia. This was the eventual outcome.

One consequence of the G7 meetings with the republics was that the IMF was given a central role in advising the republics on macroeconomic policies. The communique signed by the republics, the Union government and the G7 in November 1991 said that the republics intended, "in full consultation with the IMF, to adopt and implement during the first quarter of 1992 comprehensive and ambitious macroeconomic and structural adjustment programs, taking into account the recommendations of the IMF." They also agreed that they would seek to maintain free interstate trade. Although these commitments had no legal force, and the republics did not have formal relations with the IMF at that stage, they introduced the IMF into the thinking of the republics (most of which barely knew what the IMF was) and made it easier for us to establish close relations after they became independent countries.

Our relationship with one of the republics, Russia, began seriously even before the Soviet Union was dissolved. Yeltsin had set up a team under the leadership of Yegor Gaidar to advise on economic reforms. In a historic speech on 28 October, he outlined his economic reform intentions based on the team's advice. After that, we switched our attention to discussions with the Russian government, which was rapidly putting together plans to free prices and introduce other major reforms on 2 January 1992. I return to this in chapter 4 on Russia.

As our involvement with the Soviet Union, Russia and then the other republics grew from August onwards, we expanded our teams working on them. Most of the new recruits came from other parts of the IMF. Some of them had worked in 1990 on the study of the Soviet economy. Others had worked on other countries. A few people were recruited from outside the IMF. Most of the staff had little knowledge of Soviet-style planned economies. Only a few spoke Russian, in a handful of cases because they had grown up in Eastern Europe where they had also picked up some ideas about planned economies from the point of view of ordinary citizens. We were criticized by experts on the Soviet economy in Western universities and elsewhere for not having any depth of understanding of how the Soviet economy worked. As our job was to advise on how to make a market economy work in a situation where the old Soviet economy was collapsing, this was not in practice a major drawback.

When I went to Moscow for the first time in August 1991, we were devoting fewer than two man years to the Soviet Union. This was the time that Tom Wolf and two or three of his team spent on it. By the time the Soviet Union was dissolved in December, our staff had risen to about 60. In accordance with normal IMF practice, nearly everyone was based in the Washington headquarters from which they went to Moscow and other capitals on missions. In addition, we opened an office in Moscow in November, headed by Jean Foglizzo, a Frenchman who spoke Russian and had worked with Camdessus in the French Treasury. He was assisted by one or two Russian local employees.

Throughout the months preparing for, and then implementing, the Special Association, the Soviet economy had been collapsing at a rapid rate. As economists, we could see it in the statistics. But we could also see it in the shops and the streets. The state food shops had lines of empty shelves. A few shelves had spaced out items that no one was buying, such as cans of pineapples, which might have come as part of a barter deal with an African country. Items in short supply, such as milk or sausages, would be sold from behind the counter in limited quantities to people who had queued up, perhaps for hours. Even the kolkhoz (collective farm) markets, which were supplied by private producers, were not as well stocked as they had been. People worried openly about how they would survive the winter, and the authorities were concerned about food shortages, social unrest or worse. Many ordinary people were desperate. They scrounged what they could, including taking the property of the state or their employer.

Among the most visible signs of the economic collapse were the lines of people along the sides of the road holding up small items for sale. They might be items of clothing that they had made themselves or that they took from their own wardrobes. Or a food item in short supply, for example cooking oil. Or cigarettes. You could also find puppies and kittens, plants and tools. On the morning of 21 December, my last full day in the Soviet Union, I went with Jean Foglizzo and his wife Terri to the large market in Izmailovsky Park where there were long lines of people on either side of the footpath selling every kind of item. Most of the vendors were women, and quite a few were elderly. It was a poignant sight. Both buyers and sellers looked sad at the humiliating position they were in. The raw air and light drifting snow, which turned the ground muddy in the near zero Celsius temperature, added to the misery. I bought a fine handmade crocheted scarf for my mother and some cheap Soviet army medals to remind me of the end of the empire.

Talking of queues, Tom Wolf taught me a useful lesson. With some colleagues we went one weekend to see the famous monastery at Sergiev Posad, about 45 miles from Moscow. (Sergiev Posad was called Zagorsk then, named after a Bolshevik revolutionary, Vladimir Zagorsky. Soon after our visit, its pre-1930 name of Sergiev Posad was restored.) We saw a queue of Russian visitors, and Tom rushed off to join it. On returning empty handed, he explained that you should never hesitate to join a queue because it might be your last chance to find something in short supply. He added sheepishly that this particular queue was for religious literature in Russian.

When there are shortages and price controls, there will be black markets. Sometimes they would be operated by men in leather jackets standing on street corners. More often they existed alongside the regular state or controlled markets. I made purchases in two such markets, for caviar and taxis. The better restaurants offered caviar to their diners. The waiters might also sell it under the table for prices well below those on the menu, and further still below market prices in the West. On one occasion I was taking a few small tins of caviar home when they were confiscated at the airport. I presume that the customs officers who took them were able to sell them again, perhaps to foreigners leaving the country so that they could confiscate them all over again!

Taxi services were not always easy to find, and private car owners stepped into the vacuum. They cruised the streets looking for fares, and, of course, congregated at the airports. I took them in both situations. They were readily available, and cheap, although you had to be prepared for some difficult negotiations to secure the cheapest possible price. As I did not speak Russian, I usually paid what was asked, or a little less, figuring that the driver had probably doubled what he expected to get when setting his opening price. We heard the occasional story of unlicensed car drivers robbing their passengers, or worse. I was never threatened, but it was a risky thing to do.

The Russians had already been removing symbols of the Soviet Union by renaming places and removing statues. Leningrad had become St. Petersburg again. In between two of my visits to Moscow, the statue of Sverdlov, the chairman of the All-Russian Central Executive Committee from 1917 to 1919, which was outside the metro station nearest to my hotel, was taken down. (The plinth remained, and was soon covered with plaques commemorating pre-revolutionary heroes and groups. These too were removed after a short while.) The statue of Dzerzhinsky, the head of the Cheka (predecessor of the KGB) after the revolution, was removed from Dzerzhinskaya Square. Metro stations were renamed. I was nearly caught out by this, but was rescued by something I remembered from reading John le Carré. I had to take the metro between two meetings, and knew that I had to get out at Dzerzhinskaya to get to the next meeting. As the first meeting ran late, I did not have time in the first station to check whether the train I jumped on as it was leaving was going in the direction I wanted. On the train, I listened carefully to the announcements about the stations we were going to, but there was no Dzerzhinskaya. However, I heard that the train was going to Lubyanka. Knowing from walks in the area guided by Tom Wolf that the KGB headquarters was in Dzerzhinskaya Square, and from John le Carré that the KGB headquarters was called the Lubyanka, I reasoned that Dzerzhinskaya station must have been renamed Lubyanka. Fortunately, I was right, and I arrived at the second meeting on time.

It was often said at the time that the Soviet Union was like Burkina Faso with nuclear weapons. By this was meant that, although it was one of only two superpowers, living standards and basic infrastructure were well below those of Western countries. Staying in the Metropol Hotel, which had recently been completely modernized and brought up to the best international standards, we were not directly exposed to the poor living conditions, except when we saw the shops and people selling on the street.

However, the weak infrastructure was very apparent in the telephone system (although not the metro, which was excellent). Once, Jean Foglizzo had to make a long distance call. I went with him to the telephone office on Tverskaya Street where he first had to book the call, then come back at the appointed time and go into the designated booth to which the call was routed. It was almost impossible to make international calls from the hotel's phone system. However, a private company had installed a satellite dish on the roof of the hotel and two or three phone booths in a semi-basement from which one could dial abroad directly. There were three drawbacks: it was very expensive ($11 a minute for calls to the US); there was always a long queue of Western businessmen and others waiting to call abroad; and the semi-basement was exposed to the outside, making it increasingly cold as autumn turned to winter. In due course, the Metropol upgraded their phone system and it became possible to make international calls from the rooms.

The Metropol had an interesting history. Built in the Art Nouveau style close to Red Square and the Bolshoi Theatre, it opened in 1905. It was one of the first hotels in Moscow to have hot water and telephones in the rooms. When the Bolsheviks moved the capital from Petrograd to Moscow in 1918, the All-Russian Central Executive Committee, which was effectively the government of Russia, took over the Metropol for both offices and living accommodation. They called it the Second House of the Soviets. When I ate breakfast in the grand dining room with its fountain bubbling in the middle, I could imagine its being crowded with people listen to Lenin addressing them from one of the interior balconies that overlooked it. I had been told that he did this on numerous occasions, but did not see a picture of it. There is, however, a famous photograph of Lenin addressing a crowd in Theatre Square in 1920, with the Metropol in the background.

It was not only the physical building that had been updated to modern international standards, but also the staff. The existing staff were retrained so that they interacted with guests in a more welcoming fashion than was the tradition in communist times. New staff were hired, often much younger than the existing ones, and with language skills. As a newcomer to the Soviet Union, I was interested to see the vestiges of the old world, in which foreigners were treated with unsmiling suspicion, alongside the new world of young cosmo-politan, friendly Russians. We assumed that some of the staff were expected to spy on us, and that some rooms were bugged. I was always given the same suite, which I did not like because it was large and cold with a view only of the hotel car park. But I presumed that the bugging equipment was especially effective in that room. However, the old Soviet tradition of floor ladies who sat outside the elevators and monitored the comings and goings of the guests had been abolished. There was no one to intrude on walks through the cor-ridors, the width and height of which gave more of a feeling of being inside a palace than a modern hotel.

The death sentence of the Soviet Union was announced following a meet-ing in Belovezha in Belarus on 8 December. The leaders of Russia, Ukraine and Belarus (President Yeltsin, Chairman of the Supreme Soviet of Ukraine Kravchuk and Chairman of the Supreme Soviet of Belarus Shushkevich) issued a declaration saying that they no longer recognized the authority of the Soviet Union and would create a new Commonwealth of Independent States. Gorbachev resigned on 25 December, and the Supreme Soviet of the USSR dissolved the Union on 26 December. Although we in the IMF had not anticipated the manner in which the Soviet Union would be dissolved, we were already thinking about how to help the republics manage economic policy as authority passed to them from the center. Our discussions with Russia began a couple of months earlier, and they were soon to start seriously with all the others.

Chapter 2

Fifteen New Flags

When visiting Kiev, the capital of Ukraine, in October 1991, Jean Foglizzo and I asked our taxi driver to give us a brief tour of the city. As we passed the statue of Lenin in October Revolution Square, the driver said that we should look at it closely as it would not be there much longer. He was right; it was taken down within weeks. The Ukrainian flag was hoisted throughout the center of the city soon after. The square was later renamed Independence Square or Maidan in the shortened Ukrainian version of the name. It was where the massive demonstrations took place in 2004 and 2013–2014.

One of our earliest opportunities to meet the representatives of the fifteen republics was during my first visit to Moscow in August 1991. There was a meeting of the heads of the republican branches of the Gosbank taking place at the Gosbank headquarters. Gerashchenko invited us to come to one of their sessions. We explained the nature of the Special Association that we hoped to have with the Soviet Union, emphasizing that we would be able to provide technical assistance to the Gosbank. The World Bank representative who had also been invited explained what the Bank could do. The discussion that followed revealed that the main concern of the participants was whether the international organizations would lend them money. Our negative response did not please them. In the course of the discussion, we picked up the tensions between the republics, which wanted to print money to keep their economies going, and the center (Gerashchenko) which saw the need to keep the lid on monetary expansion. We also noted differences between their and our understanding of the role of a central bank in a market economy. The Gosbank branches did little more at that time than issue currency on demand, collect deposits from banks and lend to the government. Some republican representatives, including Leonid Talmaci of Moldova and Stanislav Bogdankevich of Belarus, seemed to have the right idea about the role of a central bank, while others were stuck in Soviet ways of thinking.

In September Richard Erb, the Deputy Managing Director of the IMF, went to Estonia where he met officials from the three Baltic countries. He was accompanied by Adalbert (Bert) Knöbl whom he sent to Latvia and Lithuania immediately after the meeting. Also in September, Kravchuk visited Washington. In order not to offend the Soviet authorities as Ukraine was still part of the Soviet Union, Camdessus, Russo and I went to see him in his hotel rather than inviting him to the IMF. Kravchuk wanted to know what the IMF could do for Ukraine; our answer was that our relations would be governed by the planned Special Association with the Soviet Union. He also sought to establish personal relations as the basis for future cooperation, and invited Camdessus to Kiev for the 50th anniversary a week or two later of the killing of over 30,000 Jews at Babi Yar early in the German occupation. Camdessus declined the invitation.

After Erb's Estonian visit, my short trip to Kiev with Jean Foglizzo in October 1991, a few days before the Special Association agreement with the Soviet Union was signed in Moscow, was the first trip that IMF staff made to republics other than Russia. The Supreme Soviet of Ukraine had voted for independence on 24 August, just after the failed coup in Moscow, and a referendum about independence was set for 1 December. We met the head of the Ukraine branch of the Gosbank but nobody from the government. Again, we were pressed for money, and again we observed how limited was their understanding of the role of a central bank in a market economy.

We were reminded of the poor state of the Soviet economy and the low priority given to service in the Soviet Union when we had lunch in a restaurant in the center of the city. There was no choice of menu, the waitress was rude and the single meatball in the bowl of very thin broth was past its best. Jean suffered a little afterwards as a result.

We met some representatives of the republics at the Annual Meetings of the IMF and World Bank in Bangkok. Erb had a joint meeting with the representatives from Estonia, Latvia and Lithuania, who were there as observers. The independence of the three countries from the Soviet Union had recently been recognized by the other republics and the Union itself, and they each applied to join the IMF in September. Their representatives in Bangkok were so different from the Soviet bureaucrats we met in Moscow that it was difficult to believe that they came from the same system. They were in their 30s or, at most, 40s and spoke English. But what mattered most to us was that they intended that their countries should move as rapidly as possible to market economies. We wondered whether they appreciated how difficult this might be but could not fault their determination.

Also in Bangkok, I met Oleksandr Savchenko, the recently appointed deputy chairman of the National Bank of Ukraine, which was the renamed Ukraine branch of the Gosbank. He was an economist who had studied at Harvard and the London School of Economics. As such, he showed a considerable understanding of what had to be done to move from a planned to a market economy. He gave a completely different impression of the ability of the leadership of the National Bank to manage its role in the transition to a market economy from that which we had received during our visit to Kiev only a week or so earlier. The tensions between bureaucrats familiar with the Soviet economic system and those, usually younger, who knew a little about market economies, was something we were to become all too familiar with in the coming years.

From October to December, we sharply increased our interactions with the republics. I have already mentioned the intensification of work with Russia. We also sent teams to as many of the other republics as we could. In October, Tom Wolf, who was in Moscow with a mission at the time, took a large team of economists from many departments of the IMF to Kiev and Alma Ata, the capital of Kazakhstan, on short exploratory visits. He went alone to Minsk, the capital of Belarus, as well. Other missions followed in November and December. Adalbert (Bert) Knöbl took a team to the three Baltic countries in November. In December, a team led by Hans Flickenschild went to Azerbaijan, Georgia, Armenia and Moldova. Peter Hole led a team to Ukraine and Belarus, and Ishan Kapur took a team to the Central Asian republics of Kazakhstan, Kyrgyzstan, Tajikistan, Turkmenistan and Uzbekistan. Missions also went from the TA departments to prepare the ground for providing advice on central banking, fiscal issues and statistics. All the missions explained what the IMF could do for the republics within the terms of the Special Association, collected whatever information they could about economic conditions and prospects and established personal connections in anticipation of a closer relationship in future.

The IMF was one of the first international financial organizations to visit many of the republics, which was a gesture much appreciated by their leaders. Up till then, their international relationships had all been handled by the Soviet government in Moscow. Being able to talk directly to us was a sign to them that the world was interested in them as countries in their own right, even though legally they were still part of the Soviet Union. Our gesture paid off in terms of the goodwill that surrounded our relations with the new countries after they became independent.

With the collapse of the Soviet economy, fuel shortages and other difficulties made flights between the republics unpredictable. Most of our missions in the final months of the year travelled on Aeroflot, the Soviet flag carrier airline. Missions to the Baltics travelled on western airlines, some of which had already started regular flights. For some journeys, however, the IMF chartered planes from a company in Geneva to take our teams around. Ishan's mission to five Central Asian countries travelled that way. It was much easier to arrange multi-country trips on a chartered plane than on scheduled flights on Aeroflot. In most cases, the teams visited three or so countries on their trips, as we did not anticipate that much time was needed in each country, and we were rather short of staff on our side.

The disintegration of the Soviet Union in December 1991 meant that the fifteen newly independent countries were free to join the IMF and other international organizations. They were quick to make their formal applications. The Baltic countries had already applied in September, Ukraine applied before the end of December, and another six, including Russia, did so in January 1992. The remaining five countries applied to join by early March. The Board of the IMF had to approve membership on the basis of reports about their economic situation. It also had to set the quota for each country, which determines how much it pays into the IMF and can borrow, and its weight in the governance of the IMF.

The Special Association that the Soviet Union had with the IMF lapsed with the dissolution of the Union. This did not significantly affect our work. We continued to provide technical assistance and prepare reports on the economies of the countries as before but justified now by the fact that they were in a premembership status.

My staff had the responsibility of preparing the reports about the economic situation; other parts of the IMF staff advised on the quotas. We therefore had to mount longer missions than in December to get a fuller understanding of the economic situation in each country. Longer missions and the need to understand the economies of fifteen new countries and to prepare for more work if the countries asked to borrow from the IMF, called for a further increase in manpower. Camdessus decided in December to create a new department to manage the work on the fifteen countries with effect from January 1992. I was appointed its first director with Eduard Brau and Ernesto Hernandez-Catá as the deputy directors.

The IMF is divided into area departments, primarily responsible for the IMF's relations with member countries and for analyzing their economies, and functional departments, namely the TA departments, treasurer's department, and departments for legal affairs, policy, external relations and administration. In 1991, there were five area departments, covering Europe, Africa, Asia, the Middle East and the Western Hemisphere. The new department made six. It was decided to call it the European II Department, and to rename the existing European Department the European I Department. The new name was geographically unsound because some of the countries were in Asia, not Europe. Alternative names were rejected for one reason or another. The IMF-sponsored history of the IMF in the 1990s, written by Jim Boughton, says that the obvious name, Eurasian Department, was rejected because of its earlier association with colonial regimes. Camdessus had made the point more colorfully when I had suggested the name to him: "In France, when people hear the word Eurasian, they think of a beautiful woman of mixed race."

Another tricky question that arose after the dissolution of the Soviet Union was what to call the group of countries covered by our new department. We began with Former Soviet Union, abbreviated to FSU, as it was in common usage in academia and the Western media. But the governments of the Baltic States objected on the grounds that they had never been part of the Soviet Union. They had been occupied by the Soviet Union, which was a different thing altogether. Some organizations, including the US government, used the term Newly Independent States (NIS). This did not seem permanent enough, because the states would not be new after some years had passed. It could also refer to countries anywhere in the world. We considered the Baltics and the Commonwealth of Independent States (CIS), but the question of permanence arose again. It was unclear whether the CIS would always comprise all the twelve former Soviet Union countries, other than the Baltics, which never joined. In the end we chose the Baltics, Russia and other former Soviet Union countries, abbreviated to BRO, a remarkably clumsy but uncontroversial name. Within the IMF, we often referred informally to EU2 countries, a more convenient handle.

Although the new department did not yet exist, Brau joined me in December to organize the recruitment of staff. He had spent his whole career in the IMF and knew many people. He was also interested in management and was well suited to the role of the department's personnel manager, which he was to become. He worked hard and successfully built up our comple-ment in the closing weeks of 1991 and the first few months of 1992. Some people wanted to work on the former Soviet countries because of some prior experience or knowledge, including knowledge of Russian or Russian studies at university. Others were attracted by the particular challenges of working on economies that were in transition from planned to market economies. A few came because their careers in other parts of the IMF were not progress-ing and they hoped for a new beginning. Whatever their backgrounds and motives, our new recruits were all enthusiastic, an attitude that carried them through a number of years of hard work, difficult travel and complex eco-nomic problems.

I first heard about the plan to create the European II Department from Erb, who came in December 1991 to Moscow where I already was. We had a number of meetings with Soviet and Russian counterparts, not least a memorable one with Yeltsin and others, which is described in chapter 4. One evening we were invited to a symphony concert performed by the European Community Youth Orchestra, conducted by its director, Claudio Abbado, at the Tchaikovsky Conservatory. The musical highlight was the 20-year-old Yevgeny Kissin playing Chopin's first piano concerto. The non-musical high-light was the presence in one of the boxes of Gorbachev. It was a poignant moment because he and we all knew that the Soviet Union and his reign over it were coming to an end within days.

We sent missions to all fifteen new countries in the first few months of 1992. Their task was to explain what membership of the IMF involved and collect information about the economies to report to the IMF Board. The isolation of many of the leaders of the countries from the world outside the Soviet Union contributed to a number of misconceptions about the IMF which we sought to correct.

There was also limited understanding in many countries about the policies that they should pursue to create market economies. A few people in influential positions in central banks or the parts of government dealing with the economy had been exposed to market economics. They were usually younger people and had often spent time in universities or research institutes in Russia where there were others who were studying market economies. Naturally, there were more people with such backgrounds in Russia itself, but they were rarer in the more remote countries. For a number of years, some of our counterparts had difficulty thinking in terms of market economics. A signal that one might be meeting such a person was when the business card of an older man or woman announced that he or she had a PhD in Marxist-Leninist economics.

Our missions in early 1992 did not have much time to spend on discussing future economic policies, except in Russia and the Baltic countries. Our emphasis was on making contacts and collecting information so that we could prepare the reports that were a requirement for the forthcoming membership decisions. We started from a position of considerable ignorance, except for those of us who had studied Russia or the Soviet Union outside the IMF. I myself looked at maps and read general books about the republics of the Soviet Union. A deeper understanding of their economies would have to follow the work that our teams were embarked upon.

As in the missions in 1991, travel to most of the new countries was by charter flights. This avoided the problem of uncertain commercial flight schedules. (There were stories of Aeroflot planes being impounded wherever they happened to land, as the countries grabbed whatever they could of the assets of the former Soviet Union.) But it did not prevent some hardship that resulted from the breakdown of trade and relations in general within the former Soviet Union.

A major problem in those months was a shortage of fuel because Russia, the main supplier, was unable to meet all demands. When I was in Moscow in February 1992, I tried to phone Donal Donovan in Yerevan where he was leading our mission in Armenia. I phoned his hotel, but no one picked up for a very long time. Eventually a sleepy voice answered and told me that Donal was not there. Why not, I asked. Because there are no guests here, we have no heating or light, was the answer. He was unable to tell me where Donal was. However, a day or two later, Donal phoned me. He explained that he would have called earlier but he could not find a phone that would connect him to Moscow. Eventually his counterpart arranged for him to phone me from the offices of the KGB, which had one of the few working connections to Moscow.

As an international institution, member countries collectively determine its policies. The ultimate authority in the IMF lies with the Board of Governors, who collectively represent the member countries and usually meet twice a year. The day-to-day work of the IMF is overseen by its 24 Executive Directors who meet in Washington as the Executive Board a few times a week. The Board, as I refer to it from here on, is supported by the permanent staff, of which I was one. The Managing Director is the head of the staff and chair of the Board. The policies that the Board decides are made operational through the criteria and rules that govern the IMF's activities and the work of the staff. The predictability this gives to the IMF's behavior is helpful to both member countries and the staff.

However, there is some flexibility in the implementation of the criteria and rules. The staff, with its detailed knowledge of the economies and policies of individual countries, uses this flexibility to recommend actions by the IMF that it judges are best for the countries. Member countries which want to change the IMF's behavior also exploit such flexibility. They can also change the policies and the rules themselves through decisions of the Board. As we will see in later chapters, both routes were used by the US and other G7 countries in the case of the former Soviet Union countries. In 1993, a new lending vehicle, the Systemic Transformation Facility (STF), was introduced, with G7 support, so that the IMF could lend to countries in transition on the basis of weaker policy conditions than were required for regular Stand-By Arrangements (SBAs). In addition, in the years up to the crisis in Russia in 1998, G7 countries pushed for the IMF to use the flexibility in existing policies to lend more to Russia than it might have otherwise done. Other member countries, especially those that themselves came to the IMF for loans, resented what they saw as unequal treatment. Many staff members were also unhappy about the pressure to lend to Russia when program conditions had not been met.

Before the former Soviet Union countries could become members of the IMF, the Board had to decide on the countries' quotas and their representation on the Board. A country's quota is based on the size of its economy, as indicated by gross domestic product (GDP), international trade and reserves. Many of the relevant statistics were not readily available for the former Soviet countries. Such as there were suggested a quota of about 3.7 percent of the IMF total for all the countries together, and 2.3 percent for Russia alone.

The Russians considered this unacceptably small as it put it below China, Netherlands, Saudi Arabia and all the G7 countries. (The quota for the Soviet Union that was agreed at Bretton Woods in 1944 was 13.6 percent of the IMF total, the third largest after the US and the UK. As it never became a member, this was of no practical importance.) It found sympathetic supporters among the G7 countries, especially the US, which wanted to support Yeltsin who was soon to face serious criticism from the Russian parliament. Another motive was to reduce the pressure on the US to assist Russia financially by increasing its access to IMF financial resources, which was determined by the size of the quota. The Board eventually agreed that Russia's quota should be 3 percent of the IMF total, and the other countries should have quotas that represented their size relative to Russia's. In support of this, the staff produced revised estimates of the statistically based quotas, using somewhat dubious calculations of trade between the countries. It was not a glorious moment for the staff's reputation for intellectual rigor. But political considerations sometimes had to be taken into account. The Russian authorities considered the outcome successful and announced it ahead of the Congress of People's Deputies meeting in April to reduce some of the opposition to their economic policies.

Related to the quotas was the issue of representation on the Board. At the time, there were 22 members of the Board. Seven members represented only their own countries: China, France, Germany, Japan, Saudi Arabia, the UK and the US. The other fifteen members represented groups of countries: three members for the Americas apart from the US; four for Europe apart from France, Germany and the UK; three for the Middle East apart from Saudi Arabia; three for Asia and Oceania apart from China and Japan; and two for Africa. Russia became the eighth single country member. It did not want to include any of the other former Soviet countries in a group. Nor did they want to be in a group led by Russia. They therefore joined the European groups, including a new one led by Switzerland, which joined the IMF for the first time in 1992. The number of Board seats was increased to 24 to accommodate these changes.

The Board approved the membership of the fifteen former Soviet countries, and their quotas, in time for the Governors of the IMF, the ultimate authority, to approve the membership resolutions by the end of April 1992 (a few days later in the case of Azerbaijan). The prospective members were invited to send representatives to the Board Meetings at which their requests for membership would be considered. I was anxious on their behalf because few officials in many of the countries could speak about their economies in terms that would be meaningful for the Board members. In the event, only a few countries sent representatives, and they acquitted themselves well.

Membership actually took effect only when a country signed the Articles of Agreement of the IMF. These were housed in the United States State

Department. The IMF staged a little ceremony for the representative of each new member country before he or she went to the State Department to sign the Articles. It revolved around the flag of the new member which was added to the flags of all the existing members displayed in the atrium of the IMF headquarters. The Managing Director or the Deputy Managing Director made a speech and the country representative replied. Photographs were taken, with the new flag being prominent in them. All countries except Tajikistan became members by the end of September. Tajikistan, which was in the middle of a civil war in 1992, joined in July 1993.

The fifteen new flags had various origins, reflecting the complex history of the countries before they became parts of the Soviet Union. The new Russian flag had been the old Imperial Russian flag until 1917. The Baltic countries similarly restored the flags from their period of independence between 1918 and 1940. Belarus, Ukraine, Armenia, Azerbaijan and Georgia brought back the flags from their very brief periods as independent countries between the collapse of the Russian Empire and their becoming part of the Soviet Union. This period lasted only a year or so in Belarus and Ukraine, and 2–4 years in the three Caucasian countries. (Belarus and Georgia changed their flags again: Belarus in 1995 to reintroduce some elements of its Soviet-era flag, and Georgia in 2004 when the flag of the mediaeval Kingdom of Georgia was restored as the national flag.) Moldova based its flag on the tricolor of Romania, with the addition of the national arms of Moldova in the center. The Central Asian countries (Kazakhstan, Kyrgyzstan, Tajikistan, Turkmenistan and Uzbekistan) did not have historical flags to fall back on and designed completely new ones.

Apart from Russia, which had its own Board seat, the other new members were represented on the Board through the seats led by the Nordic countries (Estonia, Latvia and Lithuania), Netherlands (Ukraine, Armenia, Georgia and Moldova), Belgium (Belarus and Kazakhstan) and Switzerland (Azerbaijan, Kyrgyzstan, Tajikistan, Turkmenistan and Uzbekistan). Konstantin Kagalovsky and Aleksei Mozhin were the Executive Director and his alternate for Russia. We had known them since our discussions about economic reforms in Russia had started towards the end of the previous year and had a high regard for their abilities. By agreement among the countries led by Netherlands, the alternate to the Dutch Executive Director was a Ukrainian. The first to hold this position was Oleh Havrylyshyn, a Ukrainian-born Canadian who was a professor of economics at George Washington University. After a few years as alternate he transferred to the IMF staff and worked with me in European II Department. The other countries were too small to be in a position to provide the Executive Director or alternate in their groups. However, they did send younger people who acted as assistants in the Executive Directors' offices.

The staff of the IMF is recruited from all member countries. There are no country quotas, and so there is overrepresentation of people from countries whose citizens have opportunities to be educated up to the level that the IMF looks for. In the case of economists, the level in my time was a PhD or equivalent from a respectable university for young recruits, or relevant education and experience for mid-career recruits. Very few people from the former Soviet countries could meet these standards. However, a growing number of people were studying economics in Western universities, and after a few years we were able to recruit young people from these countries. In the meantime, I was keen that we should hire mid-career people who had relevant experience, even if they did not have much of an education in market economics. Mid-career recruits without an advanced education in economics were able to take advantage of the IMF's program of paid study leave to catch up. Among the first two in this category were the deputy governors of the central banks of Moldova (Veronica Bacalu) and Estonia (Peter Lohmus). They had impressed our teams working on their countries, and we were happy to take them when they expressed an interest in joining the staff. Russia, with a quota of 3 percent of the IMF total, was naturally concerned to see more Russians in the staff. One of the men from the Russian embassy who had hand-delivered the letter in January applying for membership joined the staff early on. He worked in the external relations department and I did not see much of him. It was a number of years before there were many Russians in the staff.

During the first half of 1992, we continued to build up our staff. Especially important was the recruitment of people to live in the countries. The IMF assigns resident representatives to live and work in those countries where there is a special need for close contact with the authorities. The most common situation is where a country is borrowing from the IMF and we have to monitor its economic performance and policies closely. The objective is to confirm that it is keeping to the commitments it made when it started borrowing and that it discusses with us any adjustments to policies necessitated by unexpected developments. As we were still at an early stage in understanding how the economies and economic decision-making worked, having someone on the ground was essential. Resident representatives had considerable responsibility and delegated authority, with their independence enhanced by the time difference from Washington, ranging from 7 hours in the most western countries to 11 in the most eastern ones, which reduced their exposure to interference from their superiors in Washington. There was only one resident representative in each country, except Russia and Ukraine where there were more. The resident representatives had small offices, often inside the central bank buildings, with local support staff (mainly interpreters, secretaries and drivers) and usually one or two economists. The local staff made valuable contributions to our knowledge and effectiveness. Many resident representatives became attached, beyond their professional work, to the countries where they were posted. In a few cases they married local women (nearly all the resident representatives were men) and sent their children to local schools.

Ed Brau was active in searching for suitable candidates for resident representative positions. The ones he found had various motives. Some had a prior interest in the region, perhaps because they had taken Russian studies. Some, perhaps the largest group, wanted an adventure and work in our region looked as though it was going to be exciting. A few wanted to get away from the routines of IMF headquarters to a situation where they could be their own bosses. We filled most of the resident representative positions by the middle of 1992, although some took longer. The civil war in Tajikistan made it difficult to send someone to live there; the position was not filled until 1995.

Taking account of the positions in headquarters and the resident representatives, the complement of the department had grown to about 100 by the middle of 1992, including support staff in Washington but not those in the field. It had grown rapidly from two man-years in July 1991 to about 60 at the end of 1991, and then to about 100.

WORK WITH THE FIFTEEN COUNTRIES

We turn now to the nature of our work. The major attraction of IMF membership for the former Soviet countries was the access it afforded to foreign currency credits. Most directly, it gave countries the right to request loans from the IMF itself. It also opened the door to loans from the World Bank, the European Bank for Reconstruction and Development (EBRD), the Asian Development Bank (ADB) and bilateral governmental lenders, many of whose loans were conditional on the country's policies being approved by the IMF. The IMF does not require collateral for its lending. Instead, it agrees to lend only when it is satisfied that the borrower's economic policies are the right ones to deal with the situation it is in. Most of the negotiations between the IMF and a member country in the lead up to a loan are therefore about the country's economic policies, which are brought together into a comprehensive macroeconomic policy program. The policy discussions between the IMF and a member take place within the context of the program that the country hopes will qualify it for a loan from the IMF.

There is an important human side to relations between the IMF and its staff and a country. While the policies of the two parties are the dominant determinant of interactions between them, individual people and their personalities can make a difference. On our side, some mission chiefs were more able to persuade their counterparts of the merits of a particular policy proposal than others. In some cases, they were natural negotiators, in others they were better able to understand the cultural context of their counterparts and in still others they were imaginative about adjustments and compromises that could help their counterparts accept our proposal. In considering whom to appoint to lead missions, I and my senior staff took account of the personalities of the possible candidates as well as their competence as economists, managers and communicators. Promotion should depend on more than just the technical abilities of a candidate as an economic analyst; something that I knew from earlier days in the UK Treasury was not always understood by younger economists.

We began discussions about economic policy programs with the Baltic countries and Russia even before they formally became IMF members. As a result, they were able to borrow their first loans from the IMF in 1992, within six months of becoming members. Programs with Moldova, Kyrgyzstan, Belarus and Kazakhstan were agreed in 1993; with Armenia, Georgia and Ukraine in 1994; and with Azerbaijan, Tajikistan and Uzbekistan at the end of 1994 and in 1995. We did not lend to Turkmenistan at all, mainly because its foreign currency position was strong. One reason for the delay in some cases was that the country had not clarified its monetary arrangements, specifically whether it wanted to continue using the ruble or to introduce its own currency. Another reason in the cases of Armenia, Azerbaijan, Georgia and Tajikistan was that there was civil strife and political instability.

I will come to specific features of our relations with individual countries in later chapters. In the rest of this chapter, I will describe common aspects of our work with the countries, and also two problems arising from the economic relations between the countries: whether and when to leave the ruble zone and introduce national currencies, and the accumulated debts some countries owed to others.

In many ways our work was similar to the IMF's work in other countries around the world. As elsewhere, we collected data to enable us to understand the economic situation. We helped the authorities devise monetary, fiscal and other policies to achieve and maintain macroeconomic stability. When a country was seeking a loan from the IMF, we agreed a set of policies that the authorities had to implement as a condition of the loan. This could involve some difficult negotiations if we thought that the country should be doing things that the government did not want to do. The work was conducted by our missions from headquarters which typically lasted about two weeks, supported by our resident representative on the ground. After each mission, our teams had to analyze the material they had collected and prepare reports for the Board.

There were various ways in which our work in the new countries differed from that in other countries. The central issue was that the countries were going through an extraordinary transformation. The transition from a planned to a market economy was only one of three major elements. Most of the countries were also building democratic institutions–elections, a free press, and parliaments that were more than rubber stamps–to replace the communist system. It is true that many of them preserved the authoritarian character of the old system, with the democratic institutions being somewhat constrained. But, except in Belarus after 1994, Turkmenistan and Uzbekistan, there was a loosening of the old authoritarian structures, to differing extents depending on the country.

Nation building was the third element. Although Russia had always been a nation in its own right and the three Baltic countries had been nations in the interwar period, most of the others had limited, if any, experience of being independent countries. Nation building went well beyond designing the national flag and writing a constitution. In the economic area, it required creating a central bank that could manage monetary policy and oversee financial markets. The finance ministry, which in Soviet times was not much more than the accounts department of the government, now had to manage fiscal policy. In the Soviet Union, the finance ministers of the republics were not politically important or influential. It took time after independence for them to acquire the status and influence in the government that they have in most market economies. New legislation regarding property rights and the operation of markets and companies, among many other things, had to be written.

The IMF provided considerable amounts (224 man-years from 1991 to 2000) of technical assistance (TA) for central banks, finance (including tax) ministries, statistics agencies and others to all the countries of the region. My colleagues in the TA departments were in charge. Naturally the impact of the TA varied from case to case. At one extreme were first rate resident advisers who transformed the areas they were working in. At the other extreme, reports were shelved without being implemented and there were advisers who did not convey much useful advice. However, in general the IMF's TA efforts made an important contribution to the nation and institution building of the new countries. As well as technical assistance, the IMF also provided training for government and central bank officials in various aspects of macroeconomics and monetary, fiscal and tax policy and operations. Together with the World Bank, EBRD, Bank for International Settlements, Organisation for Economic Cooperation and Development (OECD) and the government of Austria, it founded a training center in Vienna in 1992 for officials from countries in transition in Europe and the former Soviet Union, called the Joint Vienna Institute (JVI). It had a permanent staff of trainers from the sponsoring institutions and visiting speakers. I went there on a few occasions to talk about our views of the transition process in our countries.

There were advantages and disadvantages of the simultaneous pursuit of economic transition, democratization and nation building. It released great enthusiasm and energy. It also brought younger people into influential positions earlier than would be the case in more static conditions. We found that the younger economists were quicker to understand the basic features of macroeconomic policies in market economies than older people who had worked in the previous system.

On the other hand, the absence in the early years of established practices, market economy institutions, relevant laws and regulations and a modern judicial system meant that policies we agreed to with the authorities were not always implemented smoothly. The old command-and-control methods sometimes had to be deployed. Over time these were gradually displaced by mechanisms based on the rule of law, at least in those countries, notably the Baltic States, that moved in a "European" direction. In countries at the other extreme, especially those in Central Asia and Azerbaijan, the external appearance of democratization in the form of elections and other institutions was often merely a front behind which the top man and his associates exercised total control. In the first group of countries, we could have some confidence that policies we had agreed to would be implemented. In the second group, implementation could be interrupted by a change of heart by the leaders, or perhaps because they never had any intention of implementing them. We were not well equipped to understand the internal power structures and decision-making processes of each country. Our resident representatives did their best to collect relevant intelligence. But, in the end, it was not difficult for countries to mislead us if they chose to do so.

In the early years, our work also differed from the work of IMF staff in other countries in that our counterparts in the countries did not usually have any background in market economics. For example, Marxist-Leninist training, and the way the Soviet economy worked, led them to think of inflation as a problem of increases in costs rather than a monetary problem. Increases in interest rates which tend to restrain inflation in market economies were, on the contrary, seen as inflationary because, from an enterprise's point of view, they raised costs which would then have to be passed on in higher prices.

Another example comes from the experience of living in an economy with shortages, such as during Soviet times. People hoard when there are shortages. At the country level, countries restrict exports—in its final years, the Soviet Union cut back on oil and gas exports to its Eastern European partners. The mindset of exports=bad and imports=good carried over into the early years of independence. By contrast, exports in a market economy are encouraged because they earn foreign exchange with which to buy imports. The collapse in trade between the new countries after the disintegration of the Soviet

Union was perhaps worse than it might have otherwise been if there had been more of a market economy approach and less retention of exportable goods.

Our communication with government and central bank officials in the early years was not only a matter of economic understanding, but also of ordinary language. They all spoke Russian, and documents were usually in Russian. Although a few of our team members knew Russian, we mostly had to operate in English, the official language of the IMF, with interpreters. IMF staff use English in most member countries, although they sometimes use Spanish or French in Spanish and French speaking countries. Elsewhere the country officials speak English to us, or there are interpreters. The Russian interpreters who worked with us were very good. Some of them lived outside the former Soviet Union, but most of them lived in Moscow or one of the other capitals. The language training in the Soviet Union had been of high quality, and our interpreters quickly learned the relevant economic terms that arose during our meetings. Sometimes, we would meet an official who was happy to talk in English. The few places where this occurred were Russia, the Baltic States, Armenia and Georgia. Over time, some of the countries conducted business primarily in their own languages and dropped the use of Russian. The Baltic States were the first, and local languages also became more widely used in Ukraine, Georgia and Armenia. Interpreters were essential in these cases except when our interlocutor spoke English.

In the first few years of our work in the region, many policy makers did not fully understand the details of the policies we were recommending. This was especially true of the older ones who had held senior positions in the Soviet system. They wanted their country to move to a market economy without quite understanding in detail what this involved. This placed a heavy responsibility on us to explain the reasons for our recommendations, and to persuade our counterparts that they were good for their country, not just to insist on them as the IMF is sometimes accused of doing. I tried to appoint as mission chiefs people who could communicate economic ideas to people without an economic background. But, in the end, it came down to trust. Did the country officials trust us (or not) to have their best interests at heart? The absence of any history of relations with the IMF, and our efforts to visit all the countries in 1991 before the Soviet Union was dissolved, worked in our favor. There was no baggage from the past, nor a perception that the IMF was an enemy, as has been the case in many other parts of the world.

We also had to trust them. They were anxious to borrow from us and were sometimes a little too willing to agree to whatever policies we recommended. This raised questions in our minds about whether they understood what they were agreeing to, and, if so, intended to implement the policies after receiving the money. We tested their understanding as much as we could, but in the end had to make a judgment about whether the policies would be implemented.

This required an assessment of the political as well as economic pressures on the authorities. I saw it as part of my job to establish relations with the top leaders to assist us in deciding on their commitment. But this, and the assessments of our teams and, especially, the resident representative, could only take us so far. In the end it was a matter of trust. Sometimes the desperate economic conditions of the first decade or so did cause a country to mislead us deliberately to secure another loan. However, after a short period of disengagement and measures to reduce the likelihood that there could be a recurrence, we resumed an amicable working relationship in such cases.

When the IMF started lending to the former Soviet countries in the early 1990s, there were enormous uncertainties. These included the state of their economies; how quickly they could switch from the prior system to a new one in which markets, prices and private decisions played a larger role; the impact of the disruption of economic links between the countries; and the effectiveness of government policy. We and the policy makers in the countries could not hope to plan the perfect route to a market economy. Although the impact of the macroeconomic stabilization policies that we recommended was somewhat more predictable than that of policies to change the whole economic system, we certainly recognized that they might not achieve their goals. The IMF's lending programs allow for mid-course corrections in response to unexpected developments. We took full advantage of this when lending in the 1990s, as the outcomes were often rather different from what we had predicted. IMF lending programs always have an element of risk attached to them; countries usually turn to the IMF only because private lenders are not prepared to take on the risk themselves. The risks were greater on average in the former Soviet Union countries than in most others.

One frequent error that we made in designing the programs was to predict a faster recovery in output than occurred. This is a common bias in economic programs that countries adopt when they are borrowing from the IMF. There are pressures on the sides of both the borrowing country and the IMF that contribute to it. Both of them want to show that the program is going to have good results. Domestic and international support for it depends in part on its showing that economic growth will be restored within a reasonably short period. This is especially the case if there is expected to be an unavoidable, initial reduction in output and incomes, which is often the case. In addition, the borrowing country wishes to minimize the increases in taxes or declines in government expenditure that might have to occur, and higher predicted output growth contributes to this end. In the former Soviet Union countries, the extreme uncertainty about the likely evolution of the economies added to the difficulty of predicting output growth.

An unfortunate consequence of the overestimate of output growth was that some countries accumulated more debt than was desirable. By the beginning of the 2000s, the CIS-7 group of countries, as we called the group with low national incomes (Armenia, Azerbaijan, Georgia, Kyrgyzstan, Moldova, Tajikistan, and Uzbekistan), had high ratios of external debt to GDP, having risen from very low levels after independence. In the case of Kyrgyzstan and Tajikistan the ratio was over 100 percent. Had output grown at the rates predicted in the programs, the ratios would have been considerably lower.

Our work with the countries of the former Soviet Union also differed from that in other countries in our degree of openness with the press and public. In previous decades, the IMF had preferred to operate in private as much as possible. The aim was to preserve the confidentiality of our interactions with member countries. As time went on, especially under the leadership of Camdessus and Stanley Fischer, the First Deputy Managing Director from September 1994, the IMF opened up more, with press conferences, publication of reports to the Board, articles in newspapers and media interviews of staff members. In the European II Department, we were able to move ahead of the IMF-wide trend because our countries generally did not object. In many cases they encouraged our mission chiefs and resident representatives to explain the government's economic policies to the local media. The trust between us and the authorities stemming from the absence of historical baggage helped in this area too. It is telling that one of the few objections we received to our openness to the media came not directly from the countries but from their Executive Director in Washington. Onno Wijnholds, the Dutch Director, complained on a couple of occasions about press briefings that we had given on Ukraine and Moldova, two countries that he represented on the Board.

A different aspect of openness was the security of our internal communications. Our staff in Washington had frequent communications with missions and resident representatives in the countries by email, a special phone line to our Moscow office and public phones (for example in hotels). Given the history and technological sophistication of the Soviet Union, it was wise to assume that the local authorities were capable of intercepting our communications. (We did not go out of our way to find out whether we were being overheard. The discovery of a microphone behind a radiator in the Kiev apartment of our resident representative to Ukraine was an accident, and we never found out whether it was active or left over from a previous occupant.) As far as possible, we therefore tried to say the same things in our internal communications as we were saying face to face to the authorities. While this occasionally hampered our negotiations, it could also help. For example, I once told Leif Hansen, our mission chief in Uzbekistan, who was speaking late at night from his hotel room in Tashkent, that he should stand firm on some position where the government wanted us to shift. The government opened the meeting next morning by offering to come into line with our position.

NEW CURRENCIES

When they emerged as independent countries at the end of 1991, few countries had given much thought to when and how, or even whether, to introduce their own currencies. The Baltic countries, which had their own currencies in the interwar period, were clear that they would issue their national currencies as soon as possible. Ukraine also favored introducing its own currency and had even printed new bank notes in Canada. Russia's situation was more complex. The team of reformers working with Gaidar in 1991 recognized that it would be difficult to bring about macroeconomic stability unless Russia controlled its own monetary policy and hence currency. But they thought that it would take too long to separate the bank accounts of Russia from those of the rest of the former Soviet Union to enable Russia to convert the Soviet ruble into the Russian ruble by January 1992 when the key reforms were to be implemented. The other countries mostly did not want to leave the ruble area, fearing that it might damage trade with each other and with Russia, and that it might reduce Russia's financial transfers and provision of oil and gas at below world market prices.

Our first reaction on hearing that some members of Gaidar's team were pushing for Russia to have its own currency was concern that the other countries were not yet in a position to introduce their national currencies. I had a conversation with Aleksei Mozhin in a car in Moscow in November 1991 when he forcefully made the case for Russia to have its own currency. I was surprised that Gaidar's team was thinking along those lines, and probably reacted in a way that suggested that we opposed it. The reality was that we were not opposed to national currencies in principle but thought that it would take time to create the conditions for their successful introduction. As early as February 1992, we showed that we were ready to help countries introduce their own currencies when Ernesto Hernandez-Catá explained the principles of doing so at a meeting in Brussels attended by representatives of most countries. The first country to introduce its own currency was Estonia. Even though it moved as quickly as possible, it was June before the new currency, the kroon, was issued.

In the meantime, the Central Bank of Russia (CBR), which had effectively replaced the Gosbank of the Soviet Union at the end of 1991, was struggling to keep monetary conditions in the ruble area under control. Inheriting the old Gosbank system in which imbalances between republican branches of the Gosbank were settled automatically, it did not have the instruments to control monetary and credit emissions in the non-Russian countries. Some of these countries were issuing money freely, undermining the efforts of the CBR to manage ruble area monetary conditions. One instrument available to the CBR was the distribution of banknotes, which were printed in Russia. It reduced the supply, but countries managed to get round this by issuing their own coupons and initially making them interchangeable with rubles.

It was apparent that new arrangements had to be made if the ruble area was to operate efficiently, and monetary conditions brought under control. The option of a system controlled by the CBR, with powers to dictate monetary and credit emissions in the other countries, was politically unacceptable to countries that had just broken free of Moscow's grip. An independent central bank, perhaps similar to the European Central Bank, which was created much later, was also politically impossible because of the lack of trust between the countries. The alternative was a cooperative arrangement in which all participating central banks would have a say in credit and monetary policy in the ruble area. The central banks of the new countries set up a Coordinating Council in March 1992, with the aim of trying to bring the policies of the members into line. We were invited to their meeting in Tashkent, the capital of Uzbekistan, in May.

Ernesto prepared a paper setting out how a cooperative arrangement might work. As was always the case in the IMF, the paper was discussed with other interested parties before being finalized. The Research Department, headed by Michael Mussa, responded by saying that the ruble area would break up anyway and the IMF should not be trying to devise ways of keeping it going. But the balance of opinion in the management and staff of the IMF was that we should try to help the countries operate the ruble area efficiently until such time as they were ready and willing to introduce their own currencies. A consideration that influenced some people was that a breakdown of the ruble area would damage trade between the countries and create even more hardship on top of the serious economic problems they were already having.

The Tashkent meeting was memorable. The IMF team consisted of myself, Ernesto, Ishan Kapur who was mission chief for Uzbekistan and Sami Geadah from the European II Department; Charles Adams from the Policy, Development and Review Department; Warren Coats from the Monetary and Exchange Affairs Department; and Malcolm Knight from the Research Department. I flew from Moscow on a chartered plane (some team members had come from Geneva on the plane), returning there two days later. It was my first experience of a charter plane. Ishan, who had had many such flights to Central Asia by then, arranged for me to sit in the pilot's cabin to watch the landing in Moscow.

On the first day in Tashkent, Ernesto and I met privately with Georgy Matiukhin, the Chairman of the CBR. Without Russia's agreement, our proposals for a cooperative arrangement would go nowhere. However, he disappointed us by saying that his concern was that Russia should be able to control money emission throughout the ruble area, which was not consistent with the cooperative arrangement we were proposing.

The real excitement came the next day at the full meeting of all the central banks. (The Baltic central banks were not members of the Coordinating Council but sent observers.) The representatives of the central banks, other than the CBR representative, spoke in turn. There was not much discussion of what we were proposing about how the cooperative arrangement should operate. Instead, the speakers mostly attacked the CBR for not sending them enough banknotes, and for trying to restrict their money emissions in other ways, ineffectually in reality. They were also much exercised about the governance arrangements for the proposed system. As Russia accounted for well over half of the region, whether measured by population or GDP, there was no way that it was not going to have the dominant voice. The others were not prepared to accept this. The Russians at the meeting kept quiet, but their faces revealed their disapproval, not only of the attacks on them but also of our proposals. Matiukhin had prepared us for this.

After the meeting on the first day, we prepared a draft communique that would be discussed the following morning. Our work was interrupted by having to attend a dinner arranged by our Uzbek hosts in a pavilion overlooking a fish pond at a fish farm on the edge of Tashkent. It was my first experience of the large official meals that were often laid on for us, especially in the Caucasian and Central Asian countries but rarely in Russia or the Baltics. There was usually a certain amount of formal toasting when you were expected to empty your shot glass full of vodka after each toast. As every delegation to the Tashkent meeting made a toast, and I and one or two others also did, I must have consumed at least ten glasses of vodka, even allowing for some discreet spillages and failures to empty my glass each time. On returning to the guest house where we were staying, we had to finalize the draft communique and have it translated into Russian. Our interpreter and translator was Galina Lagveshkina from Moscow. She was excellent and continued to work for the IMF in the region and elsewhere for decades. She became a good friend. Despite the lateness of the hour, she produced a Russian draft of the communique, which we distributed to the meeting next morning.

The communique basically said that the participating central banks agreed to set up a system for coordinating monetary policy in the ruble area along the lines of our guidelines. The Russian delegation was now led by Sergei Ignatiev, Matiukhin having already returned to Moscow. He was part of Gaidar's team of reformers who favored separate currencies for all the countries. He thought that our proposal for a cooperative system would not work because the participating central banks would not stick to the agreed limits for monetary emission and the enforcement mechanisms were weak. To the Russians it looked as though we were trying to push an arrangement onto them against their will to allow other countries to continue to print money and undermine the stability of the ruble. (Despite this disagreement, we worked closely with Ignatiev in subsequent years, when he was First Deputy Finance Minister and, especially, from 2002 when he became chairman of the CBR.) Although most participants were willing to agree to the draft communique, the Russians could not. In some other cases, the participants felt that they did not have the authority to agree and had to consult with their governments first. It was decided not to issue the communique that day. Instead, the Uzbeks would collect signatures over the coming days and issue it later. But as Russia refused to go along with it, the communique was never issued.

A week or two later, Camdessus again pressed Russia to cooperate in promoting a good monetary policy throughout the ruble area. He was meeting with Kagalovsky, who was in Washington to sign the Articles of Agreement for Russia. Kagalovsky, who could be blunt as well as charming, made clear that Russia was not willing to sacrifice its own reforms for the sake of foreign countries. This was in line with what we had heard from other members of Gaidar's team of reformers. In conversations I had had with him at various times earlier in the year, Kaglovsky had gone further. He had made clear that he thought that we were too concerned about the economic fate of other former Soviet Union countries and were unfair to Russia.

With the hardening of the Russian position against a cooperative system for operating monetary policy, the obvious solution was for all countries to introduce their own currencies, as they were not willing to submit to a ruble area controlled entirely by Russia. But some of them were reluctant to go that route because they feared that it would damage their relations (economic and political) or financial position vis-à-vis Russia, or because they were generally unprepared to take such a major step. For several months after the Tashkent meeting, we felt that we could not take a firm line with them and insist that they introduce their own currencies. For one thing, it was difficult to insist on anything until they became members of the IMF. We were also inhibited by concerns about their technical abilities to operate their own monetary policy. The choice of currency would ultimately be a political one and was therefore outside our terms of reference. This was something that Camdessus always emphasized. He was also aware of the mood among various major Western countries, especially in Europe, which was moving in the opposite direction, namely towards monetary union. They feared the disruption to trade and output from the disintegration of the ruble area.

By the autumn when all but Tajikistan had joined the IMF, we were privately encouraging countries to introduce their own currencies. They were making progress in strengthening their institutional capacity for sound monetary policy making based on national currencies. As Russia was not succeeding in stabilizing the ruble, it became less likely that inflation would be any worse with their own currencies than with sticking to the ruble. In July, Russia had made clear that debts to Russia that had been created by the automatic transfers from the CBR to the central banks of other countries would have to be honored and, in future, credits from Russia would have to be agreed in advance. This was another disincentive to remaining in the ruble area. Once all countries, except Tajikistan, had become IMF members, a new element came into play. We told countries that we could not lend to them unless they either had their own currency or monetary policy in the ruble area was governed by clear and stable institutional arrangements. All these developments led a number of countries to make preparations for introducing their own currencies over the coming months. Ukraine did so in November and Kyrgyzstan was next, in May 1993. (The three Baltic countries already had their own currencies.)

In July 1993, Russia demonetized ruble banknotes issued before 1993 and said that it would deliver new ruble banknotes only to countries that agreed to the rules of a new ruble area. This was a sensible attempt to establish a ruble area that was fully under its control to replace the unsatisfactory, unco-ordinated arrangements of the previous year and a half. Despite the disadvan-tages for them, five countries (Armenia, Belarus, Kazakhstan, Tajikistan and Uzbekistan) decided to join the new ruble area. By now it was clear to us that such a system would not work given the lack of will to cooperate on monetary policy, the resistance to Russian dominance in the other countries, and the different external financing needs. We conveyed our doubts to the countries, and within a few months all but Tajikistan withdrew from discussions about the new ruble area. All former Soviet Union countries, except Tajikistan, had introduced their own currencies by the end of 1993, counting the Russian ruble after July as a new currency. Tajikistan, which did not have an effective government because of serious civil conflict, eventually introduced its own currency in 1995.

The Russian government and some of their foreign economic advisers criti-cized the IMF for trying, in the first half of 1992, to find a way to preserve the ruble area, as in the guidelines we presented in Tashkent. My conversations with Mozhin and Kagalovsky might have contributed to their perception that we were opposed to countries introducing their own currencies. Messages they were receiving from European governments might have strengthened the perception. It was true, of course, that we were concerned about the abil-ity of the other countries to manage an independent monetary policy without some preparation. We also did not want to see an additional barrier to trade and economic relations between the new countries. More generally, our role was to support our members in whatever feasible currency arrangement they adopted. This included a cooperative monetary policy for the ruble area if it could be made to work. It also included the introduction of own currencies, as in Estonia which we actively assisted with the introduction of the kroon in June 1992. After the failure of the Tashkent meeting, a cooperative monetary policy for the ruble area looked unlikely to work. But, as many countries still wanted to have it, we felt that we could not rule it out completely. Nevertheless, within a few months we started to encourage countries to introduce their own currencies.

Our critics said that we should have realized from the beginning of the year that the cooperative system could never work. We should have pushed for separate currencies early on. Perhaps they were right; some IMF staff thought so. It is certainly true that Russia would have avoided a part of the rise in inflation during the year, and that the IMF would have been able to lend more to Russia. (I say more about these issues in chapter 4 on Russia.) On the other hand, there could have been problems in other countries if they proved unable to manage their own currencies and monetary policy in the absence of any preparation. For a few months there seemed to be a chance that there could be a successful cooperative system, and many countries appeared to want it. With our obligations to all our members, we had to explore it.

EXTERNAL DEBTS

Another issue that caused friction between former Soviet Union countries was external debt, both that which was inherited from the Soviet Union and new debt incurred after the Soviet Union was dissolved.

The system set out in the Memorandum of Understanding agreed with G7 representatives in 1991 soon broke down. Not all the countries signed the MOU, and fewer still signed the interstate agreement that defined each country's share of debt service payments and assets and established a committee to manage them. Russia, which was the only country that had set aside any foreign exchange to service Soviet debt, proposed to the other countries in 1992 that it assume sole responsibility for all Soviet Union external liabilities and assets. It was motivated by the desire to place relations with external creditors on a sound footing so as to facilitate future borrowing from them. A number of the other countries resisted Russia's proposal. Among the arguments they made were that the Soviet assets, for example gold reserves and embassies abroad, were much more valuable than Russia was telling them, and that Russia was the main beneficiary of the original Soviet borrowing and so should inherit all the liabilities and none of the assets. We supported Russia's proposal, saying that there was no merit in these arguments, and urged the other countries to agree to it. In time, enough of them did agree, and Russia took over all the Soviet liabilities and assets. It also reached agreements with external creditors to reschedule the debts.

Apart from those inherited from the Soviet Union, the new countries started with no external debts. But they quickly acquired them. In the first year or two, most of the external financing came from other former Soviet Union countries, especially Russia and Turkmenistan, which were the major sources of oil and gas in the region. After the period of ruble area chaos, Russia moved to consolidate outstanding interstate balances in the central bank payments system into long-term state debt. A new source of debt was interenterprise arrears, which were essentially just unpaid bills. Many of these arose from oil and gas exports from Russia and Turkmenistan, especially after both countries began to raise energy export prices towards world levels. Russia managed its claims in a fairly orderly way, with a mixture of new credits, refinancing, write-offs and barter arrangements.

Turkmenistan did not have the same leverage over its debtors that Russia had. Yet it continued to export gas to its neighbors even though their payments for it were increasingly in arrears. As IMF policy prevented our lending to countries that were in payment arrears, we pressed the debtors to reach agreements with Turkmenistan about schedules and other terms for paying their debts. In order to speed up the process, we invited Turkmenistan and its debtors to a meeting during the World Bank and IMF Annual Meetings in Madrid in October 1994. The purpose was to explain why it was important that debts owed to Turkmenistan were regularized, and to offer our assistance. The meeting was chaired by Stanley Fischer, who had recently taken up his position as First Deputy Managing Director of the IMF. As I had expected, there were accusations and counteraccusations thrown about between creditors and debtors in language that was much blunter than was usual among international financial officials. The low point in this respect was when Viktor Yushchenko, the Chairman of the National Bank of Ukraine and later Prime Minister and President of Ukraine, said that it was the Turkmens' own fault if they exported gas without being paid for it. (Ukraine was Turkmenistan's biggest debtor.) Fischer was shocked, as was I, even though I had some experience in the region of such insulting exchanges. It was disappointing to hear this from Yushchenko, who was a supporter of economic reforms in Ukraine, and with whom we worked well for many years.

Over the following months, Turkmenistan worked out debt arrangements with most of its debtors, even if some of them were rather unusual. For example, rather than repay its debt to Turkmenistan, Georgia agreed to service, free of charge, Turkmenistan's Sukhoi fighter planes that had been inactive since the end of the Soviet Union. A few years later, with David Owen, our mission chief for Georgia, I visited the factory in Georgia where they did this work and saw some planes being repaired. We were told that, when the Georgian engineers went to Turkmenistan to inspect the planes, they found birds nesting in some of the engines. It was a poignant reminder of the demise of one of the two superpowers of the Cold War.

Chapter 3

Stop Doing Whatever You Were Doing Before

When I started working on former Soviet Union countries, I asked an economist friend what he thought were the most important reforms to be implemented at the beginning. He replied that I should say to them "you should just stop doing whatever you were doing before." Much later, I read that Mart Laar, the prime minister of Estonia who presided over the rapid transformation of that country in the 1990s, had a snappier version of the same message: "Goodbye Lenin and just do it." Laar admired Margaret Thatcher and said after she died in 2013 that she had taught him decisiveness. She told him that "if you want to do something, just do it, do not stand there trembling."

Of course, the transition from the Soviet system to a market economy is infinitely more complicated than that. Dismantling the old system is the easy part, although difficult enough. Building the institutions and implementing the policies to make a market economy function properly is complex, takes many years and requires new ways of thinking and behaving. The transformation of planned economies to market economies was a new experience for the world. As it accompanied the break-up of the Soviet Union and the end of communist party rule, it represented one of the most important and challenging economic transitions of modern times. Not surprisingly, many talented economists around the world were attracted to the new field of transition economics and a lively debate ensued about economic policy choices and courses of action. Economists in the IMF contributed to the debate and, in their operational work, drew on it.

The transition raised questions about many different policy issues. The emphasis between them changed over time as the transition progressed. Much of the debate in the early years was about the overall strategy and sequencing of reforms. Macroeconomic stabilization policies were also a major concern of the IMF in those years. Other important and controversial issues, such as methods of privatization, were not central to the IMF's activities. As inflation came down, first in the Baltic countries beginning in 1993 and then in CIS countries, the IMF's focus shifted to policies that would bring about a recovery of the supply side of the economy. This led to an increased focus on structural and institutional reforms. The problems that governments encountered in implementing agreed policies led to greater emphasis being placed on governance and administrative reforms.

OVERALL STRATEGY

The first major statement by the IMF about the strategy for the transition in the Soviet Union was in the study of the Soviet economy by four international institutions mentioned in chapter 1. The conclusions were published in December 1990. They proposed a radical approach that combined a strong macroeconomic stabilization program, immediate decontrol of most prices, the privatization of small-scale enterprises and the beginning of major structural reforms. It contrasted this with a conservative approach in which price decontrol and macroeconomic stabilization would be spread over a period of two to three years and structural reforms would proceed on a slow track. The radical approach was favored because it was more likely to succeed. The authors argued that, while the output and income losses that were an inevitable part of the transition might be lower in the short term under the conservative approach, the postponement of major systemic changes would in turn postpone the restructuring of the economy and the higher living standards that could be expected eventually. The outcome would be worse still if macroeconomic policies were too loose, prices were still largely controlled and shortages and rising black market prices developed. Even without these additional problems, the credibility of the reforms under the conservative approach would be damaged by the failure of the economy to recover and the strategy might have to be abandoned.

The authors proposed measures to mitigate the short-term squeeze on households and enterprises under the radical approach. Controls should be kept temporarily on the prices of public utilities and housing rents. The prices of some traded goods, particularly energy, should be moved gradually rather than immediately to world levels, budget funds should be made available to help enterprises restructure, and viable enterprises should be enabled to write down past debts.

In broad terms, the radical approach was not too different from that proposed in some of the plans produced by Soviet economists in 1989 and 1990. The most prominent of the plans were the 500 day program based on the work of a team led by Yavlinsky and the program produced by a team headed by Stanislav Shatalin. However, many Soviet economists preferred a more conservative approach, as did some Western Sovietologists, such as Marshall Goldman of Harvard. The latter were very concerned about the massive disruption that radical reforms would bring and tried to plot a gradual path towards a market economy. As we have seen, Gorbachev also turned away from a radical approach towards the end of 1990, at the same time as conservative political forces were building up against him. Not surprisingly, our proposals in December for a radical approach fell on deaf ears.

Then came the dramatic events of 1991: the coup against Gorbachev in August, Yeltsin's successful power grab, his endorsement of Gaidar's radical economic reform program for Russia, and the dissolution of the Soviet Union in December.

With the new countries becoming IMF members in 1992 (Tajikistan in 1993), we were able to give more detailed policy recommendations than was possible in the earlier study of the Soviet economy. We were even more convinced that the radical approach was essential, as the old structures of the planned economy had broken down in the chaotic conditions of the previous year or two. One of the first public statements of our views was Camdessus' speech at Georgetown University in April 1992. He called for a bold and comprehensive approach including the speedy adoption of the legal and institutional framework for a market economy, the early liberalization of prices (including the exchange rate and interest rates), macroeconomic policies to contain inflation, opening up the economy to world trade and prices, and early steps to privatize the state sector.

In July there was a special meeting of the Board to discuss the reform strategy in the former Soviet Union, drawing on the experience so far of reforms in Eastern Europe. The staff paper for the meeting repeated the arguments of the study of the Soviet economy that a radical strategy was preferable to a gradualist one because the recovery of output and incomes would come sooner and there would be less risk of losing political support for reforms. It made two additional points. First, a gradualist strategy would call for external financial assistance over a longer period of time and this was not likely to be forthcoming. Second, the risk of macroeconomic instability would be greater under a gradualist strategy because the government would have no firm arguments against pressures to give temporary financial assistance to enterprises. Special interest groups would apply pressure to delay reforms that affected them adversely. This second point turned out to be all too true in Russia and many other countries. The Board endorsed the strategy, although not without misgivings on the part of some directors who were concerned about the short-term costs in terms of lost output and incomes but were unable to offer a superior alternative strategy.

The contrast between the radical and gradualist strategies echoed the public debate that was taking place among academics and others about "big bang" versus gradualist strategies for the reform of centrally planned economies. The main supporters of a "big bang" in the West were economists such as Stanley Fischer and Jeffrey Sachs. Fischer had worked on the study of the Soviet economy in 1990 when he was Chief Economist at the World Bank. He worked in 1991 on the Grand Bargain for the Soviet Union described in chapter 1 and co-authored a seminal article with Alan Gelb of the World Bank. He was a consultant to the IMF on the Soviet Union in 1991 and became First Deputy Managing Director of the IMF in 1994. Sachs, an economics professor at Harvard, had advised Poland on its initial market reforms in 1989 and 1990. Liberal economists in the centrally planned economies, such as Gaidar, supported the "big bang" approach. They had seen that gradual reforms in Eastern European countries and the Soviet Union in the 1980s had often been reversed or caused new problems.

The recent successful stabilizations of some Latin American economies provided a model for the macroeconomic part of the transition strategy. Sachs had been an adviser on the Bolivian reforms of 1988 and 1989. Rapid liberalization of prices and external and internal trade together with privatization and the securing of property rights were critical elements of the structural part of the strategy.

The advocates of a gradualist strategy argued that there would be less economic and social disruption and smaller output losses with such a strategy. It was also argued that radical reforms would not work because the new institutions of a market economy would take time to build. In the meantime, the benefits envisaged by advocates of rapid reform would not materialize. Dissatisfaction with the failure of the economy to recover would lead to the abandonment of reforms.

As 1992 developed it became clear that output and incomes were falling much more steeply than most people inside and outside the former Soviet Union countries had expected. Enterprises were running into financial difficulties and were not paying their bills. Gradualists interpreted these developments as a sign that the economy was unable to adjust to the new conditions that the reforms had created. They argued that a more gradual approach to macroeconomic stabilization and structural market economy reforms was needed.

The IMF and most other supporters of the radical reform strategy had a different interpretation. Our view was that a fall in output was inevitable, and it would undermine the reform strategy to resist it. The end of central planning led to disruptions in linkages between enterprises which had to learn to replace government coordination with direct enterprise-to-enterprise purchasing, selling and marketing activities. Changes in the structure of demand and relative prices caused output to fall because of the gap between when traditional sectors and products became obsolete and new sectors and products were able to expand to fill the gap. For example, the large cuts in defense expenditures in Russia in 1992 had repercussions throughout the economy and were estimated to have reduced overall GDP by 3–4 percentage points. The sharp rise in energy and some other prices as economies opened up to world trade caused a deterioration in the terms of trade of energy-importing former Soviet Union countries. It was estimated that this amounted to about 13 percentage points of GDP in the fourteen countries other than Russia.

Further output losses arose from the disintegration of the Soviet Union. The dissolution of the Council for Mutual Economic Assistance (COMECON) in 1991 before the end of the Soviet Union had already disrupted trade between Soviet enterprises and those in other COMECON countries. Trade between the countries that emerged from the Soviet Union was disrupted even more when they introduced quotas and licenses for trade with each other and were slow to create effective payments mechanisms. The collapse in interstate trade among former Soviet Union countries in the early 1990s was much greater than the collapse of output. This did not necessarily mean that the output decline was mainly attributable to the breakup of the Soviet Union. The structural changes in the economies were responsible for much of the output loss in individual countries and this was carried over to reductions in interstate trade. There was an additional negative shock from the breakup of the Soviet Union that went in the other direction, from trade to output.

Another burden on some of the poorer countries was the discontinuation of the large transfers that they had received from the Soviet budget. Finally, a few countries, especially Armenia, Azerbaijan, Georgia, Moldova and Tajikistan experienced civil strife after the Soviet Union broke up, with adverse consequences for their economies.

It was not difficult to list the reasons why output would fall during the transition. But we at the IMF, along with most other people inside and outside the transition countries, did not expect the collapse to be as big as it was. Attempts were made in 1992–1994 in many countries in the region to mitigate the collapse by providing subsidies and credits to producers. As discussed in the next section, they were not successful. Our policy advice was to continue macroeconomic stabilization and to speed up the reforms so as to arrive as quickly as possible at the point where economies started to grow again. The only countries in the region that did this were Estonia, Latvia and Lithuania. As a result, they experienced a steeper decline in output in 1992–1993 but they were the only countries to start growing again in 1994. They were also the only countries that could be said to have persisted with a radical reform strategy. The others, including Russia, pursued policies that were effectively gradualist.

Our views and advice about economic strategy for the transition were communicated to the authorities of the countries through our regular interactions.

We addressed a wider public through articles, conference papers and speeches, in the latter case especially those of Camdessus and Fischer (after he came to the IMF in 1994). One of the more comprehensive presentations of our approach was a paper, mostly written, I must confess, by my colleagues, that I gave at a conference in Brussels in 1994. The other participants were mostly Europeans, both government officials and academics and policy analysts. Many of them were skeptical of the radical approach that we advocated for the transition, but their arguments did not cause me to change our views. I cannot say whether I convinced them to change theirs.

In the same year I gave a paper, mostly written by Tom Wolf, at a seminar in Moscow on the experience of economic reforms to date. The paper separated out short-term, medium-term and long-term objectives of transition, with the last of these involving changes ranging from industrial restructuring to developing a market culture and showed that these various objectives could be pursued simultaneously. It proved useful in subsequent discussions with some government officials who argued that, because some aspects of the transition would take a very long time, there was no point in embarking on even the short-term reforms. There was a Russian language version of the paper that we could hand out round the region.

At the end of 1995 the IMF published an important Occasional Paper, edited by Dan Citrin and Ashok Lahiri, that brought together various papers written over the previous year or so on the main problems experienced so far, including the decline in output, interenterprise arrears, and the decline in tax revenue. Some of the papers had been presented at a meeting of the Board in March 1995. The conclusion of that meeting was that the Board endorsed the IMF's policy of emphasizing early macroeconomic stabilization and rapid structural reform.

As the 1990s unfolded, evidence accumulated about the relative merits of radical reform and gradualism. The countries pursuing a gradualist strategy did not reduce the cumulative output cost of the transition compared with a radical strategy, and the output recovery was almost always preceded by macroeconomic stabilization. We concluded from this that bold and rapid stabilization, liberalization and reform measures were conducive to sustained recovery of economic activity. Others came to the same conclusion, notably the World Bank in its *World Development Report* in 1996 and the EBRD in its annual *Transition Reports*. As time passed, it became clear that the gradualist strategy that most countries were pursuing in practice had allowed powerful vested interests to become entrenched. They used their position to undermine attempts to continue the reform process. We became increasingly concerned about this. Oleh Havrylyshyn and I wrote a short article on the political economy of stalled reforms in 2000. Oleh later wrote a book that expanded on the idea and examined it in the broader context of an evaluation of all the reasons for the successes and failures of different countries in the reform process.

Despite the accumulating evidence for the relative success of the radical approach, the financial crisis in Russia in 1998 and growing awareness of the scale of corruption and cronyism in the countries of the region gave new encouragement to its critics. One of the most influential of them was Joseph Stiglitz, Chairman of the Council of Economic Advisers in the US in 1995–1997, Chief Economist of the World Bank in 1997–2000 and winner of the Nobel Prize in economics in 2001. With reference mainly to Russia, he argued that the rapid reform strategy had led to the collapse of output, much social distress, and the dissipation of existing institutions that enabled the economy and society to operate. A gradualist strategy, which maintained these institutions and went slowly on privatization and other structural reforms until new market institutions were introduced, would have been better. He cited the Chinese model as the way to go, as many gradualists had done before.

The IMF was not impressed by these arguments. For one thing, Stiglitz was wrong to claim that countries in Eastern Europe and the former Soviet Union that had adopted gradualist strategies had done better than radical reformers. The only countries in the former Soviet Union that unambiguously took the radical route were the three Baltic States (Estonia, Latvia and Lithuania). They freed prices, introduced their own currencies, introduced restrictive macroeconomic policies and privatized before all the other countries. The result was that they went through a very difficult couple of years or so, with big falls in output and incomes, and shortages of goods, including energy. But the price was worth paying, as inflation fell faster than in the other former Soviet Union countries that chose more gradualist paths, and output began to grow again before it did in the others. In some cases (Ukraine, for example), years before.

In our discussions with the other countries, we would point to the Baltics as examples of the benefits of a radical reform strategy. Our counterparts in a few cases tried to learn from the Baltic experience, even consulting with Baltic officials. More often, however, they were defensive, and persuaded themselves (but not us) that the Baltics could do things that they could not. They cited the fact that the Baltics had experience of market economies until the Soviet occupation in 1940, and that they were given more financial and other assistance from the West, especially the Nordic countries. While it was true that these factors made the transition a little easier for the Baltics, they did not fundamentally alter the balance of arguments about the radical versus gradualist choice. I was grateful that we could point to the Baltics as illustrations of the advantages of radical reforms in countries that were hesitant to take the plunge, even with modest reforms.

China had, of course, done well. But it was a completely different case. Most importantly, the communist state and the discipline it imposed on society and the economy had not collapsed as it had in the Soviet Union by the end of 1991 when the IMF became involved. The former Soviet Union countries had to conduct their reforms in the absence of strong state structures. (The few countries that tried to rebuild state structures before undertaking major economic reforms, especially Belarus, Turkmenistan and Uzbekistan, had somewhat better results than the others in the early years, but not over the 1990s as a whole and beyond.) When its economic reforms began, China was an agricultural country, more like the Soviet Union in the 1920s than in the 1990s. Less than 20 percent of the workforce in China was in non-agricultural state enterprises compared with over 85 percent in the former Soviet Union. It was therefore possible to move gradually with state enterprise reform and focus initially on the agricultural sector. The former Soviet Union countries had no alternative but to tackle the state enterprises from the beginning if any progress was to be made. The attempts in the 1980s under Gorbachev to do this in gradual steps had failed. Finally, China benefitted greatly from the proximity of highly dynamic economies with plenty of excess capital to invest, especially Hong Kong and Taiwan, and from a large Chinese diaspora.

There was a lack of realism in Stiglitz's vision of a carefully sequenced series of gradual reforms. The old communist institutions had collapsed quickly. Even if they had not done so, it is difficult to imagine that they could have continued to function efficiently while new market economy institutions that operated in completely different ways were being introduced. Moreover, the development of new institutions cannot be done entirely on the drawing board. They have to be tested in action and gradually improved, and the process will not always be smooth.

Our attitude to the issue of sequencing was a pragmatic one. We did not believe that it was possible to design an optimal sequence of reforms. There were too many unknowns, such as how long it would take to plan and implement particular reforms, the way in which different reforms would fit together, the social and political acceptability of reforms that reduced or redistributed real incomes and, of course, the unintended consequences. The reforms that could in principle be implemented quickly and that would create the basic elements of a market economy, especially the liberalization of prices and trade and macroeconomic stabilization, should be done as quickly as possible. As private property is also important for a successful market economy, we advocated rapid privatization, especially of small enterprises. Otherwise, our advice was to proceed as quickly as possible with all the other legal, institutional and administrative reforms that were needed without too much regard for precise sequencing. There would, of course, be difficulties along the way which would have to be sorted out at the time. But it was better to deal with such problems in a dynamic context where continuous progress was being made towards a market economy than to postpone everything until the ideal sequence, whatever that was, could be implemented. The major delays that the latter approach would involve would give the opposition to reforms time to mobilize and would almost certainly mean that they would never happen.

The IMF was far from alone in favoring a radical rather than a gradualist strategy. The other international financial institutions that were active in the region, the World Bank, the EBRD and the ADB, took the same view, as did the OECD. After all, the IMF, the World Bank, the EBRD and the OECD had together signed up to the radical approach back in 1990 as joint authors of the study of the Soviet economy. Most governments of their member countries supported the strategy. Although there were no doubt misgivings in a few of the governments, these never affected the commitment of the institutions to the radical strategy. The only international organization that favored a gradualist approach was the United Nations Economic Commission for Europe. Based in Geneva, it was the only international organization during the Cold War that had analyzed and discussed economic policies in communist countries and trade between East and West. Its staff, which included many nationals of Soviet Bloc countries, had greater expertise on those economies under central planning than the staff of the IMF or the other international organizations. They were perhaps more aware of the scale of the disruption that dismantling the old system and building a new one would create. But they also had more faith, unjustified in our view, in the ability of governments to manage a gradual transition successfully.

A major task for the IMF was to persuade the governments in the region that radical reforms were better than gradual ones. No effort was needed in the Baltic countries whose governments were more than ready to undertake rapid and comprehensive reforms. It was also fairly easy in Russia where most of the governments in the 1990s were committed to making radical reforms. However, in some quarters in Russia there was opposition which the IMF tried to sway. For example, Camdessus and Fischer both met with parliamentarians, who opposed many reforms, on a number of occasions. More importantly, Camdessus established a close relationship with Viktor Chernomyrdin, who was prime minister from 1992 to 1998, and was not initially a supporter of radical reforms. Helped in part by his conversations with Camdessus, Chernomyrdin came to accept the need for macroeconomic stabilization along the lines we were recommending. In most of the other countries in the region there were usually some people in government who favored radical reform, and the official policy, at least in dealings with the IMF, was often a radical one. But the commitment to such strategies was shallow and the prevailing sentiment much of the time was for gradualism. As a result, the planned reforms were only partially implemented. In Belarus,

Turkmenistan and Uzbekistan, the authorities were quite explicit about favoring gradual reforms. In reality, they reformed very little.

In general, our efforts to persuade governments that radical reforms were in their best interests were unsuccessful. The programs that we helped to design to produce a rapid transformation were often only partially implemented, at best. The outcome in such cases looked more like a gradualist strategy than a radical one.

The collapse of the economies and the hardship endured by the people during the 1990s caused many both inside and outside the countries to question whether they were on the right path. When people were struggling to survive with greatly reduced real incomes, with public services such as education and health less accessible except at a high price, and with a less effective law and order system failing to stem the rise in crime, it was inevitable that some people would conclude that the reforms had gone wrong. I myself sometimes had doubts. But once the old planning system had collapsed in 1990–1991 and the price liberalization had begun (just as the IMF was arriving on the scene) in 1992, there really was not a more gradual strategy that would have led eventually to a market economy but with much less pain. It would have been possible to postpone, or even reverse, some of the reforms and this might have reduced the fall in output initially. But there would have been a price to pay, in shortages, queues and black markets, and, more fundamentally, a postponement of the day when the economy would recover, and the benefits of the reforms be reaped. Moreover, once the pace of reform slowed down without the economy having recovered, there was a strong likelihood that support for reforms would fade and they would never be completed.

In talking to the governments of countries where reforms were lagging, and to others, I used to put the case for radical reforms in as simple terms as I could:

- The transition is bound to involve a temporary fall in output and incomes and considerable disruption in the economy. (Just as doctors often minimize the side effects of treatment they believe is in the best interests of their patients, for example talking of discomfort rather than pain, so I was inclined to understate the temporary costs so as not to discourage governments and others from undertaking radical reforms.)
- The faster reforms are implemented, the sooner output and incomes will recover. The Baltic States have shown this.
- By delaying difficult reforms, you are just prolonging the agony and increasing the risk that you will never get to a functioning market economy.

This argument fell on deaf ears in Belarus, Turkmenistan and Uzbekistan which feared the consequences of the government's losing control over the economy. It might have had some minor impact in a few of the other countries.

MACROECONOMIC POLICY

Macroeconomic stabilization was an essential component of any strategy for reform. All economies need to aim for price stability to provide a predictable environment for investment and growth. But the liberalization of prices, which was part of the transition from central planning to a market economy, posed an additional challenge for macroeconomic policy. The serious shortages in the final years of the Soviet Union reflected the fact that prices were fixed at too low a level to bring supply and demand into balance. Economists talk about there being a "monetary overhang," meaning that people were obliged to hold more money, as cash or bank accounts, than they wanted because the things they would have purchased were not available. When prices were freed, they would have to jump to bring supply and demand into balance, or to eliminate the monetary overhang, to put it another way. Consumer prices jumped three and a half times after the liberalization of most prices in Russia in January 1992. Other countries in the region were forced to liberalize their prices soon afterwards and experienced similar jumps. The challenge of macroeconomic policy was to prevent these jumps from leading to entrenched inflation as could occur if the initial price jumps produced knock-on increases in wages and other costs that fed back into higher prices.

The IMF's advice to former Soviet Union countries was to set monetary and fiscal policies to bring monthly inflation down from the very high level at the beginning of 1992 to low single digits by the end of the year, and lower still in subsequent years. We recommended reducing fiscal deficits because they were being financed mainly by borrowing from central banks and were thus making it difficult to control monetary growth. In most countries these recommendations were accepted in principle but were not implemented in practice. The main problem on the monetary side was the delay in resolving the ruble area question, which meant that countries still using the ruble could not use monetary policy effectively to contain inflation. On the fiscal side the desperate situation as economies collapsed, and government revenues with them, placed enormous pressure on governments to find money to try to mitigate the collapse and to keep public services going.

In time, with much advice from the IMF and encouragement through the conditionality attached to our loans, most countries brought inflation down successfully during the course of the 1990s and output began to grow. It took a little time in some countries for policy makers to understand the role of restrictive macroeconomic policies in stabilizing the economy. Acceptance came first from young, technically qualified people but eventually spread to the political class and the highest levels of government. Events, especially the failure to achieve growth through loose monetary policies and the exchange rate crises in Russia, contributed as much to the learning process as anything that we or other foreign advisers said. By the mid-1990s, the necessity of restrictive macroeconomic policies to stabilize the economy and the mechanisms for operating such policies were fairly widely accepted by policy makers. Of course, accepting them in principle did not always mean that they were implemented in practice. The political and other obstacles to implementation were considerable.

We turn now to some problems and controversies that arose in discussions about macroeconomic policy in the early years of the transition.

An early debate we had with a number of officials in countries in the region was about the nature of inflation. We argued that inflation was essentially a monetary phenomenon and could be controlled through restrictive macroeconomic policies. As mentioned in chapter 2, in a planned economy prices were fixed as a mark-up over costs and money was little more than a unit of exchange. To people brought up in this environment, inflation could only occur if something was pushing up costs. They sometimes argued that the problem was the existence of monopolies, which had the power to set prices and make excess profits. They also resisted increases in interest rates as part of a tighter monetary policy because interest payments were a cost and higher rates would push up costs and hence prices, the opposite of what was intended. We explained that, while monopolies can lead to high prices for certain goods, they cannot cause a continuously rising price level. A similar argument was made about interest rates. More generally, we tried to explain the role of macroeconomic rather than microeconomic factors in determining inflation. Fortunately, most of our interlocutors understood this very quickly, if they had not already done so before we came on the scene.

A more serious debate was about the impact of macroeconomic policies on output. Many people argued that the restrictive monetary and fiscal policies that were needed to reduce high inflation would damage output, which had already collapsed as part of the transition. There were two strands to this position. One, which was more common among Western economists, was the conventional argument about the short-term impact of macroeconomic policy on output. The other strand, which came from a Soviet view of the role of money, was the belief that there was too little money in the economy to provide working capital for enterprises. The shortage of money was the main reason why enterprises were not paying their bills and interenterprise arrears were rising. The Central Bank of Russia under Gerashchenko in late 1992 took this position and saw it as its responsibility to issue credits to refloat the economy and monetize arrears. In his book, Gaidar reported Gerashchenko as presenting his case roughly as follows: "Well, look. Prices have gone up fourfold, but the money supply only twofold, which means there isn't enough money in the economy, which means that output is declining because of an insufficient money supply, so let's increase the money supply and grant more credits to the republics and to enterprises."

Within a year or two developments in the real world sidelined the first argument. The countries with lower inflation and money growth tended to be the ones with higher output growth. More systematic analysis later over longer periods of time and including Eastern European as well as former Soviet Union countries confirmed that there was no clear evidence that disinflation had compounded output losses. On the contrary: those countries that experienced the earliest disinflation resumed growth first.

The argument that there was too little money in the economy was superficially attractive. But we did not believe that this was the explanation for the output collapse or that more money would increase output. The output collapse was the result of the breakdown of the planning system, the changes in relative prices and demands that followed the reforms, and the disruption following the disintegration of the Soviet Union as already discussed. It was not generally caused by a shortage of money or credit although this might have been a contributing factor in specific cases. The rise in interenterprise arrears occurred because managers of state enterprises were slow to switch from a culture of production to one of profit. In the jargon of the time, they had lost the hard administrative constraints of the planned economy but had not yet accepted the hard budget constraints of a market economy. Had there been hard budget constraints, managers would have been under greater pressure to avoid losses and arrears. Those whose enterprises had been badly hit by the structural changes in demand and relative prices would have tried harder to adjust. A policy of pumping more money into the economy would just perpetuate the soft budget constraints, create inflation and postpone the transition at the enterprise level to the new market realities. We made these arguments in our discussions with the authorities but, with the exception of the Baltics, most countries continued until at least the mid-1990s to provide credits from the central bank or subsidies from the budget to help enterprises in difficulty. In an article in 1995, Ernesto Hernandez-Catá gave a vivid description of the scramble by special interest groups in Russia for more credits.

Another debate concerned the advisability of government borrowing abroad or from domestic financial markets to finance budget deficits. In the early stages of the transition there was no possibility of borrowing from anywhere except the central bank. But this was inflationary and macroeconomic stability required that such borrowing be reduced as much as possible. As domestic financial markets developed and borrowing abroad from private as well as official (including international financial institutions) sources became feasible, governments were tempted to ease their budgetary problems by borrowing in non-inflationary ways. The increase in debt could be justified if the borrowing was used to finance structural changes that would improve growth prospects and thus capacity to service the debt. Jeffrey Sachs was a strong advocate of this and advised Russia and Ukraine to borrow as much as they could.

The IMF agreed in principle with the case for more borrowing if the finance was available. We encouraged countries to create markets in treasury bills partly for this reason as well as to improve the operation of financial markets and monetary policy. In Russia we supported the government when it wanted to open the treasury bill market to non-residents against the advice of the central bank. As things turned out, especially the crisis of 1998, it might have been better not to have liberalized the market. Despite all this, many in the IMF staff, including Ernesto Hernandez-Catá, were uneasy about the rise in borrowing to finance the government. They were concerned that this was merely postponing the need to reduce the structural fiscal deficit. It was not solving the problem and there was no evidence that the breathing space it allowed was being used to speed up reforms and hence hasten the recovery of growth. In these circumstances a rising debt burden would cause difficulties in the future, especially if maturities were short and interest rates high as they would probably have to be. How right these concerns were! The unresolved fiscal problem was at the heart of the financial crisis in Russia in 1998 and the need to reschedule debts in Ukraine and some other countries in the region in subsequent years.

The choice of exchange rate regime was an issue that was debated throughout the first ten years of the transition and more. In the early years the question was whether it would be better to bring inflation down from initially very high levels by fixing the exchange rate or by allowing it to float. These alternative approaches are called exchange rate-based stabilization and money-based stabilization. The choice only made sense in countries that had their own currencies. In countries still using the ruble, there was little possibility of implementing either type of stabilization because of the difficulty of coordinating the monetary policies of the ruble area countries.

The case for an exchange rate-based rather than a money-based stabilization was that it would have a more certain impact on inflation because of the stronger connection between the exchange rate and prices than between the money supply and prices. In addition, the cost of failing to stick to an exchange rate target would impose discipline on the government and central bank and add to the credibility of the policy. But, if the authorities would be unable to stick to an exchange rate target, perhaps because their commitment to implement tight monetary and fiscal policies was weak, it would be safer to opt for a money-based stabilization policy.

By the time these questions arose in former Soviet Union countries, evidence was accumulating of the success of different approaches in Eastern European transition countries. Czechoslovakia and Poland had some success with exchange rate-based stabilizations and Slovenia with a money-based stabilization. However, Yugoslavia had failed with an exchange rate-based stabilization, after an initial success, as had Bulgaria and Romania with money-based stabilizations. No clear conclusions could be drawn from these experiences. The IMF had been willing to support both approaches provided the supporting policies, especially fiscal policy, were in place.

IMF staff working on former Soviet Union countries tended to favor money-based stabilizations because of uncertainty about the commitment to, and ability to implement, strong stabilization policies, especially fiscal policy. But they were prepared to support countries that preferred an exchange rate-based stabilization and that were prepared to complement it with the necessary supportive policies. In the first round of stabilization in 1992, only Estonia chose to fix the exchange rate in the form of a currency board arrangement, the strongest type of exchange rate discipline. Latvia and Lithuania chose a money-based stabilization, although in 1994 they both adopted variants of fixed exchange rate regimes. Although only Estonia initially chose a fixed rate regime, there was an expectation that some of the other countries in the region might do so later as they strengthened their control over monetary and fiscal policies.

Russia in particular was expected to adopt a fixed exchange rate at some point. Early in 1992, it requested $6 billion from the IMF to create a Currency Stabilization Fund (CSF) to bolster a fixed exchange rate. The impetus for the request came from the success of Poland's exchange rate-based stabilization, supported by a CSF, in 1990. Sachs, who had worked on the Polish case, helped to persuade the Russians that it would be good for them too. The G7 promised a CSF in a major statement about financial support for Russia in April. In June 1992, Camdessus agreed with Gaidar that the IMF would contribute funds for a CSF only in the third stage of three planned stages of cooperation between the IMF and Russia, by when monetary and fiscal policies to support a fixed exchange rate would be in place. Ukraine also expressed an interest in a CSF. As it turned out, no country borrowed from the IMF to set up a CSF. The main reason was that the interest in a CSF in Russia and Ukraine waned when they realized that it was intended as a reserve cushion to strengthen the credibility of an exchange rate peg and was not available for financing the balance of payments. Also, the terms for setting up and drawing on such funds from the IMF were rather onerous.

After the three Baltic countries in 1992, five more countries launched stabilization programs in 1993, all of which were money-based. Only two programs were successful, those of Kyrgyzstan and Moldova. Belarus, Kazakhstan and Russia were unsuccessful because they were not able to contain monetary growth as envisaged initially, partly because of lack of budgetary discipline.

In a paper written for a Board meeting in March 1995, the staff recommended a case-by-case approach to exchange rate policy. Directors agreed, although most directors leaned towards flexible exchange rates, the US Director being the main exception. The version of the paper that was edited by Dan Citrin and Ashok Lahiri and published in December named the countries that might be ready to fix their exchange rates (Armenia, Georgia, Kazakhstan, Russia and Ukraine) and those where the preconditions were unlikely to prevail in the near future (Azerbaijan, Belarus, Tajikistan, Turkmenistan and Uzbekistan). With respect to the first group, it commented that "whether or not a peg would ultimately be warranted would depend crucially on whether the fiscal adjustment set out in these programs was sufficiently deep–and the likelihood that it would be followed through sufficiently high–to give to the exchange rate peg a reasonable chance of success." These were prescient words especially as applied to Russia which introduced an exchange rate peg in July 1995 but had to abandon it in August 1998 because of a failure to carry through the fiscal adjustment that was needed to support the peg.

The IMF continued to give advice on exchange rate policy on a case-by-case basis until the crisis in Russia in 1998. It supported both countries that had chosen some kind of peg, including Estonia, Latvia, Lithuania, Russia and Ukraine, and those that were nominally floating, including Armenia, Azerbaijan, Georgia, Kazakhstan, Kyrgyzstan, Moldova and Tajikistan. (The IMF did not endorse the policies of the other three countries in the region, Belarus, Turkmenistan and Uzbekistan.) However, it must be admitted that the floaters were obviously trying to keep their currencies as stable as possible. In most cases they were pursuing a de facto fixed exchange rate policy while retaining the freedom to change the exchange rate if it suited them. In general, this policy worked rather well.

When the ruble depreciated sharply after the peg was abandoned in August 1998, the IMF advised CIS countries to allow their currencies to depreciate to avoid a loss of competitiveness against Russia. Almost all of them did. (The Baltic States were determined to stick to their fixed rate policies and make the necessary adjustment in other ways, which they did.) Subsequently, nearly all of them, including Russia, pursued a policy that they described as floating. In practice, however, they allowed very little flexibility in the rate. They liked the predictability of a steady rate, especially against the ruble, as

Russia continued to be the largest trading partner for most of them. In some countries, including Azerbaijan, Kazakhstan, Russia and Ukraine, strong balances of payments were pushing up the international reserves and making it difficult to control money growth and inflation. The IMF advised these countries to allow the exchange rate to appreciate but they were reluctant to do so because of opposition from exporters and holders of foreign currency assets.

The best way to summarize our advice on exchange rate policy in the 1990s was that it was pragmatic. There was no ideological commitment to either fixed or flexible exchange rates. It was responsive to countries' circumstances and preferences although that is not to say that we did not sometimes try to talk countries out of particular policies. There was a cycle in our receptiveness to different exchange rate regimes. In the first few years we favored flexible exchange rates in many countries because of doubts about their capacity to implement suitably strong monetary and fiscal policies to support fixed rates. Then for a few years we were more supportive of countries that wanted to peg their exchange rates. However, the Russia crisis in 1998 revealed the vulnerability of fixed rate regimes, especially when fiscal policies led to too much debt. After 1998, we therefore again favored more flexible regimes.

To some extent this cycle reflected fashions among economists and policy makers. Following the successful exchange rate-based stabilizations in Israel and some Latin American countries in the 1980s, there was increasing interest in fixed exchange rates in countries that wanted to bring down high inflation. The big increase in international financial flows and the Asian, Russian and Brazilian crises in 1997–1998 focused attention on the problems of fixed rate regimes, a major one being the difficulty of choosing the right moment to exit from them. In a general review in 2000, the IMF took a balanced view of the choices that countries might make depending on their circumstances; it concluded that no single exchange rate regime was best for all countries. In 2001, Fischer wrote an article arguing that adjustable pegs do not work; countries faced a binary choice between a rigid peg and a free float.

In remarks I prepared with Richard Haas and delivered at a conference at the Bank of Estonia in 2002 to mark the tenth anniversary of the reintroduction of the kroon, I suggested that the choice of exchange rate regime was less important than the quality of other policies, especially fiscal policy and structural policies designed to create more flexible and efficient markets. Andrew Crockett, who was General Manager of the Bank for International Settlements and had been a senior member of the IMF staff many years before, objected to my presentation of the issue. He said that the choice of exchange rate regime was important but, once the choice was made, then the other policies became more important. Our positions were not fundamentally different. He thought of policies being adopted sequentially: first the exchange rate regime, and then appropriate monetary and fiscal policies. My view was that the authorities should think of them simultaneously, even if implementation would take place over different time scales.

Meanwhile, the countries of the former Soviet Union had a broad preference for fixed exchange rates throughout the period. The Baltics exercised their preference successfully. A few other countries operated with formal pegs for a few years until the crisis in Russia. But, even when their exchange rates were floating, most of them aimed to keep their exchange rates fairly stable, while retaining the possibility of allowing some flexibility if necessary.

STRUCTURAL AND INSTITUTIONAL REFORMS

While we focused primarily on macroeconomic policies, we were well aware that by far the greater part of the transition to market economies involved reforms of a structural and institutional nature. Lenin's legacy, which Mart Laar was keen to vanquish, was more apparent in areas such as the ownership of the means of production and government control of the economy through the planning and administrative systems than in the macroeconomic field. Camdessus' Georgetown speech in April 1992 emphasized the speedy adoption of the legal and institutional framework for a market economy and privatization at least as much as price and trade liberalization and macroeconomic stabilization.

However, the sharp rise in prices throughout the region that followed price liberalization in Russia at the beginning of 1992 pushed macroeconomic stabilization to the top of the policy agenda in the early years. Without a reasonable amount of price stability, there would be little investment, output and incomes would not grow and the political will to undertake the difficult structural reforms would weaken. While the early focus on macroeconomic stabilization was essential, there was a legitimate worry that it might be drawing the attention of the authorities away from structural reforms. We were criticized for prioritizing macroeconomic stabilization, more by Western commentators, especially those who favored a gradualist strategy, than by people in the countries themselves. But it was unavoidable.

Some structural issues fell into the IMF's area of competence. The most important of these were tax policy, tax administration, Treasury functions, central banking issues, the introduction of new currencies and reforming the statistical services. Our advice was delivered primarily through technical assistance (TA) managed by my colleagues in the technical assistance departments of the IMF. We were sometimes able to give the reforms in these areas a push by requiring certain changes as preconditions for receiving IMF loans.

Most IMF technical assistance was uncontroversial. There was, however, some tension between the advice of TA experts to reduce tax rates and expand tax bases, and worries in my teams that this could lead to lower revenues in the short term. When revenues were already low or declining, we insisted that tax rates should be maintained until the fiscal situation had been brought under control. Our tax TA experts were naturally disappointed.

The expert tax advice was also challenged in some countries. One criticism was that the advice to replace the type of sales tax that was inherited from the Soviet Union by VAT was premature, given the lack of administrative preparedness in the tax administration department and businesses. Another was that we failed to appreciate the likely increase in revenues that would come from better compliance and the shrinkage of the informal economy after tax rates were reduced or made more uniform. We were therefore reluctant to support reductions in tax rates or moves towards uniform rates. Nevertheless, some countries went ahead against our advice. Even after the event, it was not easy to say whether there were significant reductions in revenue, but, if there were, they were not large. There was no ambiguity about the consequence of our insistence in Russia in 1996 that the oil export duty should be replaced by excise duties. There was a big drop in revenues. We were wrong to insist on it at that time as the government was not able to administer an efficient excise duty regime.

In the first year after Fischer came to the IMF as First Deputy Managing Director in 1994, he asked me why the economies of countries that had brought inflation down, such as Moldova, were not growing. He and we had expected growth to follow the achievement of low inflation fairly soon afterwards. My answer was that the resumption of growth also depended on privatization and structural and institutional reforms to create a framework for a market economy, and these were progressing slowly. Of course, we understood that some of the necessary changes would take years, even decades. Nevertheless, it was disappointing that they were not moving ahead faster. Without growth, countries would find it difficult to hang onto the macroeconomic stability they had achieved.

We considered what, if anything, the IMF could do to speed up structural and institutional reforms. The expertise for advising countries on such reforms lay in the World Bank, not the IMF. With help from our World Bank counterparts, we identified structural and institutional reforms that we could ask countries to implement as conditions for borrowing from the IMF. Privatization was, of course, one of the most important structural reforms. There was much discussion among economists and others about the best way to privatize, for example sales to stakeholders such as employees, giving vouchers to the population that could be used to buy state assets, or through sales on the market. We did not get involved in these debates which we left to our colleagues in the World Bank. However, we did urge countries to move as quickly as possible with their privatization programs, sometimes specifying benchmarks they should meet as conditions for our loans.

Structural conditionality, as it was called, was only partly successful. One problem was that we were reluctant to interrupt our lending if the macroeconomic conditions were met but the structural conditions were not. In other words, structural conditionality did not always have teeth. Another was that it was difficult to monitor. Unlike most macroeconomic conditions where we could easily ascertain whether, say, the budget deficit was above or below the agreed target, it was not always apparent whether, say, a new law was being implemented properly after it had been enacted. Because of the wide range of needed reforms, we sometimes imposed a large number of structural conditions. Although governments were prepared to sign up to them in order to obtain our loans, their ownership of the reforms was often weak, and they were unwilling or unable to make the effort–which usually required spending political capital–to implement them. Despite these drawbacks, some reforms were made that, in the absence of our structural conditionality, might not have been made. I supported it for another reason as well. I believed that the process of identifying structural reforms and discussing them with the authorities gave the reform minded members of the government an authoritative road map that they could follow in their internal planning and policy discussions.

At the same time as we were increasing our use of structural conditionality in the 1990s because of the importance of structural and institutional reforms in our countries, IMF lending to countries in other regions of the world was moving in the same direction. By the end of the decade, pressure was building up in borrowing countries and the Board of the IMF to limit the extent of structural conditionality because it took the IMF into too many policy areas and undermined the authorities' ownership. One of the early changes that Horst Köhler made after arriving as Managing Director in 2000 was therefore to streamline conditionality so that it would apply only to areas related to macroeconomic stability. My staff had mixed views about this. Some welcomed it, while others thought that it weakened their ability to persuade countries to reform. I was in the latter group.

As sister institutions that were set up following the Bretton Woods conference in 1944, the IMF and the World Bank work closely together. Being located side by side in Washington makes this easier. They have different mandates, with the IMF being responsible for macroeconomic analysis, policies, institutions and lending, and the World Bank for sectoral analysis and lending. There is inevitably some overlap, leading to occasional turf wars. The formal agreements between the two institutions about how they should work together help to contain these, but just as important are the attitudes and behavior of individuals. One or two of my senior staff members harbored a deep distrust of their World Bank counterparts. In some cases, this was because they had past experience of World Bank staff encroaching on the macroeconomic work that was the responsibility of the IMF. At least as often, I regret to say, it was because my colleague was defensive and reluctant to share information and views with his World Bank counterpart. Fortunately, my opposite number at the World Bank, initially Wilfrid Thalwitz and then, for many years, Johannes Linn, was very cooperative and we were usually able to maintain good relations between our teams.

One feature of the different mandates of the IMF and World Bank caused some tensions. We relied on the World Bank to recommend the structural and institutional reforms that our countries should undertake. Most such reforms could only be implemented over a period of months, if not years. It was therefore not easy to incorporate them, whether as structural conditions or in other ways, into our agreements with countries that typically had much shorter time horizons. We sometimes felt that the World Bank was being unhelpful in not suggesting reforms that could take place within our time horizon. They felt that we were unrealistic and did not understand the nature of structural and institutional reforms. At best, the inevitable tension in such situations was creative in that it led to improved cooperation between us, and better advice to the countries. But it sometimes had the opposite outcome.

We had much less interaction with the EBRD, mainly because its mandate was to lend for private sector projects. Our main counterparts were the economists in the Chief Economist's office which was responsible for analyzing the economies of the EBRD's borrowing countries. It also published an annual *Transition Report*, which combined material on macroeconomic developments in the countries in transition with assessments of their progress in moving towards market economies. The Chief Economists for most of my time were Nicholas Stern and Willem Buiter, with whom I had an understanding that their staff would not knowingly and publicly contradict our position on macroeconomic issues. The exchange of information and analysis between us was probably more beneficial to us than to them because we used in our research and analysis the transition indicators that they devised to measure progress towards market economies. I also had contacts with the Presidents and Vice-Presidents of the EBRD, one or two cases of which I describe in later chapters.

The European Commission had lending programs in some of the low income countries in the region, other than the Baltic States which were in line to become EU members. As with the EBRD we expected the Commission to follow our lead on macroeconomic issues. In practice, the Commission backed up our conditionality by tying their lending to a country's compliance with the IMF's conditions. My counterpart there was Joly Dixon, the Director of International Affairs in the Economic and Financial Affairs Directorate.

We had known each other for many years and established an excellent working relationship.

WHAT WENT WRONG: VESTED INTERESTS, OLIGARCHS AND CORRUPTION

The fifteen former Soviet Union countries can be divided into three groups from the point of view of economic reforms and successful outcomes. The three Baltic States reformed early in a radical way and were the first to experience renewed growth. Their levels of economic development have been catching up with those of western European countries. Nine of the twelve CIS countries chose a more gradual reform path, although with bursts of more rapid reforms in one or two cases, especially Russia and Kyrgyzstan. The remaining three CIS countries, Belarus, Turkmenistan and Uzbekistan, opted for minimal reforms because their leaders wanted to maintain as much of the old system as they could.

I will discuss the countries in more detail in separate chapters. Here I propose a general explanation for why the reforms in the nine intermediate CIS countries were not more rapid and successful, namely that their leaders were ambivalent about their support for market reforms. Unlike the leaders of the three laggards, they wanted to create properly functioning market economies, but they put the brakes on when their own economic interests, or those of their associates or political supporters, were threatened by the reforms. Examples of reforms that were threatening included transparent and competitive government procurement arrangements, competitive market rules (for example, allowing free entry of new businesses, constraining monopoly behavior), level playing fields in taxation and regulation, anti-corruption legislation and institutions, and an independent and impartial judiciary. The vested interests that stood to lose from such reforms, and therefore worked to prevent them, were able to exert their influence on the governments in these nine countries.

These vested interests emerged in various ways. Even before the end of the Soviet Union, many people in the business and political elites, that is the enterprise managers and senior party and government officials, saw the end coming and arranged to acquire state assets for themselves. They did this in various ways. Some set up cooperatives after the 1988 law permitted them, into which they were able to transfer the profits of the state corporations that they managed. Others acquired licenses, perhaps by bribing the officials responsible for allocating them. The licenses allowed them to export products at world prices, for example minerals or energy products, which they had purchased at controlled domestic prices. These and many other forms of asset stripping, as it was called, mainly benefited the old managerial, party and government classes. They were able to do it when previous generations could not because of the breakdown of discipline in the economic system, the freedoms afforded by the new legislation of the Gorbachev years and the opportunities for arbitrage between different markets because of the price differentials resulting from incomplete reforms.

The old elites from Soviet times were joined by a younger group of entrepreneurs at the end of the Soviet period and during the early years of independence. People who later became known as oligarchs started with cooperatives that did business with state enterprises from which they managed to skim the profits. For example, Mikhail Khodorkovsky, a PhD student at the chemical technology university in Moscow, established a cooperative to provide consulting advice to state enterprises on chemical processes. Boris Berezovsky set up a management consulting firm which advised Avtovaz, a major car company. Somehow, the profits of Avtovaz found their way into Berezovsky's firm.

After independence, most of the nine CIS countries implemented programs for privatizing state enterprises. Unfortunately, they were not always carried out in a transparent and fair way. There were many cases of insider privatization in which the existing managers became owners at prices well below any likely market price. Other well-connected businessmen and politicians acquired assets cheaply. They were sometimes assisted in this by government officials. The loans for shares operation in Russia in 1995–1996 was a notorious example of non-transparency and unfairness. I return to it in the next chapter.

The complicit involvement of government officials in the processes by which some people became very wealthy was a form of corruption. I think of it as grand corruption. There was also plenty of small-scale corruption, such as when an enterprise paid a regulator not to enforce a regulation, or a tax collector to reduce its tax liability. The culture of small-scale corruption was inherited in part from the Soviet Union where bribes were common. Indeed, they were often necessary to enable the inefficient planning system to work as smoothly as it did. After independence, small-scale corruption was more likely where there was little competition, no free press or judiciary, complex regulations and discretion given to the regulators and tax administrators. Countries that reformed quickly, such as the Baltic States, avoided some of these pitfalls.

The growth of vested interests and corruption was a consequence of incomplete reforms. The connection also ran the other way round: the vested interests put pressure on the government to slow down the movement to a competitive market economy system. Vested interests and corruption were the single most important reason why the nine CIS countries did not move more rapidly to market economies, with adverse consequences for the longer-term growth of output and incomes. They also created a large rise in income and wealth inequality and gave market reforms a bad name. Some of the stories recorded by Nobel Prize winner Svetlana Alexievich in *Secondhand Time: The Last of the Soviets* capture the resentment of those left behind by the economic changes.

We were well aware of the malign influence of corruption and vested interests on market reforms. Tom Wolf and Emine Gürgen published a booklet in 2000 setting out the connections between governance and corruption and explaining how corruption exacts high economic costs. They also described the reforms that the IMF recommended to improve governance and reduce the opportunities for corruption. In lending programs, we often insisted on such reforms as conditions for loans. However, it was easy for governments to carry out the agreed measure, whether it was a legal or regulatory change, or a change in practices, but subsequently to negate its effects through administrative or other means. In countries where the government was reluctant to tackle corruption or vested interests seriously, our efforts to change things had little impact beyond signaling what we thought was good for the country.

During the course of the 1990s, the IMF, in common with the World Bank and other international organizations, became increasingly concerned about corruption and governance issues more generally. The Board decided in 1997 that the staff should look into economic governance issues that had significant macroeconomic implications and raise their concerns with the authorities of the country concerned and report to the Board. This strengthened our hand in pursuing these issues in our countries.

Camdessus was himself very engaged in using the influence and leverage of the IMF to help countries improve governance. Two occasions in Moscow illustrate this. In April 1997, he gave a speech at the Moscow State Institute for International Relations, an important university and think tank. His theme was the crisis of the state. He urged the acceleration of institutional reforms of the state, the separation of the state from business interests, and the institution of the rule of law, as well as reforms to the tax administration and control of government expenditure to reduce corruption. In February the following year he made the same point directly to Yeltsin. He came to Moscow straight from Asia where he had been dealing with the serious crises in Indonesia, South Korea and Thailand. He told Yeltsin that Russia was suffering from the same kind of crony capitalism–abnormally close links between the state, the banks and enterprises–that was at the heart of the Asian crisis. His message was that oligarchs in Russia were cornering the wealth of the country, capturing its media and attempting to take over the state in a climate of corruption. Yeltsin seemed to be angry, not with Camdessus but because he knew that the oligarchs were too powerful. He agreed that there should be a proper distance between political power and business, and that small and medium sized firms should be able to operate freely subject to the law. But in practice he was not able to do much about it.

I felt that we should keep the spotlight on the problem of vested interests and corruption. At a conference in Vienna in November 2000 on *Completing Transition*, I therefore gave a presentation that had been prepared mainly by Tom Richardson, on "Transition and Vested Interests." I explained how vested interests opposed key reforms, had excessive influence on policymaking, reduced competition and created an unfriendly business climate. The problems were not easily solved given the power of the vested interests. Among the solutions were a stronger and more independent judiciary, deregulation and anti-monopoly measures and greater transparency in all public financial activities. Horst Köhler, who had recently succeeded Camdessus as Managing Director, spoke forcefully on the same theme in his keynote address at the same conference. He criticized "grand corruption wherein vested interests in effect 'capture the state,' and then use their power to preserve monopolies, hinder competition and inhibit reform, including the establishment of the legal and regulatory system needed for a well-functioning market economy. Russia and Ukraine have been unhappy examples over the years. In such situations, the authorities must be prepared to challenge the vested interests, in part by being fully committed to transparency in policymaking and public sector operations."

Oleh Havrylyshyn did important analytical work on the role of vested interests in holding back reforms, slowing down the transition to competitive market economies and hence damaging the prospects for better economic growth. Following the article we wrote together in 2000, he went on to look more deeply into the issue and published a book in 2006 that expanded on the idea and examined it in the broader context of an evaluation of all the reasons for the successes and failures of different countries in the reform process. He returned to the subject with a longer time perspective in another book he published a few months before he died in 2020.

My final attempt to persuade the governments in the region to tackle vested interests and corruption came when I visited many of the countries in November 2003. It was my last trip, and, having already announced that I was retiring, I had nothing to lose from speaking frankly. In meetings with the most senior person I had access to, in most cases the president or prime minister, I went through the usual arguments for restraining vested interests and corruption. Everyone listened politely, without showing much emotion or, in most cases, having much to say by way of a response. I doubt that my speeches caused my principal interlocutors to change their minds, but they might have emboldened more reform-minded officials to push a little harder for better policies. There was, however, little public sign of this in the years that followed. The truth was that by 2003 crony capitalism and corruption had become a way of life in most countries. The leaders of the government were probably all caught up in it in one way or another. The opportunity to create a transparent and competitive market economy by rapid reforms, as in the Baltic States in the early 1990s, had been missed. It would be extremely difficult to climb back onto such a path now, and no one was prepared to attempt it.

While in Armenia on that trip, I was invited to a seminar to mark the tenth anniversary of the introduction of Armenia's national currency in 1993. I took advantage of the occasion to spell out in public our concerns about the malign influence of vested interests and corruption, and the need to transform the role of government in the economy into one supportive of a competitive market economy. As written with the help of Henri Lorie, my speech listed what governments should do, and also what they should not do. It ended with the usual warnings:

> Tolerance for corruption and its adverse effects on business and investment is the single most important factor holding back the more rapid economic growth that many CIS countries could achieve . . . More needs to be done within the CIS, where political systems have too often allowed a few to capture the state and its resources for their own benefit.

I have already said that our efforts to speed up structural and institutional reforms were only partly successful because we gave priority to macroeconomic stabilization and could not easily monitor whether agreed structural and institutional reforms had been implemented in the spirit as well as the letter of the original intention. This was also true of reforms that might have curbed some of the abuses arising from vested interests and corruption. Governments that were corrupt or had surrendered some power to vested interests were able to continue on their chosen path despite our disapproval and attempts to stop them. The IMF is in a strong position when lending money to insist that countries pursue appropriate macroeconomic policies. It is much less able to influence other policies for creating successful market economies unless the government itself really wants to go in that direction.

Friends who worked on human rights issues in transition or developing countries sometimes asked me why the IMF did not use its leverage to improve human rights in countries which it was supporting financially. Our formal position was that there were other international organizations that were concerned with human rights, and our mandate was strictly economic and financial. I also added that our leverage was much less effective than observers might imagine. Even in the economic area, we could not always persuade reluctant governments to implement important reforms. Or they would agree on paper but not follow up in practice. In international affairs, it is generally the case that outsiders cannot make countries do what they do not want to do without applying enormous pressure, which can be done only in extreme circumstances.

Similar arguments apply in the case of leaders of countries and their families, friends and associates becoming extremely wealthy at the expense of the state. There were a number of countries in our region where this occurred, especially the natural resource rich ones. The term kleptocracy, literally meaning rule by thieves, became increasingly used around the world in the 1980s and 1990s. An academic at an American university, Karen Dawisha, published a book in 2014 called *Putin's Kleptocracy: Who Owns Russia?* The sums of money she alleged Putin and his associates had extracted improperly from the state were enormous.

The IMF has always opposed such corruption. Indeed, one of the motives behind the increased attention paid to corruption from the 1990s onwards was the damage to the public finances and the economy, not to mention the IMF's reputation, caused by President Mobutu's "kleptocratic" rule in Zaire. But our ability to prevent it was limited. The illicit flows of money were hidden from us as much as they were hidden from the population. We therefore could not apply quantitative limits to them as we did to budget deficits, credit growth and other measurable financial flows. As long as the macroeconomic conditions we insisted on were met, it was difficult to deny financial assistance on the grounds that the leaders were becoming wealthy in mysterious ways. Our attempts to improve the transparency of public financial operations and governance more generally may have helped to limit the corruption. But we had no way of stopping it entirely in countries where the leaders and their associates intended to continue their corrupt practices.

Chapter 4

Russia: It Turned Out as Always

Viktor Chernomyrdin, who was prime minister of Russia for five years from late 1992 to 1998, had a reputation for malapropisms. After an unsuccessful monetary reform in 1993, he said "we wanted the best, but it turned out as always." Although he was ridiculed for this, both at the time and in later years, it was certainly true that the well-intentioned economic reforms during the 1990s failed to change things as much as the reformers had hoped, mainly because they were undermined by vested interests and their political backers.

EXTRAORDINARY POLITICS, 1991–1992

The phrase "extraordinary politics" was first used by Leszek Balcerowicz, the leader of economic reforms in Poland, to describe the early months of the reform process when the political situation is very fluid and the opposition to reforms has not yet crystallized. Anders Åslund has dated the equivalent period in Russia as August 1991 to March 1992.

Our first substantive encounters with the Russian authorities took place in November 1991 after Yeltsin's speech on 28 October in which he revealed his intention to introduce major economic reforms at the beginning of 1992. A week or so later he announced a new government of reformers led, on the economic side, by Yegor Gaidar as deputy prime minister and Minister of Economics and Finance.

Then in his mid-30s, Gaidar had lived in Prague and Cuba where his father, a journalist, was posted. (His grandfather, Arkady Gaidar, was a famous writer of children's stories.) His prior experience had been as an economic researcher and writer, and in 1990 he was appointed the first director of the Institute for Economic Policy under the Academy for the National Economy of the USSR. He was a very impressive figure who seemed to understand many of the complexities of economic policy in a market economy despite having had little personal experience. He formed a good relationship with Camdessus who later wrote of his subtle mind, courage, and eyes that "sparkled with intelligence." For us, he was an amazing contrast with most of the Soviet officials we had dealt with up till then, with the exception of Grigory Yavlinsky. He was communicative where they were monosyllabic; he was prepared to discuss economic reforms where they stuck to platitudes about current policies; and he wanted to change things where they wanted to preserve the status quo and not risk their jobs. He was clearly the intellectual leader of the group of reformers he brought together under Yeltsin. Although he had a senior position in government for only a short time, he had a huge impact on the course of economic reforms. Unfortunately, he became very unpopular because the economic collapse of the early 1990s was incorrectly attributed to the reforms rather than to the inherent difficulty of moving to a market economy, not to mention the failure to follow the radical reform path that he himself favored. After he left government, he continued to lead his research institute and write books and articles. The institute was renamed the Gaidar Institute for Economic Policy in 2010 after he died.

Before Yeltsin's speech in October, Gaidar had been preparing the Russian government's plans for major economic reforms with a small team of market-oriented reformers and a few foreign economists. Clearly the time had come for the IMF to engage with the new Russian authorities. We sent a mission that arrived in Moscow on 10 November and stayed, with a changing composition, for 6 weeks. This was an unusually long time for an IMF economic mission, which typically lasts about two weeks. The length reflected in part the amount of work that was needed, given the IMF's limited knowledge of and access to data about the Russian and Soviet economies. However, there was at the time strong pressure from the G7, especially the US, to do something about Russia and the Soviet Union, and the length of the mission was also intended to show that we were responding. In addition, with things changing rapidly in Russia and the Soviet Union, it would be important to have people on the ground to keep up with developments. Jean Foglizzo was the only person we had based in Moscow, although Augusto Lopez-Claros and others joined him the following year.

During this mission we met for the first time many of the young economic reformers whom Yeltsin had brought into government, including Sergei Aleksashenko, Pyotr Aven, Konstantin Kagalovsky, Vladimir Mashits, Aleksei Mozhin, Andrei Nechaev and Andrei Vavilov, as well as Gaidar. We were impressed by the understanding that they showed of the key economic reforms that were needed and especially the importance of ensuring macroeconomic stability after the initial jump in prices when controls were lifted. The meetings were enhanced by the presence on our team of Stanley Fischer who knew some of the Russians from academic conferences and other occasions. He was then a professor at MIT but had previously been the Chief

Economist at the World Bank where he had coauthored a pioneering article about the transition from a planned to a market economy. He joined the IMF mission for a few days as a consultant and helped us improve our understanding of the situation. After he became the First Deputy Managing Director of the IMF in 1994, he was deeply involved in our policy towards Russia.

Most of our meetings took place in government buildings but we met Kagalovsky, who had not yet been assigned an office, in one of the dachas in the village of Arkhangelskoe on the edge of Moscow where Gaidar's team had prepared all their plans. It was remarkable to think that crucial decisions about the future of Russia had been taken in such modest traditional wooden houses surrounded by typical Russian woods of birches and conifers.

Although the IMF did not have a formal relationship with Russia as it did with the USSR, nearly all the contacts during this mission were with the Russian rather than the Soviet authorities. During this period, power was shifting rapidly from the Soviet Union to Russia, with Russia effectively taking over the Finance Ministry of the Soviet Union and the Central Bank of Russia (CBR) taking over the State Bank (Gosbank) of the USSR. The efforts of Grigory Yavlinsky to forge an agreement about the economic and monetary arrangements defining relations between the republics of the Soviet Union were going nowhere. With the collapse of the Communist Party and the growing independence of the Union republics, the Soviet Union's economic system was imploding and its political leaders were incapable of rescuing it. There was little to be gained from a dialogue with the Soviet authorities.

Despite the length of the mission, we achieved less than we had hoped. We had planned to find out exactly what economic policies the Russian government was proposing to introduce, and to help its technocrats develop a quantified and consistent set of monetary and fiscal policies. However, the government's plans were still being developed and were known to relatively few senior people who were too busy to spend much time with the IMF team. The more junior people, who in normal circumstances would often be able to brief the IMF team, were not always themselves well informed. They were also in the middle of major upheavals as Russia took over Soviet institutions, and, as former Soviet bureaucrats, were uncomfortable giving information to or receiving advice from foreigners.

Another major barrier to preparing a quantified financial program, one that persisted for another year or more, was that the ruble was the currency of the whole Soviet Union, not just Russia. Finally, the absence of a formal relationship between the IMF and Russia meant that the IMF could not insist on a closer dialogue with its authorities, although the November agreement between the G7 and Russia and other CIS countries committed Russia to consult the IMF in preparing its economic program for 1992. The consequence of these constraints on the November/December mission was that the IMF had virtually no input into the economic reforms that were initiated in January 1992. However, we fully supported the broad reform strategy which was in line with our view of what was required.

As part of the preparations for the reforms, Yeltsin invited the foreign economic advisers who had been working with Gaidar and his team to a discussion about the reform plans. Anders Åslund, Marek Dabrowski, Rudiger Dornbusch, Richard Layard, and Jeffery Sachs were among the foreign advisers. Erb and I also attended. Yeltsin led most of the discussion and showed a keen interest in the economic reforms. He was well aware of the enormity of what was being planned as was revealed by his passing comment that he had ensured that the military and the security services would remain loyal. He asked sensible questions of the kind that astute leaders ask their economic advisers when they are assessing the political consequences of economic policies. How much will prices go up? When will there be more goods in the shops? Which groups will be hardest hit by the reforms? There was a longer silence than usual when he asked the most difficult question: "I know that what we are doing will depress living standards for a time; how long will it be before people will start to see an improvement?" The silence was partly explained by genuine uncertainty because none of us had experience of policy changes on the planned scale although Poland and other Eastern European countries were helpful examples. But I guess that others were thinking what I was thinking, that it could be a number of years. Gaidar broke the silence by saying that he thought it would be at least six months and perhaps a year. Yeltsin seemed reassured, although it was not clear whether he fully believed Gaidar. In reality, it turned out to be a number of years before living standards for the average person started to rise.

The meeting in December between Yeltsin, Kravchuk and Shushkevich, the leaders of Russia, Ukraine and Belarus, which led to the dissolution of the Soviet Union, took place during the IMF mission to Moscow. It clarified our task, as we could now focus fully on Russia and not seek to continue a dialogue with the Soviet Union. One positive outcome of the mission was that broad agreement was reached with the Russian authorities on the next steps in the relationship. As soon as it was recognized as a country by the international community, Russia would apply for IMF membership. During the months that would elapse before membership became effective, the IMF staff would assist the authorities in developing a program that would guide macroeconomic policies for the year of 1992. This program would be revised as the year progressed so that it could be the basis upon which the IMF could lend money as soon as Russia became a member and thus eligible to borrow.

The foreign economic advisers, especially Jeffery Sachs, were influential in persuading the government that they should engage with the IMF in this way. Sachs thought that the IMF's professional knowledge would be useful to

Russia, although he also had his eyes on a bigger goal. He wanted to persuade the G7, especially the US, to lend many billions of dollars to Russia, and he knew that this would require, among other things, that Russia would agree to its macroeconomic policies with the IMF. He encouraged the Russians to ask the G7 in December for a currency stabilization fund of $4–5 billion. His experience in Poland led him to believe that the existence of such a fund, which would be available to support the currency after the initial jump in prices, would calm the foreign exchange market and might never have to be used (as it was not in Poland). However, the G7 were not inclined to provide money on that scale. They insisted instead that Russia should join the IMF as quickly as possible and thus become eligible to borrow from the IMF. Only then could the G7 consider lending more money.

The price liberalization and other reforms that were introduced on 2 January brought the anxious waiting period to an end. Consumer prices jumped three and a half times on average, almost wiping out the real value of households' savings. However, together with the liberalization of imports and a Presidential decree at the end of January liberalizing domestic trade, the freeing of prices gradually brought goods back into the shops and to informal kiosks which sprouted up everywhere. While real incomes and wealth were squeezed and production continued to fall, the fear of total collapse engendered by empty shops and a downward spiraling economy was eased.

The IMF focused on helping the government prepare an economic program for 1992. We sent missions to Moscow in January and February to discuss the program with the government. The February mission concluded with an agreement between the IMF and the government and CBR on a Memorandum of Economic Policies (MEP) which was published in Russia and summarized in English in the IMF's *Economic Review of the Russian Federation* published in April.

In large part the MEP was merely a codification of what the government planned to do. We were broadly supportive of their plans and did not seek to second guess them in most areas. However, we were concerned about two critical determinants of macroeconomic stability, the budget deficit and control over monetary policy. We projected that there would be a budget deficit of over 10 percent of GDP in the first quarter of the year and we urged the government to take steps to bring the deficit down over subsequent quarters. With expenditures having been severely cut already, achieving this would require a big increase in tax revenues. After much discussion the government agreed to raise taxation on various products, especially domestic sales and exports of oil and gas, and imported goods.

There were various angles to the problem of monetary control, including the apparent existence of excess reserves at commercial banks, an enormous settlement account at the CBR because of the inefficient payments system, and the weak instruments available to the CBR for controlling monetary emissions in other former Soviet Union countries, all of which were still using the ruble. Moreover, it proved impossible to create a consistent set of monetary accounts that would enable us and the authorities to be precise about the desired scale of credit and money growth during 1992. Rather than set out quantitative targets for credit and money, the MEP therefore promised that the situation would be closely monitored against certain broad criteria. The CBR also undertook to coordinate its monetary policy with other central banks in the ruble area.

There was a somewhat surreal atmosphere surrounding the talks we had with the authorities in January and February. There we were, in the government offices in Old Square (Staraya Ploshchad) that had housed the Secretariat of the Central Committee of the Communist Party of the Soviet Union until just a few months before, calmly discussing the details of a coherent set of macroeconomic policies with our Russian counterparts. Meanwhile, only a few streets away people were standing on the sidewalks in the freezing cold selling a few possessions to get money to live. Throughout the country, production and living standards continued to fall drastically. While those of us in the room believed that what we were discussing had the potential to improve the situation gradually as market-based incentives altered behavior, we did not expect to see a quick turnround in the economy. Nor could the IMF provide any money to ease the immediate hardship until Russia became a member, and even then the amounts would not make a big impact. The challenge for Yeltsin and the rest of the leadership was to persuade people to accept the temporary hardships until the new policies produced results.

Another disconnect was between the policies being discussed and the preparedness of the government machine to implement them. The lower level officials we met were intelligent, competent administrators and mostly willing to implement the government's economic reforms, although a few no doubt resisted the changes on principle. But we realized that they did not always have sufficient understanding of the reforms to make the necessary administrative arrangements quickly. Gaidar's team of reformers was largely drawn from academic institutions and did not have much administrative experience. They therefore underestimated the amount of time and work that were required to ensure that their bold policy ideas were translated into action.

An example was the introduction of value added tax at 28 percent in January 1992. The law authorizing this was passed on 6 December 1991 but there were delays in issuing supplementary instructions. Not surprisingly, VAT receipts were very low at the beginning of the year; more than half of the enterprises had not paid any VAT by the middle of February. More seriously, almost no revenue from the export tax, also introduced in January, had been collected by the middle of March, a shortfall of over 10 percent of GDP compared with the budget. The main reason was that the credit mechanism to enable exporters to pay the tax in advance of receiving payment for the goods had not been put in place. We were not always aware of the administrative shortcomings and even when we were, we were perhaps too quick to accept the Russians' promise that everything would work out all right. The problem of poor implementation and IMF tolerance of it were to plague economic reforms throughout the 1990s.

After the February mission, the IMF was worried that the CBR was not fully committed to the strict monetary policies that we and the government believed were necessary to bring inflation down after the price jump in January. The CBR reported to the Supreme Soviet, not the government. (Gaidar had tried and failed in November 1991 to change this.) The Chairman, Georgy Matiukhin, had been nominated to his post by the Chairman of the Supreme Soviet, Ruslan Khasbulatov, who was not generally supportive of the government's reforms. As interenterprise arrears rose during the first few months of 1992 and enterprises sought more credit from banks, he came under increasing pressure from banks and enterprises, backed by the Supreme Soviet, to ease monetary policy.

Camdessus invited Matiukhin to Washington for a few days in March to give him some relief from the pressures of Moscow and enable us to spend time explaining why tight monetary policy was essential. He was friendly and listened to us, without showing any of the resentment we sometimes encountered among Russians who did not think they had anything to learn from foreigners. He mostly kept his views to himself, perhaps because he lacked confidence in discussing monetary policy. (He had been at the CBR only since August 1991. Although a professor of economics, he had little experience of central banking or market economies.) We thought he understood what the CBR should be doing about monetary policy, although the political constraints on him at home were considerable and the lack of coordination with the other countries in the ruble area was a major problem. In the event the CBR did fairly well in the first few months of the year. Base money growth and inflation both fell, though the latter did not fall as rapidly as it did in Eastern European countries at the same stage of their reforms. However, this gradual improvement was not to last.

Opposition to the reforms grew rapidly during the first few months of 1992. Most of the powerful groups in the country were adversely affected by the reforms. The military-industrial sector had its budget cut drastically. Industry suffered from the cuts in the state capital budget. Public sector wages did not rise nearly as much as prices, seriously squeezing the real incomes of teachers, doctors and other government workers. The real value of savings had been almost wiped out by inflation. The sharp changes in relative prices, coupled with the continued fall in production, created large losses and

liquidity problems in some enterprises, to which they responded by not paying suppliers and sometimes even workers. Arrears accumulated throughout
the economy.

Not surprisingly, there was much lobbying of Yeltsin, the government
and the CBR to give special concessions and financial support to one
group or another. Opposition to the reforms at the political level was led by
Khasbulatov and Aleksandr Rutskoi, the Vice-President, and came to a head
at the 6th Congress of People's Deputies of the Russian Federation in April.
Although overwhelmingly hostile to the government's economic policies,
the Congress passed a resolution supporting the reforms after Gaidar and the
government threatened to resign. But this was only a tactical retreat because
the Congress did not want to have to take responsibility for economic policy
and so a compromise was found that enabled Gaidar and his team to remain
in the government. Pressures for a change in direction continued unabated.

It was during the weeks leading up to the April Congress meeting that the
IMF began to be blamed for the policies of the government. Such accusations
were in the tradition of the Russian political debate in which it was always
popular to blame foreigners and their lackeys in government for undermining
the Russian state for their own nefarious purposes, regardless of whether it
was true or not. Russia's long history of duplicitous leaders had understand-
ably inclined its people towards conspiratorial rather than straightforward
explanations of events. The Soviet era had added a deep suspicion of foreigners to the mix. The government was castigated by its opponents in the
Congress as monetarist, in part to suggest that it was doing our bidding. From
our point of view, the accusations of an IMF plot were absurd because the
economic reforms were obviously fully owned by the government and our
influence on them at that stage was only marginal. But the idea stuck in the
public's consciousness, and we had to live with it for the next decade or more.

The major Western powers were, of course, intensely concerned about
developments in Russia. The government sought large scale financial
assistance from them. The G7 recognized the importance of supporting
the unprecedented economic transformation taking place in Russia but it
responded cautiously. This reflected doubts about whether the reforms would
succeed even with their help, as well as fiscal problems at home. Moreover,
unlike at the end of the second world war when the US set up the Marshall
Plan, there was no one ready to take the lead in crafting an imaginative solution. President Bush was in the last year of his first term and was preoccupied
with his reelection. One thing everyone could agree on was that the IMF
should have a major role, both to convey policy advice and to provide money.

President Bush and Chancellor Kohl eventually announced in early April
1992 a $24 billion package of assistance. Over $10 billion of this was to come
from a $6 billion stabilization fund to be financed by loans from rich IMF

member countries and linked to an IMF loan, and $4.5 billion from international financial institutions (IMF, World Bank and EBRD). Another $11 billion was to come from bilateral creditors, mostly G7 countries but including some other countries, and the rest from debt relief. Although the details were never made public, it appeared that the bilateral credits were to be mostly disbursements from existing commitments to the Soviet Union. Most of these were tied export credits and not the kind of assistance that would help the government ease the pain of the reforms, although there was some humanitarian assistance, mostly grain and other foods. With a stabilization fund not being available to finance the government, and the money from the international financial institutions depending on conditions that would take months to agree and implement, the great bulk of the eye-catching $24 billion could not reach Russia immediately, or even by the end of the year. The government needed money quickly to prevent a massive collapse in the economy and cushion the fall in living standards. The failure of the G7 to provide this was a disappointment to Yeltsin and Gaidar, and was much criticized by their foreign economic advisers, especially Sachs and Åslund.

There were various consequences of the IMF being given a leading role by the G7. First, the Russians knew that they had to agree their macroeconomic policies with us if they were to obtain G7 financial assistance. As a result, we had good substantive policy discussions with them. Secondly, the G7 wanted to keep tabs on our activities. In practice this meant more reports by the staff and management, not only through the normal route of the IMF Board but also through ad hoc channels. For example, I was asked at a couple of days' notice to attend a meeting of G7 deputies in London in January, and I visited Bonn in February to brief German officials (Germany held the G7 chair in 1992).

Thirdly, the western media took a close interest in IMF activities in Russia. For example, in 1992 the *New York Times* reported whenever the IMF had a mission in Moscow and when senior Russians visited the IMF in Washington (although they missed Matiukhin's visit). They noted some of the measures that the IMF urged Russia to take, such as raising energy prices more rapidly and cutting the budget deficit. The tone of much of the reporting implied that the IMF already had much more influence in Russia than we knew to be the case. This in turn may have contributed to the exaggerated perceptions in Russia of the IMF's role. The western media coverage was more extensive than was the case with IMF work in most member countries. We responded by being more open with the media than was traditional in the IMF at that time.

I headed missions to Moscow in May and June 1992 to try to agree with the Russians on a detailed program of policies that would be the basis for financial support that Russia's membership, finalized on June 1, made possible. There was ready agreement on many reforms, including the important unification of the exchange rate which took effect in July. There were two main problem areas, the ruble area and the budget.

The Russians wanted either to control monetary policy and emission throughout the ruble area through the CBR, or for the other countries to introduce their own currencies. As we saw in chapter 2, they opposed a cooperative approach to monetary policy in which control was shared between the countries in the ruble area. And they were not ready, either politically or technically, to force the other countries out of the ruble area. For our part, we could not support a Russia-run ruble area as it was opposed by the other countries. Nor were we willing to put pressure on the others to introduce their own currencies, which the Russians would have liked. The rather feeble compromise we settled on was that Russia would seek to make a series of bilateral agreements with other ruble area countries on their monetary policies and emissions. In practice this did not happen.

As Russia did not have full control over monetary policy, the IMF's loan to Russia in 1992 was limited to only $1 billion. Camdessus and Gaidar agreed in Washington on 17–18 June that this loan would be the first stage. It would be followed by a second stage in which Russia would have obtained full control over monetary policy and the IMF would lend a much larger amount, and a third stage in which Russia would peg its currency to a suitable major currency and the IMF would lend money for a currency stabilization fund.

The growing opposition to the government's economic policies had caused a sharp rise in expenditures in the second quarter, especially in the defense sector and subsidies to producers and consumers. The government was reluctant to agree to increases in revenues, especially from the oil and gas sectors, to bring the budget deficit for the year as a whole down to a reasonable amount. While the reformers, including Gaidar, favored higher oil and gas prices and higher taxation, the increasingly powerful energy and industrial lobbies were opposed. We were prepared to raise the planned budget deficit for the year from the level agreed in February, but we felt that we could not raise it as much as the government proposed because of the implications for inflation. No agreement on policies was therefore reached in my June mission.

After I returned to Washington, G7 leaders privately urged the IMF to settle with Russia. (In the US, where Yeltsin was on a successful state visit, some of the pressure was public.) In response, Camdessus went to Moscow in early July and told Gaidar that he would need to produce a stronger program to obtain IMF support. The next day Yeltsin told a press conference that the IMF was trying to force Russia to its knees. A meeting between Camdessus and Yeltsin, their first one, lowered the temperature and eventually a compromise was found. But the economic policy program that was agreed was much weaker than had been envisaged in February, or than I had sought in the negotiations in the preceding weeks. The target for monthly inflation at the end of the year was raised from 1–3 percent in the February MEP to 10 percent and that for the budget deficit for 1992 from 1 percent to 10 percent of GDP. These changes were a measure of how far stabilization had fallen short of earlier intentions and of the government's reduced ability to bring the situation under control. We had experienced the first of many episodes in which "we wanted the best, but it turned out as always."

Throughout the year, but especially after April, the government was losing ground in its struggle with those who were opposed to macroeconomic stabilization and economic reforms. After the 6th Congress of People's Deputies in April, Yeltsin felt that he had to compromise with the opposition. In April he dismissed Gennady Burbulis as first deputy prime minister, which meant that Gaidar had less political cover, and in May he fired the fuel and energy minister, Vladimir Lopukhin, who had been advocating energy price liberalization. He brought Viktor Chernomyrdin, the chairman of Gazprom, into the government as deputy prime minister for fuel and energy and elevated Gaidar to be acting prime minister.

In June the Supreme Soviet fired Matiukhin as chairman of the CBR because he refused to reduce interest rates. Gaidar asked Camdessus whether he thought that Viktor Gerashchenko would be a suitable replacement. On the basis of our limited knowledge of Gerashchenko's apparently competent management of the State Bank (Gosbank) of the USSR in 1991, Camdessus did not raise any objection. Gerashchenko was appointed chairman of the CBR and turned out to be a major obstacle to macroeconomic stabilization in the next two years. Immediately after his appointment in July, he raised CBR money emission sharply because he believed that the decline in production and the rise in interenterprise arrears were the result of excessively tight money supply. The federal government and the CBR succumbed to pressure from virtually all sectors to provide more money. Inevitably inflation began to rise again a few months after the increase in monetary growth, and the threat of hyperinflation reappeared. Gaidar subsequently wrote that the government was in retreat between May and August and stabilization was coming apart at the seams. He also wrote that supporting Gerashchenko's appointment was one of his most serious mistakes of 1992.

The Board approved the first loan to Russia of $1 billion on 5 August on the basis of the macroeconomic policies that had been agreed in July. The implementation of these policies continued to deteriorate, and it became clear that even the weak targets agreed in July would not be met. However, there was an improvement in the fiscal and monetary situation in the last few months of 1992 and hyperinflation was averted.

Looking back at the first momentous year of economic reforms in Russia, the IMF's role was modest. We helped the government and CBR formulate their macroeconomic policies and communicate them to other governments through the documents prepared for the IMF's Board. We strengthened the government's hand when it was resisting pressures to loosen fiscal and monetary policies, especially in the difficult months leading up to the IMF's decision in August to lend the first $1 billion. But the government already had a reasonably clear idea of the policies it wanted to pursue. And the pressures on it to abandon or at least seriously modify those policies were too great for the IMF's countervailing weight to count for much.

I have often asked myself whether we could have done things differently during the period of exceptional politics to increase the chances that the reforms would be successful and reduce the risk of backsliding. Was our lending too little and too late, as alleged by some critics, especially those in Russia and outside who approved of our support of the government's policies? The main constraint on the size of our lending was the failure to resolve the ruble area problem. Beyond that, we were bound by the IMF's existing rules.

I explained in chapter 2 why we did not actively urge other countries in the first half of 1992 to introduce national currencies as the Russians wanted us to, nor encourage Russia to insulate itself from other ruble area countries. Even if there had been a rush of new currencies, they might not have been in place by the middle of the year to enable Russia to have full control over its own monetary policy and emissions. (Estonia, which was first to introduce its own currency, did not do so until June.) The IMF would still have been limited in how much it could lend.

We could have lent more if the IMF had been willing to relax its rules. It did just that a year later when it introduced the Systemic Transformation Facility (STF), under which it was empowered to lend more money to countries in transition on the basis of weaker policy conditions than were required for regular stand-by arrangements (SBAs). But in the first few months of 1992, the IMF's major members were not convinced that the potential gains from giving Russia, and other countries in transition, extra money through the IMF would be great enough to justify relaxing the rules. In part, this was because the seriousness of the economic situation had not been fully understood.

As for being too late, the IMF could not lend to Russia until it became a member at the beginning of June in record time. In principle, we could have approved a loan immediately afterwards, thereby saving two months, but there would have been little time for us or the Russians to craft a coherent economic program.

The truth is that the IMF was not the right instrument for channeling large amounts of public sector money into a fluid political and economic situation where the government was finding it increasingly difficult to keep its promises. Gaidar recognized this and wrote later that the IMF could not begin to handle the political problems associated with the economic policies of early 1992. The inevitable delay in Russia's membership anyway prevented the

IMF from lending during the critical months from January to April. Gaidar suggested that the G7 should have stepped forward with a bold initiative, but at the time it lacked visionary leaders. The two most important leaders, President Bush and Chancellor Kohl, were preoccupied with domestic issues that year: Bush with reelection and Kohl with unification.

My conclusion is that the IMF was not in a position to do much more than it did to support the government's reform efforts in the period of extraordinary politics in 1992. The forces undermining those efforts were already strong by May and growing all the time. Without more domestic support for its reform program, the government was always going to struggle to implement it, whatever we did. The lesson I learned then applies in most countries most of the time: foreign actors, even ones with the money and authority of the IMF, cannot always get their way. Yet it was our misfortune, and even more that of Gaidar and his team, to be blamed for what went wrong in Russia, when the blame should properly rest with the domestic opponents of reform.

AD HOC STABILIZATION, 1993–1994

Sergei Dubinin, who in 1994 was acting finance minister, in 1995 described macroeconomic policies from 1992 to the end of 1994 as gradualist, with policies being hardened in a phased manner to allow the continuation of some inflationary financing until enterprises were able to adjust to the new market conditions. I prefer to call it a period of ad hoc stabilization when the reformers were doing their best to stabilize the economy, winning battles whenever possible and otherwise retreating. The outcome was, at best, mixed. Inflation came down but remained high (an average monthly rate of more than 10 percent in 1994). The same was true of the budget deficit. Most targets in the economic programs we agreed with the authorities were missed. Output in the economy and living standards continued to fall.

Our frequent missions to Moscow to discuss economic developments and policies were led by Ernesto Hernández-Catá. He had a strong understanding of macroeconomics and the policies needed to stabilize economies in transition. He had a forthright style of communication and negotiation that went down well with the Russians. I was relieved to hand over leadership of the missions to him as I needed to pay more attention to our work on other countries in the region. I was also not as confident of my own qualities as a negotiator as I was of Ernesto's.

We found towards the end of 1992 that the government and CBR were unprepared to agree on macroeconomic policies for 1993 that would take another step towards stabilization. Yet such policies were necessary to meet the IMF's normal criteria for the larger loan that was envisaged by Camdessus and Gaidar when they met in June. Although the government officials who dealt directly with the IMF team were mostly Gaidar's people and supported tighter macroeconomic policies, they knew that effective power had shifted to political and economic interests that were opposed to such policies. They were therefore caught between the IMF that was pressing them to do what they too believed was in Russia's best interests and powerful Russian groups that had the ability to make life difficult for the officials. The tension under which they operated was to be a constant feature of the next six years or more.

For much of the 1990s, Yeltsin tried to straddle various different, often opposing, forces. In economic policy, there were the reformers who wanted to move quickly to a market economy and bring inflation under control using monetary and fiscal policies. These were our main counterparts. Opposing them were the representatives of the large enterprises that made up the bulk of the economy outside the service sector. They wanted to move to a market economy in a more gradual and controlled way that would not force sharp structural changes on enterprises or deprive them of opportunities to benefit financially from the distortions created by incomplete reforms. Although Yeltsin himself had a similar background to the latter group, he instinctively felt that Gaidar and the reformers were right. He was strengthened in this view by the support that Gaidar's approach received from the IMF, other international institutions and western leaders whom he trusted. (Yeltsin's instincts led him in surprising directions in other arenas too. For example, he was content to allow the press and TV to criticize him, which was quite unusual for a former communist apparatchik.)

One way that Yeltsin balanced the different forces was by having them all represented in the government. There was usually someone close to the enterprise view of economic policy in a senior position. For example, Oleg Soskovets, whose career had been largely spent in the metals industry, was first deputy prime minister from 1993 to 1996. When we met him on occasions, he did not disguise his disapproval of the policies that the reformers were promoting, still less that they listened to foreigners such as ourselves. Yeltsin did not insist that his governments stick to particular economic policies but rather allowed shifts to take place in response to political pressures. He usually signaled this by altering the balance of power between individuals and factions. For example, after the parliament refused to confirm Gaidar as prime minister in December 1992, Yeltsin appointed Viktor Chernomyrdin instead. Chernomyrdin had been deputy prime minister for fuel and power since May and had had a successful career in the oil and gas industry in the Soviet Union, including spells in the ministry overseeing it and as founder and first chairman of Gazprom. His views about macroeconomic policy when he became prime minister were probably similar to those of the state enterprise managers whose background he shared. Thus, he believed that the monetary economy was secondary to the real economy and money had to be provided by the government and CBR to keep production up. One of his first decisions at the end of 1992 was to freeze prices. Fortunately, wiser heads prevailed, and the decision was soon rescinded. Despite this inauspicious start, over the five years that he was Prime Minister, Chernomyrdin gradually came to understand the role of monetary and fiscal policies in maintaining macroeconomic stability. Camdessus' role in this transformation will be an interesting part of our story.

While Yeltsin was able to manage the opposition to Gaidar's reform policies within government by making tactical retreats from time to time, he faced a much bigger challenge from the opposition outside government. At the political level, it was concentrated in the Congress of People's Deputies, the highest legislative body, and the Supreme Soviet, which was the standing legislature. (These two bodies were part of the constitutional arrangements set up in Soviet times.) There was also opposition among the regional governors and from his vice-president Aleksandr Rutskoi.

As output and living standards deteriorated throughout 1992, the Supreme Soviet, led by the speaker Ruslan Khasbulatov, continually challenged Yeltsin for control of economic policy. In December, the Congress of People's Deputies refused to confirm Gaidar as prime minister, and he therefore left the government. Yeltsin and Khasbulatov agreed that there should be a referendum the following April and that Yeltsin's emergency powers should be extended until then. Yeltsin survived the vote of confidence in the referendum which also called for new legislative elections. The power struggle between Yeltsin and the parliament remained acute, with both sides attempting to make policy by issuing decrees and passing legislation. It came to a head in September 1993 when Yeltsin, with dubious constitutional authority, dissolved the Congress of People's Deputies and the Supreme Soviet. When the parliament dug in its heels, Yeltsin brought in the military in early October to shell their building. October 4 1993 was my mother's 90th birthday, which she celebrated with her children and grandchildren in Yorkshire. I spent the time shuttling between our family luncheon and the room next door where the dramatic events in Moscow were being shown on television. Although questions about what this all meant for the future of Russia and our work there were crowding into my head, I was still able to enjoy being with the family.

Yeltsin's show of force cleared the air and enabled him to consolidate power. A new constitution, the first since Soviet times, was adopted in December 1993 when elections to the State Duma, one of the two chambers of the new parliament, were also held. The outcome was not favorable for economic reforms. Gaidar's new Russia's Choice party received only 15.5 percent of the vote while parties opposed to his policies were in the majority. Gaidar had to resign from the post of First Deputy Prime Minister which he had assumed in September, only a few months before, when Yeltsin brought him back to strengthen the reform effort.

The conflict between the reformers in government and the opponents of reform in the Duma continued for many years thereafter. Although Yeltsin's instincts were to back the reformers, he continued to make compromises towards their opponents that undermined the reforms. He was also increasingly absent from the scene, partly because of health problems. I believe that the reforms would have been more successful if Yeltsin's health had been strong throughout the 1990s and he had shown the same resolution that he showed in his conflict with the parliament in 1992 and 1993.

The two years of ad hoc stabilization started well with the appointment of Boris Federov as finance minister in January 1993. He was a liberal economist who had started his career in Gosbank, the State Bank of the USSR, and subsequently worked at the EBRD. At the time of his appointment, he was Russia's Executive Director at the World Bank. Before he left Washington to take up his position as finance minister, he asked to speak to IMF staff. Ernesto Hernández-Catá and I crossed 19th Street in Washington to his office at the World Bank. We could hardly believe our ears when he told us that he intended to pursue a strict fiscal policy and he wanted our backing. The contrast between his aspirations and what was actually happening in Russia was so great that we wondered whether he knew what he was up against. But further discussion revealed that he did and that he intended to fight hard for his plans. Unfortunately, Federov only lasted a year. The failure of Gaidar's party in the December Duma elections meant that Gaidar had to resign in January 1994. Federov, who was unpopular with the parties that won the election, was forced to leave the government at the same time. He was succeeded as acting finance minister by his deputy, Sergei Dubinin.

Both Federov and Dubinin themselves favored restrictive policies and they used the need to agree with the IMF as a lever to persuade others in government and the CBR that such policies were in Russia's interests. In the early months of 1993 and 1994, Federov and Dubinin respectively were able to keep the situation under control by not paying the bills. During these periods they reached agreement with us about economic policies and the IMF Board approved loans under the STF in June 1993 and March 1994.

However, as soon as the loans had been approved, macroeconomic policies went out of control. In 1993, both monetary and fiscal policies were loosened sharply. In 1994, the bulk of the problem was on the fiscal side, with the CBR doing no more than monetizing the budget deficit. In both 1993 and 1994, it became increasingly difficult to contain the budget deficit by not paying bills as the year proceeded. A pattern became established whereby the reform-minded elements within government agreed to sensible macroeconomic policies with us in the early months of the year, and the government as a whole failed to implement those policies during the rest of the year. The main reason for this, of course, was that powerful groups within the ruling elites did not favor the policies that had been agreed to with the IMF. They took every opportunity to commit financial resources from the budget and the CBR to their favored sectors. There was also a seasonal character to some areas of expenditure, especially agriculture and the Northern Territories, with some major unbudgeted expenditures appearing after the middle of the year (supplies for the Northern Territories had to be shipped in the summer months). In addition, as we came to understand, there was a tradition inherited from Soviet times, if not earlier, that agreements on paper were not taken too seriously.

We were not the only people to have to grapple with the casual attitude at that time to honoring contracts. Many foreign organizations and companies operating in Russia were trying to deal with it. I received a visit from a British engineering consultant whose small company had invested much time and money in a project to rehabilitate a Russian port. Despite the fact that he had proper contracts and had agreements with the relevant government departments at central and local levels, a Russian company pushed him out without any payment once it saw that the project would be profitable. Such stories were common.

In addition to our disappointment because of the failure to implement agreed macroeconomic policies, our people who were working with the Russians at the operational level experienced their own frustrations. In most IMF member countries, IMF staff work closely with their counterparts on the details of economic policies. Many Russian officials, especially the younger ones who were keen to learn how monetary and fiscal policies were made in market economies, did cooperate closely with IMF staff. But in general, we were kept at arm's length from the implementation of economic policy. The main reason for this was no doubt that the government was itself unsure whether it would be able to stick to its policy commitments. It therefore did not want us to know too much about what was really going on. Another reason was that the government and CBR did not always operate smoothly. Many officials took time to understand the new policies and some of them did not like them. The reformers who agreed policies with us were not always effective at ensuring that the policies were implemented, especially when opponents of the policies were able to sabotage them. Finally, Soviet traditions of secrecy and distrust of foreigners persisted. Moreover, the humiliation felt because of the loss of superpower status, the collapse of the economy and the need to borrow from the IMF naturally created some tension in relations between the IMF and Russia.

The US administration took a keen interest in our work in 1993 and 1994. In early 1993, Clinton had succeeded Bush as US President and put renewed energy behind US efforts to ensure that Russia's market economy and democratic transformations succeeded. There was increased concern coming from the US about delays in reaching agreements between the IMF and Russia about the next loan. In addition to the usual private contacts, the US used public channels to convey its aspirations for the IMF's work in Russia. In the run up to Clinton's first meeting with Yeltsin in Vancouver in April 1993, the US coordinated with other G7 countries an announcement of a major financial assistance package for Russia, which included $7.1 billion from the IMF together with a stabilization fund of $6 billion.

Although the official US position was that the IMF should agree strong reform policies with Russia before agreeing on a loan, some administration officials were quoted as saying in private that the IMF should be less stringent in its policy demands. Vice President Gore had some sympathy for the view that the IMF was too tough on Russia. In a visit to Moscow with Gore after the elections in December 1993, Strobe Talbot, the Deputy Secretary of State, said that the US wanted to promote "less shock and more therapy." This line was opposed by the US Treasury because it undermined the position of the Russian reformers. It may, indeed, have contributed to the hardening of the government's opposition to tight macroeconomic policies, and hence to the resignation of Gaidar and Federov in January 1994.

The failure of macroeconomic stabilization policies came to a head in late 1994. The growing realization in financial markets that fiscal policy was out of control led to a sharp reduction in international reserves as market participants moved out of rubles. Eventually the CBR stopped intervening and the ruble collapsed on 11 October when it fell 27 percent in one day. There was a partial rebound in the next two days, but the damage had been done. The collapse on Black Tuesday, as 11 October came to be called, had a traumatic effect on policy makers and symbolized the end of the period of ad hoc stabilization.

Beginning in 1993 and continuing during subsequent years, we tried various ways of strengthening our influence over the implementation of policies and improving communications between us and our Russian counterparts. Increasingly over time, the IMF Board delayed giving its approval to loan disbursements until as many of the agreed policy changes as possible had actually been implemented. This insistence on prior actions was our response to the failure of the Russians to implement agreed measures once we had disbursed loans.

In 1993 we sent a very senior economist, Burke Dillon, to head our small office in Moscow. The IMF normally operates with very small local offices comprising just one or occasionally two mid-career economists from the permanent IMF staff. The bulk of the substantive work with a country is carried out by visiting missions from IMF headquarters in Washington. In Russia we hoped that a senior person would be able to establish closer relations with senior policy makers which would be mutually beneficial. Burke had worked in various parts of the IMF, knew our work well and had an outgoing personality that enabled her to establish good relations with her Russian counterparts. Unfortunately, she stayed less than two years because she was promoted to a director level position in Washington, the first woman to be a director in the IMF. She ended her career in the number two position in the Inter-American Development Bank.

We encouraged all our economists to develop good personal relations with their counterparts. Many of them were successful. For example, Piroska Nagy-Mohacsi, one of our fiscal economists, had a very cooperative relationship with Mrs. Kudelina, the head of the economics department in the Ministry of Finance (and later deputy minister of defense) between 1991 and 1994. Dubinin remarked to Camdessus during one of the latter's visits to Moscow: "There are two people in the world who understand Russia's fiscal policies and accounts: our Mrs. Kudelina and your Mrs. Nagy." Siddharth Tiwari, who was based in Moscow, spent part of each day in the CBR where he worked directly with Tatiana Paramonova at her request. He began in 1993 when Paramonova was the deputy governor with responsibility for monetary policy and continued after she became acting governor following the collapse of the ruble on Black Tuesday in October 1994. We instructed him not to tell us anything confidential about his work with Paramonova. The feedback from her was that the arrangement was very useful. Siddharth later held very senior positions in the IMF, first as Secretary and then as director of the Strategy, Policy and Review Department.

In the early 1990s, we made various attempts to explain to Russian and Western academics the reasons for our support of the policies of Gaidar and his successors who were pursuing reforms. For example, in Washington I met Leonid Abalkin, who had led a team that produced a reform program for Gorbachev. Like many of the older generation of Soviet reformers who had advised Gorbachev, he favored gradual reform. It was difficult for those people to support the radical reforms of much younger men with mainly academic backgrounds. The IMF's External Relations Department organized a seminar in Moscow in 1994 at which I and others explained why we supported the government's reforms. The main guest speaker was Nikolai Petrakov, who had also advised Gorbachev, but was not sympathetic to the government's reforms. I doubt that we speakers from the IMF caused him to alter his views. In Washington in 1997 we met Michael Intriligator, an American economist who had helped to organize a public statement in Russia by some Gorbachev era economists and American Nobel Prize winners just before the second round of the Presidential election in Russia in 1996. The extraordinary statement blamed the reformers' program for generating "economic collapse, a strengthening of the mafia and growing political instability" and called for a greater role for the government and for measures to slow down the transition. Despite its obvious political intent, it is unlikely that it had any impact on the voters who a few days later elected Yeltsin over Zyuganov, whose program was closer to that of the statement signatories than was Yeltsin's. We were unable to persuade Intriligator that the situation was much more complicated and that he and the Nobel Prize winners (Kenneth Arrow, Lawrence Klein, Wassily Leontief, Douglass North and James Tobin) were mistaken.

Michel Camdessus and, after he joined the IMF in 1994, Stanley Fischer spent a considerable amount of time talking to the Russian leaders. The relationship between Camdessus and Chernomyrdin was an important part of our overall relations with Russia while the latter was prime minister from 1993 to 1998. It did not begin well. They first met in Washington in September 1993 when Chernomyrdin was on an official visit to the US. He had obviously been briefed to complain about the delay in our reaching an agreement that would allow the IMF to lend Russia another $1.5 billion. But instead of emphasizing how much Russia had done to bring its economic policies into line with what we thought was needed, he launched into a long speech about how difficult conditions were in Russia. At one point he opened up a large map of Russia to illustrate his point that the country had a huge Arctic region, which the government had to supply with food and materials. His demand for early financial support from the IMF, expressed forcefully in a typically Russian manner, did not go down well with Camdessus. After Camdessus suggested that Chernomyrdin had as much to learn about macroeconomic policy as he (Camdessus) had to learn about Russia, they agreed to meet for mutual educational sessions.

Chernomyrdin quickly realized the need for a different approach and decided that he should seek to establish a closer personal relationship with Camdessus. He invited Camdessus to join him in March 1994 on a hunting trip outside Moscow so that they could get to know each other. The way the invitation came was interesting. It was handed over to Camdessus in February in Frankfurt, where he was attending a finance ministers meeting, by Peter Castenfelt, a foreign advisor of Chernomyrdin's. It was never clear what Castenfelt's position was. An investment banker in London, he seemed to have friends in high places in Moscow, especially the security services. He occasionally passed us messages about how unpopular the economic policies that we were supporting were in many parts of the government. This added to our picture of a divided and weak government. Chernomyrdin apparently wished to avoid committing himself to an open invitation until he knew that it would be accepted. This was my introduction to the use of back channels for negotiations.

Castenfelt's name appeared in the Western press in 1999 in connection with another back-channel operation, this time one with major international implications. The Russians sent him to Belgrade with a message for President Milošević about the limits of Russian support for the Serbian campaign in Kosovo. Soon after, Milošević received President Ahtisaari of Finland and Chernomyrdin, who had recently lost his position as Prime Minister. The outcome was that Serbia withdrew its forces from Kosovo and NATO halted its bombing campaign in Serbia.

Back channels were one of the features of Soviet negotiations that continued into Russian times. We picked up an understanding of Russian negotiating style as we went along. It was nevertheless useful to read in 1998 a new book by Jerrold Schecter that set it all out clearly. It was originally prepared for American government officials who had to deal with Soviet officials. After the demise of the Soviet Union it was deemed safe to publish it. I gave copies to all my senior staff who led missions to former Soviet Union countries.

Camdessus' hunting trip in 1994 was the first of five annual events, all in the winter months when the temperature was below freezing. I took part in the last three together with Sergei Dubinin who was chairman of the CBR in 1995–1998. It was interesting to savor for a brief moment the lifestyle of Russian and, before them, Soviet leaders. We were told that Brezhnev had been a frequent visitor to the same hunting lodge. In other parts of the former Soviet Union we were often told that Brezhnev had frequented a particular house in a local beauty spot. He certainly had a fondness for building comfortable accommodations in attractive locations, although all the stories connecting him to places might not have been true.

The main lodge was a modern, beautifully designed and built traditional log cabin on two floors. Our sleeping accommodation was in separate buildings; in the early years Camdessus and I stayed in an old fashioned one storey building that looked a little decrepit, but later we were housed in smart, newly built traditional log cabins. We each went hunting alone apart from a driver and huntsman to show us the ropes. We were driven to small clearings in the forest where we sat in raised cabins to await the arrival of the deer and wild boar, which were attracted by the food that had been scattered on the snow earlier. Sometimes the animals were reluctant to come to my clearing and I grew increasingly cold and miserable, especially after it got dark during evening hunts. The arrival of animals provided a bit of excitement even for as reluctant a hunter as me. It was nevertheless a relief when the shooting was over. The huntsman summoned the animal disposal truck on his radio after the kill, and we celebrated with bread and sausage washed down with vodka. Following the hunt, the principals all met up again for a meal and some male bonding. Sometimes we ate outside where, despite freezing temperatures, we were kept warm by huge fires and remarkably warm clothes designed for the Russian military. Once we engaged in shooting practice in the forest where targets had been placed on trees and we could choose from a bewildering variety of rifles, revolvers, pistols, and laser-guided weapons. Another time we shared a Russian steam bath where, as the temperature rose, I was reassured by the presence of Chernomyrdin's doctor. On reporting the event to my wife later, I said that it was a little embarrassing to be naked in front of my boss; but on reflection I realized that it was much more embarrassing for him to be naked in front of me. Although the tradition calls for participants in steam baths to roll in the snow afterwards, only Dubinin in our party was brave enough to do this.

While Camdessus, myself and, I suspect, Dubinin approached these trips more as a duty than a pleasure, Chernomyrdin clearly loved them and was usually in a mellow mood despite all the worries of his job. There was plenty of time for leisurely conversations about a range of issues going beyond macroeconomic policy in Russia. For example, Chernomyrdin was especially interested in Camdessus' views on international economic issues. Through their conversations they developed a mutual understanding that enabled them to communicate effectively in the many business meetings they had over the years. Many years later Camdessus wrote that, while neither of them went "beyond their mandates in the name of friendship," the humanity of their contacts made their work together easier. It was interesting for me to see Chernomyrdin's views change over the years from those of an enterprise manager concerned about maintaining production to a position where he understood the importance of containing inflation through restrictive monetary and fiscal policies. His relationship with Camdessus contributed to the learning process.

Stanley Fischer also developed close relations with Russian leaders, especially Anatoli Chubais, who took over responsibility for macroeconomic policy at the deputy prime minister level from Aleksandr Shokhin in November 1994. One of Fischer's first foreign trips as First Deputy Managing Director of the IMF was to Moscow in December 1994, where Chubais was his main counterpart.

In addition to prior actions and the efforts we put into personal contacts and close working relations with Russian counterparts at all levels, we tried one other way of strengthening our influence over the implementation of agreed policies. Beginning with the loan that the IMF Board approved in April 1995, we set monthly targets for the key monetary and fiscal policy variables for which targets in IMF agreements would normally be set quarterly. The idea was that monthly targets would oblige the government and CBR to strive harder to keep policies on track. Unlike with quarterly targets, they could not risk allowing deviations in the hope that they could be brought back into line by the end-of-month deadline. Monthly targets also meant that IMF teams would go to Moscow each month to check on performance and would recommend that the next monthly tranche of the loan would be disbursed if the targets were being met. We could warn the Russians about pending problems before it was too late.

But we are getting ahead of the story. Up to the end of 1994, the implementation of macroeconomic policies agreed with the IMF was poor. The underlying problem was that the government was divided. It contained both reformers whose policies we supported and people who believed that the government should provide more finance to enterprises, through tax holidays, credits and subsidies, in the difficult conditions they faced. Chernomyrdin, whose own commitment to the restrictive monetary and fiscal policies that he signed up to in agreements with the IMF was weak, usually gave way to the latter factions.

We were not successful in significantly improving the implementation of macroeconomic policies. However, we were developing closer relations with our Russian counterparts and were disseminating knowledge about how to design and manage macroeconomic policies to a growing number of officials, not just the top few reform-minded people. Our technical assistance experts were also helping with the modernization of the CBR, tax policy, tax administration, the creation of a Treasury and other reforms. Over time these efforts contributed to better macroeconomic policies.

While our team working on Russia had to work hard, and had plenty of frustrations and disappointments, the knowledge that their work was very important for the IMF as well as for Russia provided some compensation. They did, however, have some time to relax. One valuable outcome of conversations that took place during their off-duty times in Moscow was the discovery that a number of them were amateur musicians. Led by Ernesto, the mission chief and a bass guitarist, they formed a small blues band in Washington called The Fundamentals. (Economists refer to the underlying economic forces behind observed developments, such as exchange rate movements, as the fundamentals.) The band played at social functions in the IMF, such as the annual party for all the staff at the end of the year, as well as at private events. In addition to Ernesto, it included Robert Rennhack, Brian Aitken and, as vocalist, Dan Citrin, all of whom were members of the Russia team.

FLAWED STABILIZATION, 1995–1998

The Russians' response to Black Tuesday in October 1994 was swift. Both Yeltsin and Chernomyrdin were determined to avoid another currency collapse. Yeltsin initiated personnel changes and endorsed changes in economic policy. Gerashchenko resigned from the CBR and was replaced by Paramonova as acting chairperson. Shokhin and Dubinin were fired from the government, and Chubais was promoted to first deputy prime minister with responsibility for all economic policy, not just privatization as before. Macroeconomic policy was tightened significantly. Most striking was the decree preventing any CBR financing of the budget deficit. From now on, any deficit had to be financed by borrowing in domestic markets or abroad. Monetary policy was also tightened through higher interest rates and reserve requirements. Although we did not know it at the time, such changes in policy had been under discussion before Black Tuesday but they were overtaken by events. Now the political moment was ripe, and Yeltsin was prepared to back tighter policies. Moreover, for the first time the government and CBR agreed on the objectives of macroeconomic policy. Chubais and Paramonova were committed to bringing macroeconomic policies under control and were tough enough to withstand some of the pressures.

The policy shift worked. The budget deficit was reduced in 1995. Money supply decelerated and inflation declined. The tighter monetary policies led to an inflow of foreign exchange, appreciation of the ruble and a rise in the foreign currency reserves of the CBR. The exchange rate was fixed in a corridor in July 1995 to prevent too much appreciation that could damage competitiveness, and also to guard against a subsequent depreciation. However, all was not well. Output and living standards continued to decline. And, in the macroeconomic policy area, the government failed to raise revenues as much as planned. It was therefore forced to hold expenditures down, which it did in part by allowing its wage and pension payments to fall into arrears. This was merely a way of postponing the problem and it came back to haunt them.

Faced with continued shortfalls in revenues throughout the period from 1995 to 1998, the government responded by running bigger deficits than planned and borrowing to finance them. Unlike in 1992 to 1994 when much of the borrowing was from the CBR, this time the borrowing was from financial markets in Russia and abroad, as well as from the IMF and other IFIs. At least this allowed the CBR to pursue a tight monetary policy that sustained a strong ruble and brought inflation down further. But it stored up trouble for the future and was an important cause of the crisis in August 1998. Much of the market borrowing was at short maturities and high interest rates. Markets' skepticism about the government's ability to solve its fiscal problem grew, especially after the Asian crisis broke in 1997 and focused attention on other vulnerable economies. In these conditions of dwindling confidence, the government found it increasingly difficult to roll over its debts and the CBR was losing foreign currency reserves rapidly. By the middle of August 1998, the crisis was unavoidable. One bright spot in this sorry story was that inflation continued to decline because of tight monetary policy centered on the ruble peg. But this stabilization was seriously flawed because of the inadequate fiscal policy that eventually brought it to a crashing halt.

The IMF was more closely engaged with the Russians in 1995–1998 than had been the case in 1992–1994. Chubais and Paramonova understood better than their predecessors how to use the IMF to improve policy making and implementation. They embraced monthly monitoring by the IMF because it strengthened their hand within the government. Personal relationships, such as those between Chernomyrdin and Camdessus, and Chubais and Fischer, and Tiwari's role as an adviser to Paramonova also helped communications between us and the Russians. Yusuke Horiguchi, who led our monthly missions to Russia in 1995–1997, became a familiar and trusted figure in Moscow and, with his team, was very effective in ensuring that the IMF's position was understood. Tom Wolf, who succeeded Burke Dillon as head of our Moscow office in 1995, and his team comprising (at different times) Alejandro Santos, Siddharth Tiwari, Augusto Lopez-Claros, Gunnar Tersman and Tom Richardson, maintained good communications with our Russian counterparts at a lower level. Finally, of course, the larger sums of money that the IMF was able to disburse in these years than in 1992–1994 helped to keep us in the picture in Russia.

While the bulk of the credit for the improved performance of economic policy in 1995 was attributable to the Russians, we felt that our advice and the discipline provided by the monthly targets and disbursements of our money played a role. The polite and quietly spoken Horiguchi was most persuasive when explaining the importance of achieving the monthly targets for the budget and monetary aggregates. Not that everything was to our satisfaction. We would have preferred the planned budget deficit to have been lower so as to leave less need for fiscal consolidation in later years. We were disappointed that revenue collections were lower than planned, and that wages, pensions and other important expenditures therefore had to be postponed. But on balance, our assessment was that macroeconomic policy was implemented fairly well in difficult circumstances in 1995.

Two important developments in 1995 deserve special mention because many people have criticized the IMF's support for the government's policies. In July the government and the CBR announced that they would hold the exchange rate within a preannounced corridor. The IMF staff were divided on the advisability of this. Some feared that weak monetary and fiscal policies would eventually undermine the attempt to hold the exchange rate. Others believed that pegging the exchange rate would itself provide additional discipline so that monetary and fiscal policies would be stronger than otherwise. Fischer held this view, partly because of the success of exchange rate-based stabilization policies in Israel and some South American countries.

As discussed in chapter 3, our general approach to exchange rate policy was pragmatic. We were ready to accept Russia's choice of exchange rate regime provided that monetary and fiscal policies supported whatever regime was adopted. Thus, although the IMF advised the Russians to retain the floating rate for the time being, we also made clear that we would officially support the pegging of the ruble if that was the route the authorities chose. After the Russians decided to hold the rate in a corridor, Horiguchi's mission in July worked with them to design a monetary policy framework to accompany the new exchange rate policy. As shown by the 1998 crisis, the skeptics were right. But in 1995 when Chubais and Paramonova seemed to be getting macroeconomic policies under greater control, it was difficult for the IMF not to support them.

Towards the end of 1995, the government announced a scheme, subsequently called loans-for-shares, under which banks lent money to the government on the security of attractive state assets such as oil enterprises. When the government failed to repay the loans a year later, the banks took possession of the assets. As the market value of the assets rose much higher than the valuation when they were first collateralized, the scheme has been heavily criticized for giving away valuable public property to a few wealthy bankers. Chrystia Freeland's book about it was aptly called *The Sale of the Century*.

We knew about the scheme some months before it was announced and expressed concerns to the government about its lack of transparency, scope for collusion in the auctions that set the prices of the assets, and asset-stripping. But we did not strongly oppose the scheme in public or in private. We viewed it as a particular method of privatization. As we supported privatization in general and deferred to the World Bank on methods of privatization, we did not put our foot down. I rarely remember the precise words I have used in a particular situation. But I clearly recall what I said to Fischer when we passed in the corridor one day. He asked me what I thought about the scheme. "It stinks," I said, but then went on to argue that it was not our business to have a big fight over it.

To some critics of economic reforms in Russia, the loans-for-shares scheme symbolizes everything that went wrong. They argue that valuable assets were given to political cronies in shady deals, thereby creating a class of oligarchs with more economic clout than the state itself. The arrogance and power of the oligarchs led in turn to their not paying taxes and hence to the government's financial problems and the 1998 crisis. Moreover, the perceived injustice of the new distribution of wealth and power helped to give economic reforms a bad name. Many of these critics would add that the IMF should have stopped the scheme. The counterargument is that it was necessary to create quickly a powerful property-owning class that would build a bulwark against the return of communism, as they in fact did by financing

Yeltsin's reelection campaign against the communist Gennadi Zyuganov in 1996. In addition to the political angle, the argument was made that the oligarchs deserved to be rewarded for the risks they were taking in lending to the government on the strength of collateral that was not obviously undervalued at the time, given the chaotic state of the economy.

One's position in this debate depends partly on the weight one attaches to avoiding excessive inequalities of income and wealth, and partly on one's assessment of the importance of a strong capitalist class to create new political and economic realities. Not surprisingly, Western observers have tended to split between traditional left and right groupings. At the time, while being concerned about the social and economic consequences of assets being concentrated in the hands of small groups of wealthy and well-connected people, I accepted the argument that it would help to prevent a return to communism and a planned economy. I hoped that Russia might evolve as the United States did at the end of the nineteenth century and the beginning of the twentieth century when trusts were broken up and legislation introduced to reduce the power of the "robber barons." The oligarchs themselves were aware that they could not expect to continue indefinitely to operate as they had done. Kagalovsky, who went into business after leaving government service in 1994, said to me over a private dinner in Moscow in November 1997: "You know, John, there are only a few more years when our business can grow by acquiring assets at very low prices. After that, we will have to operate like regular businesses in a market economy regulated by the law."

However, the power of the oligarchs was not significantly reduced over the following two or more decades. Although Putin reduced their influence in the political sphere, he allowed them to continue to exert their power in the economy. Kagalovsky himself, despite going into self-imposed exile in London and France after his boss, Mikhail Khodorkovsky, was arrested in 2003, remained very wealthy. His seventeenth century house in Chelsea in London was on the market in 2020 for £50 million. Many oligarchs have become important philanthropists, as Elisabeth Schimpfössl has explained in *Rich Russians*. But, as a class, as I explained in chapter 3, they have used their economic power and influence over policy to maintain their oligopolistic positions in the economy and limit the scope for small and medium sized enterprises to grow, with adverse effects on the growth of the economy as a whole.

I find it difficult to weigh up the malign impact of the oligarchy, and extreme inequality in general, on society and the economy now against what might have been a much worse outcome had loans-for-shares not taken place and the political and economic reforms of the first half of the 1990s been reversed. I might be uncertain about this, but I am clear that the IMF could not have done much to improve, still less prevent, the loans-for-shares scheme.

We did not have the expertise to dig into the details of asset valuations. Nor would the government have allowed us to have any influence over the design or implementation of the scheme.

The loan that the IMF approved in April 1995, amounting to about $6.6 billion, was fully disbursed over the following 12 months. During this period, we started discussions with the Russians about economic policies over the next three years that would allow us to agree to a new loan which would be disbursed over the three years under the IMF's Extended Fund Facility. The idea underlying such medium-term loans was that there would be more time to implement some of the needed structural reforms than was possible in a single year. Together with World Bank colleagues, we discussed with the Russians policies in a wide range of areas, including the banking sector, energy tax reform, agriculture, natural monopolies and health and education, and agreed on a broad policy agenda.

However, our major preoccupation was with fiscal policy. The government should not continue to hold down borrowing by failing to pay its bills. Not only did this cause distress among unpaid workers and pensioners, it also contributed to financial indiscipline throughout the economy. Enterprises reckoned that they did not have to pay their bills if the government was not paying its bills. Nor was it wise for the government to increase borrowing to finance needed expenditures. The cost of borrowing was high, and indebtedness could not rise indefinitely, as was to become all too clear in 1998. While some rationalization of expenditures was possible, especially the subsidies that still had some features of the non-market Soviet system, the main solution to the fiscal problem had to be an increase in revenue collections. Our interlocutors in the government agreed with this analysis and were willing to aim for much higher revenues and targets of 4, 3 and 2 percent of GDP for the budget deficits of 1996, 1997 and 1998 respectively. However, they must have worried in private about whether they could ever hit those targets.

Before the final agreement between Russia and the IMF about the policies to support a medium-term loan, there was a major political setback. In the Duma elections of December 1995, the Communist party came first, and another party opposed to the economic reforms that we were discussing with the government came second. Chernomyrdin's centrist party came third with only 10 percent of the votes cast and Gaidar's party failed to win enough votes to qualify for representation in the Duma. Yeltsin responded by firing Chubais from the government in January 1996 and appointing in his place Vladimir Kadannikov as first deputy prime minister with responsibility for the economy. Kadannikov was CEO of Avtovaz, one of the big car manufacturers, and had the industrialists' view that macroeconomic stabilization policies were a mistake. These policies, usually referred to as monetarism in the Russian discourse, were perceived by many to be responsible for the declining living standards of recent years. Yeltsin was going to run for reelection in June and needed to send a signal that he was opposed to monetarism.

The reassurances of our counterparts that the reforms would continue after the change of government lacked conviction. The big question was which policies was Yeltsin going to support, those in the program we were discussing with the government or those favored by the Kadannikov faction, and did he have the political authority to prevail? Our proposed EFF loan was relevant to this question. It could be used to persuade Yeltsin to stick to the reform program as continued IMF lending would strengthen his position in the election. The G7 and other countries wanted Yeltsin to prevail and were therefore pushing for an agreement between the IMF and the Russians. The US as usual made its position clear, with President Clinton saying publicly in January when Chernomyrdin was in Washington lobbying for a new IMF loan: "I believe that the loan will go through, and I believe that it should." With the pressure from the G7, the need for financial support from the IMF and other foreign sources and perhaps his own reformist sympathies, Yeltsin formally agreed to the reform program. At his meeting with Camdessus in Moscow in February, he signed a letter to Camdessus promising his complete support for the program. This enabled us to go ahead with the EFF loan. It also allowed others to lend to Russia. Two important loans were those from the French and German governments in April that Russia used to pay off arrears of wages and pensions thus improving Yeltsin's chances of being reelected.

The IMF was criticized for lending to Russia ahead of an election that would be likely to produce extravagant promises of more government expenditure that would undermine the agreed macroeconomic stabilization policies. It was suggested that we were taking sides by helping the government. We argued that Russia's good performance during 1995 and the agreed policies for 1996 and beyond, to which Yeltsin had committed himself, justified the new loan. Camdessus, always ready to stress the independence of the IMF, encouraged Shail Anjaria, the IMF's press secretary, to write in the newspapers denying that we were taking sides. On the contrary, Shail wrote, if we had refused to lend in those circumstances, that would have amounted to unwarranted political interference. We did, however, have private reservations about whether the agreed policies would be implemented.

It turned out that Kadannikov was not very effective at countering the "monetarist" policies that he himself opposed. In our meetings with him, he did not always seem to be on top of the issues. This was hardly surprising. Like many businessmen who move into government, in market economies no less than in Russia, the ways of government took time to understand and master. He did not last long. Yeltsin removed him in August and replaced him with one of the oligarch beneficiaries of loans-for-shares, Vladimir Potanin.

The main memory that I have of Kadannikov is of his agreeable hosting of an evening at the Bolshoi Theatre when Camdessus was in Moscow. We had seats in one of the best boxes and were joined by the deputy director of the Bolshoi. The production of *La Boheme* was good, although Camdessus told me afterwards that he did not like the way the performers rushed around the stage so much during the first act.

The Presidential election in June 1996 was of momentous importance for Russia and the world. In the economic area, although a victory for Zyuganov would not necessarily have brought back the whole edifice of central planning, it would undoubtedly have meant much more government intervention in the economy and the reversal of many of the market-oriented reforms. We did not think that this would be good for Russia's economy. Nevertheless, the IMF has to work with whatever governments are in place in its member countries. In contemplating the possibility of a communist government after the election, we comforted ourselves with the thought that there would not be much room for maneuver in macroeconomic policy whoever won the election. An additional reason for going ahead with our EFF loan was therefore to provide the government that would be in place after the election with a macroeconomic policy program that it would be risky to reject.

In preparation for the possibility that Zyuganov would win the election, I thought it wise to establish some personal contacts with his economic team beforehand. The idea was to try to persuade them that we were not the enemies of Russia as depicted by opposition commentators and politicians. I also hoped that we could start a dialogue about macroeconomic policies so that a communist government would not immediately reject the policies of its predecessor and go off in entirely the wrong direction. I therefore went to Moscow and met on 1 April 1996 with Yuri Maslyukov, who had been head of Gosplan in the Soviet Union in its last few years and was one of Zyuganov's main economic advisers. The meeting was not successful. Maslyukov's concept of economic policy was that the government had to keep industry going using all means at its disposal. Restricting the growth of credit and money supply was just starving the economy of the oxygen it needed. I was unable to persuade him that the problems of the economy, while very real, were the result of the complicated transition from a planned to a market economy, and from one structure with a large military industrial sector to one responsive to domestic and foreign demand. More money and credit would delay rather than speed up the transition process. But we were talking past each other. Maslyukov later characterized our meeting in a remark to a Western journalist as a conversation between an Eskimo and a man from the tropics. Although the communists did not come into government in 1996, we met Maslyukov again after the 1998 crisis when he joined the government of

Yevgeny Primakov as First Deputy Prime Minister. This time he was more open minded and ready to support restrictive macroeconomic policies.

After the IMF approved the three-year loan in March 1996, the implementation of the policies quickly started to go wrong. Yeltsin was promising more money, both budget expenditure and favorable tax breaks, wherever he went on the campaign trail. Russians with money were moving it out of the country as quickly as they could. Interest rates on Treasury bills rose sharply to stem the outflow and enable the government to finance the budget deficit. The IMF tolerated breaches of the deficit ceilings on the grounds that they were partly attributable to the new loans from the French and German governments and partly to the high interest payments that were the result of election uncertainty. The loans from abroad avoided the need for monetary financing and were therefore compatible with the original inflation targets. Borrowing more to finance higher interest payments for a temporary period was justified by the expectation that interest rates would fall again after the election. These adjustments to the original targets were just about defensible on economic grounds, although I am not sure that the IMF would always have been prepared to make them in another country where there was less of an imperative not to interrupt lending. But worse was to come.

Despite the easing of financial targets, they were increasingly likely to be missed. The CBR, which was already losing international reserves, feared that an interruption in the monthly flow of IMF lending would damage confidence so much that it could no longer hold the exchange rate within its corridor. It therefore misinformed us about some transactions that were critical to our decision to continue disbursing funds. In June it sold over $1 billion of Russian government securities to the Channel Islands subsidiary (FIMACO) of Eurobank which was a Paris bank wholly owned by the CBR. The securities appeared in the CBR's accounts as an increase in its international reserves because it received dollars from FIMACO and had at the same time reduced its domestic lending. We were told at the time that such a transaction had taken place with a foreign bank but not that the bank was a subsidiary of the CBR and thus not an independent bank. Under the CBR's agreement with the IMF, it had to keep international reserves above a certain level and domestic lending below a certain level. Had it not engaged in this phony transaction, it would have breached these limits and Russia would have been ineligible for the next installment of IMF lending. We did not learn about this deception until 1999 when the discovery damaged our relations with the Russians. Sergei Aleksashenko, the first deputy chairman of the CBR in 1995–1998, seemed to say in an interview in 1999 that the CBR assumed in 1996 that the IMF had guessed that they were engaged in window dressing but preferred not to know. This was not the case.

In the three months between the approval of the IMF loan at the end of March and the second and last round of the elections in early July, the IMF disbursed three monthly installments of the loan. Apart from the change in the targets for the budget deficit, the only formal breach of the conditions for the loan occurred when international reserves fell short of the target at the end of May. Given the goodwill that existed towards Russia among the major IMF members, generated in part by the desire not to be blamed if Zyuganov won the election after a financial crisis, the Board was prepared to overlook this lapse. Meanwhile, the CBR was pulling off the FIMACO operation to ensure that the June target for the reserves was met.

It was only after the elections that the financial mess the campaign caused became apparent. Our mission that visited Moscow in July found that Yeltsin's profligacy had led to the breaching of almost all the financial targets for the end of June. There could be no question of disbursing the installment that was due in July. Instead, we agreed with the government on some measures they would take to strengthen revenue collections, eased most of the financial targets for the rest of the year and resumed disbursements in August.

Thus began the pattern that was to characterize our dealings with Russia for the next two years. Russia would miss targets, usually those for tax collections and the budget deficit. We would postpone disbursements and urge the government to take steps to correct the situation. After appropriate promises and some actions from the Russian side we would resume lending. The saying in Russia was that "we pretend to reform, and the IMF pretends that we are reforming." This was a parody of the Soviet saying: "We pretend to work, and they pretend to pay us." From our point of view, and perhaps that of the reformers, it seemed more like a case of "we wanted the best, but it turned out as always."

Yeltsin's increasingly poor health meant less support for macroeconomic stabilization and economic reforms in general. He suffered a heart attack between the two rounds of the presidential elections in June 1996 and had major heart surgery later in the year. With attacks of pneumonia in 1997, he was out of action for long periods in 1996 and 1997. When he was stronger, he intervened in his typical way by changing personnel in the government. Thus, in March 1997 he brought Chubais, who had been head of the Presidential Administration since July 1996, back into government as first deputy prime minister and minister of finance. Boris Nemtsov, the governor of Nizhny Novgorod, was appointed a deputy prime minister and minister of fuel and energy. With reformers in other positions in government, Yeltsin hoped that reforms would get a new lease of life. But the opponents of reform in the Duma, the regional governments, the major enterprises and the new oligarchs were too strong. Yeltsin, who might have been able to push through more reforms, was insufficiently engaged on a regular basis, and became increasingly ineffective. In macroeconomic policy, especially fiscal policy, it continued to be a case of muddling through.

The rationale for the IMF to continue to lend despite the frequent missed targets was that we were helping Russia gradually improve its fiscal policy in a very difficult situation. Viewed in political terms, we were adding weight to those in the government and CBR who wanted a successful macroeconomic stabilization and more rapid market reforms. We were concerned that a prolonged period during which the IMF did not disburse any loans would weaken the position of reformers in the government, one of whose sources of influence was their ability to talk to the IMF and persuade us to disburse. The G7 also regarded continued IMF engagement with Russia as helping to establish market reforms and prevent relapses.

But there was a downside to our support for a macroeconomic stabilization process that was seriously flawed. Although our involvement caused the Russians to take some steps to improve the budgetary situation, at the same time the availability of our money reduced the pressure on the government to put its own house in order. In addition, financial markets lent more to Russia in the expectation that the IMF would ensure that the economy recovered and they would get their money back. Our continued support also had negative consequences for the IMF itself. Our reputation was damaged each time Russia failed to meet new, usually easier targets that we said they could achieve. We were also criticized, especially in developing countries, for treating Russia more leniently than other borrowing countries which failed to implement the agreed policies.

There were many voices inside the IMF that were opposed to our continuing to lend after the situation did not improve in the months following the election in July 1996. Among the staff, Michael Mussa, Economic Counsellor and Director of the Research Department in 1991–2001, was a strong opponent. Vito Tanzi, Director of the Fiscal Affairs Department in 1981–2000, challenged the realism of the assumed increases in tax revenues that were essential to justify our lending. He was often proved right by subsequent events, as he reminded readers of the *Financial Times* in 2003 in a letter to the editor after he had retired from the IMF. It was true that those of us who were working with the Russians on their economic programs were not as objective as we could have been—and as Tanzi thought we should have been—when assessing the realism of the revenue projections prepared by the authorities. We succumbed to the occupational hazard of IMF economists who are inclined to take an overly optimistic view of the economic prospects of countries that are implementing programs that the IMF supports with its funds. In addition, we were well aware that the G7, especially the US, wanted the IMF to continue lending as long as there was a reasonable chance of achieving the desired outcome.

In addition to some among the staff, many Executive Directors, other than those representing G7 countries, doubted the wisdom of continuing to lend to Russia, given the risks. Some of them were also quite properly exercised by the leniency shown towards Russia.

It is always difficult for the IMF, or indeed any creditor who is trying to persuade a borrower to reform, to decide when reforms are being hindered rather than helped by a continuation of lending. The situation is complicated by the fact that the withdrawal of financial support might cause short term economic difficulties and political disruption even if it has a salutary effect in the longer term. As it was my staff who had daily contact with the Russians, I was particularly aware of these short-term considerations and was reluctant to contemplate a major interruption of IMF lending and the unpredictable political consequences. However, not all my staff felt the same. Jorge Marquez Ruarte, who led the missions to Russia in 1997–99, was most skeptical about our lending. By contrast, his predecessor, Yusuke Horiguchi, who led the missions in 1995–97, was positive, having seen the useful role that we had played in 1995. It was Camdessus' job to decide, and he and Fischer favored continued lending as the best way to retain some influence and discourage a major reversal of economic policies. They had the support of the G7 countries, especially the US, which had many reasons for wanting to maintain good relations with Yeltsin and his government.

But withholding more money might not have had such bad effects as we feared. We saw later that the new communist-supported government after the crisis of August 1998 continued to pursue macroeconomic stability. This was partly because the loss of access to new foreign borrowing left them with few alternatives. Moreover, there was no significant reversal of reforms. This experience suggests that, although the political situation was not quite the same in the prior couple of years, it is likely that the response to a smaller stream of funds from the IMF, and consequently from financial markets which took their lead from the IMF, would not have been too destabilizing. There would probably have been somewhat higher inflation as the government relied more on CBR money creation to finance its expenditure. But its indebtedness and hence the risk of a crash when it could no longer roll over its loans, as occurred in 1998, would have been less. On balance I now believe that macroeconomic policy implementation would have been better if the IMF had withheld loans more often when monetary and fiscal targets were missed.

THE CRISIS OF AUGUST 1998

To the outside world, there were signs by 1997 that the Russian economy had turned the corner. It was beginning to grow for the first time since the 1980s and inflation was coming down, perhaps into single figures. Politically, Yeltsin had been reelected the year before, and the G7 brought Russia in to form the G8 in June. International financial markets decided that Russia had a good future and money poured in to finance the government and the private sector. Chubais was given the honorary title Finance Minister of the Year by the financial magazine *Euromoney*, which honored him at a ceremony in September 1997 in Hong Kong during the Annual Meetings of the IMF and World Bank. When he met Camdessus during the same meetings, he said that Russia was looking forward to an amicable divorce from the IMF when the EFF loan would be completely disbursed in 1999. Camdessus warned him not to be too confident as there were still many problems, especially tax collections and the budget. Less than a year later, there was a major financial crisis when Russia defaulted on its debt and the exchange rate collapsed.

Although the Russian crisis was largely homegrown, some events that contributed to it were set off by the Asian financial crisis of 1997. Some investors, including Koreans, who had lost money in Asia and had to liquidate their other assets, sold Russian government securities. The declining oil price following the Asian crisis affected Russia's balance of payments and tax revenues. International investors, having been surprised by the Asian problems, were looking round the world asking who might be next. Russia caught their eye, and some people reduced their exposure to Russia well in advance of August 1998. These developments, together with increasing concern about the size of the government's borrowing requirement, contributed to a loss of international reserves as investors reduced their exposure and hence to speculation that there might have to be a devaluation.

There were three waves of speculation, in November 1997, January 1998 and May 1998. On each occasion the CBR was able to calm the market down temporarily by raising interest rates. In November the CBR also announced that, in 1998, the ruble would be allowed to move within a wider band around a fixed central rate instead of in a narrower band around a sliding central rate. A few days later I had a private dinner with Chairman Dubinin in Moscow. Over a bottle of fine Bordeaux wine, he revealed his concerns that the pressure in the market would become increasingly difficult to manage. He was right. The political situation added to the sense that the authorities were losing control. Chubais' enemies had been seeking to oust him for some months and succeeded in November in replacing him as finance minister with Mikhail Zadornov, the chair of the budget committee in the Duma. Zadornov was knowledgeable and reform minded, but lacked the experience and influence, not least in the Kremlin, of Chubais.

In response to the increasing uncertainty in financial markets, the IMF's advice in the first half of 1998 was to tighten monetary policy and introduce new budget measures to close the gap between expenditures and revenues. We supported the government's and CBR's commitment to defend the exchange rate. We had almost reached agreement with the Russians on policies for the year by the time Camdessus visited in February. That was the visit described in chapter 3 when he told Yeltsin that there was too much crony capitalism and spoke about the excessive influence of the oligarchy. He also met with a group of oligarchs brought together by the CBR: Mikhail Fridman, Vladimir Gusinsky, Mikhail Khodorkovsky, Andrei Kostin, Platon Lebedev, Vladimir Potanin, Aleksandr Smolensky and Vladimir Vinogradov. Also present were Dubinin and Andrei Kazmin and Andrei Kostin, the heads of the state-owned banks Sberbank (Savings Bank) and Vneshtorgbank (VTB) respectively. Their response to Camdessus' explanation of the government's budget problems was that it was not their concern; they already paid too much in taxes. We were shocked, but perhaps not surprised, by their blatant cynicism and self-serving arguments. Many years later Camdessus wrote in his memoirs: "These men had gone over to capitalism in its most sordid form, without any qualms."

Two off-duty events during that visit are worth a mention. One evening we went to a restaurant that served fish that appeared not only on our plates but also under our feet. The dining area was on a glass floor under which was an enormous fish tank. As someone who suffers from a mild fear of heights, I found the deep pool under my seat and the fish darting about almost between my legs quite unsettling. Many restaurants with novel features were opening in Moscow during those years. One evening I went with Kagalovsky to a restaurant with a farm theme. There was a live cow with some sheep and chicken in the middle. Fortunately, their enclosure was sealed off behind glass walls so there was no smell. The farmyard noises were, however, piped to the diners outside.

The second event was my fall on the sidewalk when rushing to a meeting and slipping on the ice that lay hidden beneath the slush. I asked the hotel for a doctor to look at my painful shoulder. The scene that followed was symbolic of the ongoing transformation in the Russian economy and society. The elderly lady doctor who examined me spoke only Russian and gave gruff instructions which were translated for me by a young English-speaking bell hop sent by the hotel. The doctor thought that I had fractured my shoulder and advised me to get it X-rayed as soon as possible, and meanwhile to keep it in a sling. Two days later in Washington, an X-ray confirmed her diagnosis and a doctor agreed that keeping it in a sling was the only thing to do. That same evening my wife and I were at a party with other senior IMF people. Camdessus, who had also just returned from Moscow, asked my wife if I had told her what had happened to me in Russia. She thought that he must be referring to our naked session in the Russian banya and was stuck for words. But he just wanted to commiserate with us about my fractured shoulder.

While we were waiting for the authorities to implement the various prior actions that would allow us to disburse another installment of the medium-term loan, Yeltsin intervened with a major change of government. In March 1998 he dismissed Chernomyrdin and Chubais and appointed young and inexperienced men in their place: Sergei Kiriyenko as prime minister and Viktor Khristenko as deputy prime minister for economic policy. Zadornov remained minister of finance. Kiriyenko was only 36 when he became prime minister. He came to Moscow the previous year to become Minister of Fuel and Energy, having previously worked with Nemtsov in Nizhny Novgorod. In telling us his background, Mozhin pointed out his good and bad features: "The good news is that he does not go hunting. The bad news is that he likes scuba diving." As it turned out, he was not in office long enough for us to experience his hospitality, with or without wet suits.

There was a delay until the new government could operate effectively because the Duma initially resisted ratification. We had to delay any new disbursement. Financial markets were meanwhile becoming more jittery. The third wave of speculation came in May. The CBR raised interest rates again, but markets were less ready to be reassured by this than in the past. Although Chubais had no formal position in the government, Kiriyenko turned to him for help with relations with the IMF and the G7. On May 27 when I was in Kyrgyzstan with Camdessus for a seminar to celebrate the fifth anniversary of the introduction of the Kyrgyz currency, Chubais phoned Camdessus and asked him to go to Moscow to discuss additional IMF financial support and help calm the markets. Camdessus sent me instead. On May 28, the day I arrived in Moscow, there was a further crash in the market. The CBR raised its refinance rate to 150 percent and intervened heavily in the foreign exchange market. I held a press conference the following day in which I said that the IMF supported the government's new anti-crisis program. But the government mishandled the presentation of the program and my efforts to calm the situation failed. With confidence in financial markets being very fragile, calls were heard for more drastic measures, including devaluation, refinancing of government debt to extend maturities and a massive external loan.

Meanwhile, Chubais had flown to Washington where he met Fischer; Robert Rubin, US Secretary of the Treasury; and Larry Summers, the US Treasury Deputy Secretary. The US was sympathetic to the idea of a massive loan from the IMF and President Clinton's office made an announcement to that effect on 31 May. Camdessus was ready to contemplate this but only if the Russians took much stronger steps to sort out the budget than they had taken so far. As June and July progressed, financial markets came to expect a huge bailout so that a failure to deliver it would have itself caused a crisis. In the subsequent negotiations, the pressure was not only on the Russians but also on us, since we did not want to be blamed for having caused a crisis by being intransigent. Kiriyenko was himself ready to take the necessary tough measures and he was ably supported by Chubais (who was formally appointed Yeltsin's special representative to international financial organizations in June), Gaidar (in an advisory role), Finance Minister Mikhail Zadornov and CBR Chairman Sergei Dubinin. Agreement was reached in July on a package of fiscal and other reforms that, although many would take some months to implement, we hoped would restore confidence in financial markets and buy time for the government. The early signs were not auspicious. Within a week of our agreement with the authorities, the Duma had turned down two important tax raising measures, thereby sending a signal that nothing had changed and there was still insufficient commitment to tackle the budget problem. We responded by trimming the size of our proposed loan.

The IMF Board met on July 20 to approve Camdessus' proposal for a commitment of $13 billion of additional money, $4.8 billion of which would be available immediately, in support of Russia's policies. Some Executive Directors, especially those representing non-G7 European countries and countries that borrowed from the IMF, were unhappy about the continuation of what they regarded as excessive leniency towards Russia in the face of serious doubts about whether the reforms would be implemented. Nevertheless, they reluctantly agreed to the proposal with no abstentions or votes against.

The doubters' assessment was soon proved correct. Initially financial markets were reassured by the new policy measures and the IMF support, but within just a few weeks, no doubt influenced in part by the Duma's action, their skepticism about whether there really would be a change in Russia grew again. Both Russians and foreigners rushed to convert their rubles into foreign currency and the CBR's reserves collapsed. This time there was no way to restore confidence. We and the Russians had shot our bolt.

The growing crisis increasingly gripped all of us in the IMF who worked on Russia. I myself went to Moscow seven times in 1998, more than twice my annual average in the previous six years. In May and July, I gave press conferences in Moscow, the only times I did that. It fell to me to go to Moscow in August just before the collapse to liaise with the government during those critical days. I had to postpone a holiday in Italy to do so. A few days before going, I received a phone call from Summers who explained the US position in his usual direct and blunt manner. According to normal hierarchical conventions, he would have spoken to Fischer. But both Fischer and Camdessus were on vacation, and he had to make do with me. Within minutes of his ringing off, I was called to a meeting with the Acting Managing Director who wanted me to brief the G7 Executive Directors about Russia. The US Executive Director was on vacation and Mark Sobel was standing in for her. Arriving late because he had been receiving information from the US Treasury about Summers' phone call to me, he passed a note across the table which read: "I hear that Larry has been charming you again." It was a struggle to avoid giggling, but a relief to be able to relax at such a tense time.

The visit to Moscow began badly because heavy rain delayed my flight with Odd Per Brekk from Washington and we missed our connection in London. Arriving five hours late at 9 pm on Saturday 15 August, we were met by the head of our Moscow office, Martin Gilman, who rushed us to see Chubais and Gaidar who were waiting at a table in a back room of the Liberal Democratic Club. I am sure that the food and wine were very good, but I have no recollection because we were absorbed by the discussion of the momentous events that were about to occur.

The first question Chubais asked was whether the IMF would be prepared to lend any more money. They seemed to be expecting my negative answer, and none of us held out much hope that the G7 would be willing to make an exceptional loan. But as I was not sure about the G7, they checked later and did indeed receive the expected response. They then outlined the plan that was being developed by a small group of officials. The central element would be the forced restructuring of the government debt that was falling due in the coming months. As such a default would have a devastating impact on the market, there would be more massive selling of the ruble. It would no longer be possible to keep the exchange rate within its band. This presented a political dilemma because Yeltsin had only a day or two before affirming in public that there would be no devaluation. Some language had to be found that would permit a much more flexible exchange rate without using the D word. We all recognized that a government default and a sharp exchange rate change spelled the end of the flawed stabilization of the past few years. Macroeconomic policy had failed and the economic and political consequences, though difficult to predict, could be severe.

The next day, Sunday 16 August, we met the prime minister, Kiriyenko, and the senior economic policy makers, including Dubinin, Zadornov, Chubais and Gaidar. They were hoping that the IMF would support what they were doing, not with money which they understood was not possible, but with a public statement and assistance in dealing with creditors. Following what I had agreed with Fischer, and after they clarified some details of the proposed measures, I indicated our support. Kiriyenko went to inform Yeltsin and we agreed to meet again in the evening to discuss the details of the announcement to be made before financial markets opened on Monday.

I had been keeping in touch with Fischer and Camdessus by telephone. This was not easy because they were both on vacation, Fischer on a Greek island and Camdessus in France. In one conversation with Fischer, who was on his cell phone, I could hear clinking of glasses and the cheerful background voices of other diners or drinkers in the restaurant or bar where he was. In reporting to Camdessus on Sunday afternoon, I discovered that there had been a misunderstanding between the three of us. I had understood from Fischer that we would not object to the unilateral default by the government on its obligations. Regrettable though it was, there seemed to be no alternative at that stage. But Camdessus had expected that we would insist that the government enter into discussions with its creditors about a rescheduling and restructuring of the debt with a view to reaching a mutually acceptable solution. His view was that the IMF could only support an orderly agreed restructuring, not a forced restructuring on Russia's terms. He maintained this position when Rubin had phoned him just before from his airplane (he was returning from a fishing holiday in Alaska) and suggested that the IMF should support the Russians' plan. As he was the boss, I had no alternative but to tell Kiriyenko when we met again in the evening that we could not support a unilateral default. Instead, I urged that the announcement about the details of the debt restructuring should be delayed until there had been consultations with creditors. I explained that I had earlier misunderstood our position but had now clarified it with Camdessus. Naturally the Russians were angry, and my credibility took a beating. After the meeting we arranged for Chubais to talk to Camdessus on the phone from my hotel room. Both men spoke forcefully but courteously. Camdessus stuck to his position.

By now it was after midnight on what I told my colleagues had been the worst day of my professional life. I was witnessing the sad demise of the exchange-rate based stabilization policy that we had done so much to support. Our reputation was going to be severely damaged. On top of it all, I had misrepresented our position to the Russians who now had good reason to doubt my value as an interlocutor. I kept my spirits up by focusing on what we could still do to make the best of a bad situation: issue a supportive statement on Monday and help the Russians design a debt restructuring scheme and deal with Russian banks that were to be hit by the default and devaluation.

On the morning of Monday 17 August, the government announced the emergency measures with three main elements: the widening of the exchange rate band from one centered on 6 rubles to the dollar to one with a maximum of 9.5 rubles to the dollar; a compulsory restructuring of government debt; and a three-month moratorium on repayments of Russian banks' external debt. We had pushed for no upper limit to the ruble range to avoid the risk of a new crisis if and when a new upper limit was reached. But, given Yeltsin's "no devaluation" comment, the government felt that they needed to preserve at least an appearance of continuity with previous policy to limit political damage. Respecting Camdessus' request, no details of the debt restructuring scheme were given, except that domestic and foreign creditors would be treated alike. The moratorium on bank repayments was somewhat of a surprise to us although we had heard a hint of it during the meetings on Sunday. We learnt later that top Russian bankers had spent much of Sunday night with Kiriyenko and others at the White House insisting on it. I received a first-hand account of the meeting from Pyotr Aven, the Chief Executive Officer of Alfa Bank. We met by chance on Tuesday on a flight to Milan where I was to join my wife for our postponed Italian holiday. He was going to rejoin his family in Sardinia having briefly interrupted his holiday because of the crisis in Russia.

After the government announcement, we issued our statement. I had settled this in a series of telephone and fax communications with Camdessus who was in Paris preparing to fly to Washington that morning on Concorde. Its message was that the international community should show solidarity with Russia at that difficult time, and Russia should find a cooperative solution to its debt problems with its creditors and strengthen the underlying fiscal position. The Russians were relieved that we were not more critical.

One senior member of the Russian government's economic team did not think that the drastic measures announced on 17 August were necessary. Boris Federov had returned to the government in May 1998 as deputy prime minister with responsibility for revenues, a critical job that he tackled with his customary vigor. He thought that the crisis could be turned to advantage by finally insisting on proper fiscal discipline, perhaps with the help of a currency board. He recognized that more external financial assistance would be needed for a temporary period and hoped that commercial borrowing would be possible. He had been unable to persuade his government colleagues to accept his alternative plan and appeared in my hotel on Sunday 16 August to try his luck with us. To his disappointment, I explained our view that it was too late to try what sounded like more of the same, and anyway the government had clearly taken the decision, which we did not oppose, to go ahead with the default and devaluation.

Exhausted at the end of Monday, I turned on CNN in my hotel room to see how the world was responding to the government's announcement. Two dramatic stories captured the headlines. An IRA splinter group bombed Omagh in Northern Ireland, killing more people than were killed in any other single incident in Northern Ireland before or since. The other story was that President Clinton had appeared before the federal grand jury. The following morning in Moscow, CNN was to report his admission in a speech to the nation on Monday evening that he had conducted an inappropriate relationship with Monica Lewinsky. It was sobering to realize that what seemed to us to be such dramatic events in Moscow were seen by news editors and no doubt the general public as less important than these developments in Northern Ireland and Washington.

During the next week or two, IMF experts helped the government and CBR handle the aftermath of the default. Daniel Citrin, head of the Russia Division, advised the government on the terms of the compulsory debt restructuring. Among other things, we were concerned that Russia should be able to afford the debt service under the new arrangements, so that there would not be a new crisis later. We also wanted to ensure that all creditors were treated alike, a central requirement of orderly debt workouts that received IMF support. The scheme that was eventually announced on 25 August met these requirements. Another IMF team, led by Bill Alexander, together with World Bank experts, advised the CBR on banking issues.

Meanwhile, the government came under strong attack and Yeltsin dismissed Kiriyenko on 23 August. He brought Chernomyrdin back in his place, but the Duma, which had to approve the appointment of the prime minister, refused to accept him. During the short time that he was acting prime minister, Chernomyrdin turned to his friend Camdessus for advice. They met in secret on 25 August in the summer residence of President Kuchma of Ukraine in Foros on the Black Sea. This was the same residence where Gorbachev was on vacation in August 1991 when the coup against him took place in Moscow. Chernomyrdin's meeting with Kuchma had already been announced so his presence there did not arouse suspicions, while Camdessus' trip was not noticed. Federov accompanied Chernomyrdin and argued for a currency board to be imposed following a bout of money emission intended to inflate away the debt. Camdessus and Marquez Ruarte who accompanied him argued that a currency board could not work in Russia where the control of fiscal policy was so weak. But Chernomyrdin had no time or political support to initiate any coherent economic policy.

The economic situation deteriorated rapidly. The exchange rate fell quickly to 9.5 rubles to the dollar, the limit of its new band. The CBR tried to hold it by selling more of its depleted reserves of foreign currency but was forced to abandon the band altogether on 2 September. After that the ruble took no time to collapse to 20 to the dollar before settling back at about 16 by the end of September. The domestic financial system was paralyzed. Trust between banks evaporated and interbank transactions dried up. The payments system ceased to operate. Even non-monetary transactions were temporarily disrupted. As a result, there was a severe contraction in production and trade. Inflation jumped because of the devaluation, reaching 38 percent in the month of September alone. Incomes did not rise to anything like the same extent, and real incomes (incomes adjusted for inflation) fell sharply, by almost a third between the first quarter of 1998 and the same period of 1999. Living standards for much of the population were similarly hit.

There were considerable international repercussions, which were also of great concern to the IMF. Other countries of the former Soviet Union that still had close trade relations with Russia found their exchange rates under pressure and most of them had to devalue in the next few months. Inflation jumped in all cases, and output, due in part to the reduction in exports to Russia, grew less rapidly or fell more.

Major international banks and other financial institutions that lost money from the Russian default and devaluation had to retrench with knock-on effects throughout the system. The American hedge fund, Long Term Capital Management, faced bankruptcy. Because of the scale of its borrowings from financial institutions in the US and Europe, a rescue by private banks was organized by the New York Federal Reserve Bank, thereby giving LTCM time to unwind its positions. The Federal Reserve Board rapidly reduced interest rates. As a result of all this and other related action, a widespread international financial crisis was averted, but it was a close call. One of the few good things to come out of the Russia crisis at the international level was that financial markets learned that no country was too big (and, in Russia's case, too nuclear) to fail. Never again could it be safely assumed that the IMF or the G7 would continue to push out loans to prop up a country whose underlying macroeconomic policies were unsustainable.

For Russia, the August 1998 crisis was, at the time, a macroeconomic disaster. The government and CBR received most of the blame, and it was true that the failure to contain the government's budget deficit and rising debt was the main cause. But lying behind this was the government's weakness. It did not have the political authority to pass legislation through the Duma that would reduce the deficit, or to insist that major taxpayers paid what they owed. In some sense the opposition that controlled the Duma, the business-men who found ways of avoiding paying taxes, and the regional and local governments that kept as much of total central and local government revenues for themselves as they could were mainly responsible for the failure of the flawed stabilization policy.

The IMF was closely associated with the government's policy. What should we have done differently that would have produced a better outcome? I do not think that we could have recommended a markedly superior fiscal policy. The problem was not the design of the fiscal policy with which we were involved, but its implementation, which was beyond our control. Nor could it be said that we did not warn the government about the risks they were taking in not bringing the fiscal situation under control. With hindsight, as I have said, we might have had a bigger impact on macroeconomic policy implementation if we had withheld some of our loans in 1996 and 1997. But continuing to lend in order to discourage a reversal of the general trend in policies seemed the right thing to do at the time.

We did, however, make two mistakes in the fiscal area that exacerbated the situation. In March 1996 we insisted on the abolition of the oil export duty as part of the government's long-term program of removing all taxes and restrictions on exports. Unfortunately, the higher excise duties which were intended to substitute for the export duty were not implemented and the government lost revenue that it could ill afford at the time. It would have been better to have postponed the abolition of export duty on oil until the excise tax collection system and the government's authority were stronger. Also in 1996, we supported the government's wish to liberalize access to the Treasury bill market by foreign investors. Despite CBR opposition, we insisted. In early 1997 the government and CBR agreed to a phased program of liberalization to be completed in January 1998. This reduced the cost of borrowing and added a significant element to the total financial market volatility that culminated in the 1998 crisis. However, we were not wholly responsible for the liberalization. Indeed, some government officials and observers have argued that, even if the IMF had not pressed, then the government would itself have insisted on the liberalization. These two mistakes did not, of course, cause the crisis, but they made it more difficult to avoid.

Should we have pressed for an earlier devaluation or other change in exchange rate policy that would have avoided the sharp break in August 1998? So long as there was a chance that fiscal policy could be brought under control, there was a good case for maintaining the exchange rate peg. It not only provided an anchor for inflation, which continued to fall gradually towards acceptable levels. It also meant that fiscal indiscipline was quickly revealed by a loss of international reserves, and corrective fiscal action was signaled. It is never easy to spot the point at which the failure to maintain fiscal discipline has fatally wounded the exchange rate policy.

Finding the right moment to adjust an exchange rate peg always presents a dilemma. So long as exchange market conditions are benign, as they were in Russia until the onset of the Asian crisis in late 1997, there is no reason to change the policy. When market conditions worsen, any attempt to exit the peg arrangement risks creating a crisis. Nevertheless, there was probably a window from November 1997 to March 1998 when people might have been persuaded of the need for an exit, and an orderly exit might have been possible. With hindsight, it is regrettable that the IMF did not spot this opportunity at the time. Even if we had, the government would surely have resisted our recommendation to devalue because its credibility and, one of its few macroeconomic achievements, the low inflation rate, were linked to the exchange rate peg. But it would probably have relented eventually.

RUSSIA REBOUNDS

Together with many other observers, we were surprised by the good economic recovery after the debacle of 1998. My colleagues, David Owen and David Robinson, explained what caused it in a book entitled *Russia Rebounds* which was published by the IMF in 2003.

When the Duma refused to confirm Chernomyrdin as prime minister in September 1998, Yeltsin turned to Yevgeny Primakov whom the Duma confirmed on 11 September. Primakov had been Director of the Foreign Intelligence Service in 1991–1996 and Minister for Foreign Affairs from early 1996. He appointed Yuri Maslyukov, whom I had met in 1996, as first deputy prime minister for economic policy. Gerashchenko was recalled as chairman of the CBR for the second time, Dubinin having resigned on 7 September. Only Zadornov as finance minister remained from the senior economic officials whom we had worked with before 17 August.

It was difficult in September 1998 to be optimistic about economic prospects. The CBR had pumped liquidity into the monetary system to prevent it seizing up altogether. This could lead to higher inflation being sustained beyond the post-devaluation jump. The cost of servicing foreign currency debt had increased sharply with the devaluation, and it was not clear whether tax revenue collections would rise proportionate with the increase in nominal incomes. While some foreign commentators were quite gloomy and expected a return to the hyperinflation of the early 1990s, I foresaw a kind of muddling through in which inflation would be kept in check, because Gerashchenko and others had learnt from the mistakes of the early 1990s. But it would not be brought down to low levels. Nor would the real economy recover quickly from the disruption of the crisis. How wrong this turned out to be, especially the latter point.

We had frequent contacts with the new government, starting with my meeting with Primakov on 15 September and a full mission later in the month. Our main message was that the broad strategy pursued by previous governments should be maintained but that the fiscal situation must be brought under control unlike before. There was also a need to recapitalize the now insolvent banking system. We were concerned that the government might reverse many of the previous market-oriented policies. After all, Maslyukov's previous experience in government had been as head of Gosplan in the Soviet Union, and he had showed little sympathy for macroeconomic stabilization policies and pro-market reforms in my meeting with him in 1996. I was especially worried that the government might default on its $16 billion debt to the IMF. Such a huge default would be unprecedented and would create a major crisis for the IMF. But again, I was too pessimistic.

The government wanted us to release the money that it believed had been promised in July. We explained that the installments of the July loan that had not been released were conditional on the continuation of the policies agreed at that time. The crisis made it impossible to continue in the same way and so it would be necessary to agree a new set of policies suited to the new economic situation before more money could be released.

Primakov never seemed to accept this, or at least he pretended that he did not accept it. As he explained in his book published in Russia in 2001, he thought that the IMF was deliberately dragging its feet because its major members, especially the US, had political objections to helping Russia. He therefore sought to make progress through direct contacts with important foreign leaders. This did not work. Unlike in the early 1990s when the US was keen to see the IMF lend more to Russia, there had been a change of mood in western countries following the crisis and their governments were not prepared to press the IMF to ease its usual conditions. We therefore continued to discuss economic policies throughout the coming months and only reached agreement on policies that would justify a new loan in April 1999.

The CBR and the government gradually brought macroeconomic policies under control. This was partly a case of necessity because new lending to finance budget deficits had dried up. After a few months of rather easy monetary policy that led to a further depreciation of the exchange rate, monetary policy became tighter. The budget for 1999 that was approved by the Duma in February 1999 marked a break with the past with stronger expenditure controls and tax compliance measures. One important way that the budget deficit was reduced was by holding the increase in government wage and pension payments well below the increase in the price level. This made many people significantly worse off while improving the government's financial position. In the IMF we were concerned that the reduction in living standards would not be sustainable and we urged the government to increase wages and pensions by more and to raise extra taxes to pay for them. This irritated Primakov who complained to Camdessus in March that the IMF was outflanking him on the left. In an earlier meeting with Gérard Bélanger, who had taken over from Jorge Marquez Ruarte as mission chief, Primakov accused Bélanger of being a socialist. But his political judgment was sound. Helped by his credibility with the Duma and ably supported by Zadornov he successfully enacted a more restrictive budget than in earlier years. Thus, in macroeconomic policy the government managed the recovery from the crisis better than I and many others had expected. This opened the way for the agreement with the IMF after a few detailed issues had been sorted out.

Meanwhile, Camdessus had been building a personal relationship with Primakov. He hoped that this would ease the process of reaching agreement on policies as well as make it less likely that Russia would seriously contemplate defaulting on IMF loans. In Camdessus' first visit to Moscow in December 1998, Primakov took Camdessus and me after dinner to a shooting gallery in the basement of the White House where security personnel trained. Camdessus, who had done military service in the French army in Algeria during the independence struggle, was a good shot. This impressed Primakov. My own image of Camdessus' performance was his determination to save the beautiful girl represented by a cardboard cutout. She was being held hostage by a cardboard bad man who held her in front of him. The challenge was to kill the man, who was largely hidden, without injuring the girl. When I undressed in the hotel that evening, a spent cartridge case fell out of my trouser turn-ups, a souvenir of our brief pose as armed security guards.

Camdessus' second visit to Moscow in March 1999 was arranged at the last minute after Primakov had dramatically turned his plane round over the Atlantic rather than proceed to Washington when he heard that NATO had begun to bomb Serbia. Camdessus did not want this episode to prevent him from having his planned meeting with Primakov and so he and I flew to Moscow a few days later.

The relationship between the two men was cordial but did not develop the warmth of that between Chernomyrdin and Camdessus. It may, however, have helped remove some of Primakov's misunderstandings about the IMF although not all of them, as his book shows. As for the risk of default on IMF loans, we learnt later that a decision had been taken back in September 1998 to honor Russia's obligations to the IMF.

One interesting event during the visit in March was a dinner hosted by the Patriarch of Moscow and All Russia at which Primakov and Camdessus were the main guests. Camdessus, a religious man, liked to meet religious leaders from whom he picked up a different perspective about conditions in the country than he received from the IMF staff and the authorities. Apart from the excellent meal accompanied by Chateau La Mission Haut Brion, a surprise during Lent, the main interest was Patriarch Alexei II's discourse on the difficulties that ordinary people had in adjusting to the enormous economic and political changes in the country. In their memoirs, Primakov and Camdessus recalled different aspects of the conversation. Primakov was pleased that the Patriarch explained the realities of Russia to Camdessus. "This was something new; the church and state were acting together and on the same wavelength." Camdessus was impressed by the Patriarch's appeal to Primakov not to allow any Russian intervention in Kosovo to be seen as a conflict between Orthodox Christianity and Islam. The Patriarch stressed that orthodoxy must be fighting for peace in today's world and not work towards obsolete pan-Slavism.

During one of our visits to Moscow in 1998 or 1999, Camdessus and I were sitting side by side in a meeting in the President Hotel. The meeting room looked out over the Moscow River. The upper parts of the controversial Peter the Great statue that was erected in 1997 on an island in the river were visible from our seats. We could see a giant size Peter standing on the deck of a small sailing ship which in turn stood on an elaborate high plinth. The magazine *Foreign Policy* included it in 2010 on a list of the world's ugliest statues. Camdessus, who had not seen the statue before, had a similar view. He passed me a note during the meeting to the effect that he would be sick if he had to look at the statue any longer. Such light moments kept us going during tedious meetings.

Although we reached agreement with the Russians on economic policies in April 1999, the IMF did not formally approve the loan until July. One reason for the delay was that there was a need to strengthen the revenue side of the budget before the loan could be approved. Yeltsin's unexpected decision to replace Primakov as prime minister with Sergei Stepashin, and a subsequent change in finance ministers, added to the delay.

In addition, we learned in the spring about the deception by the CBR in 1996 regarding the phony transactions involving FIMACO. The IMF is not able to carry out independent checks on all the information it is given and must therefore trust its members to report honestly. When a member misreports, that trust is broken. The rules of the IMF call for it to apply sanctions in such cases, usually involving the early repayment of any loans that a country took on the basis of false information. In addition, the country is expected to put in place measures to reduce the chances that there could be a reoccurrence of the misreporting. Russia did not have to repay early because it was protected by a two-year statute of limitations. But it did have to hire an international accounting firm (PricewaterhouseCoopers) to investigate and report on the offending transactions. And it had to agree to various measures to increase the transparency of its operations, the details of which were worked out over the following months.

The FIMACO affair inevitably created some ill-feeling between the CBR and the IMF. It was apparent at the highest level when Camdessus expressed his displeasure at the CBR's deception to Gerashchenko at a meeting in St. Petersburg in June 1999. Gerashchenko was not personally involved in the FIMACO affair in 1996. Nevertheless, he was not comfortable being at the receiving end of Camdessus' reprimand. It was not easy for Russians, especially those who had, like Gerashchenko, been in senior positions when the Soviet Union was a superpower, to take criticism from international institutions.

There were also tensions subsequently at a lower level when we had to persuade the CBR to be more transparent. It was particularly resistant to being more open about certain operations that provided it with income that it feared the government would try to take. The most extreme example was the precious metals market. The CBR still operated the old Soviet system whereby companies mining platinum and other precious metals had to sell them to the CBR which then sold that part not needed in Russia on the international market. At a time of rising world prices this was a very lucrative business, but not the sort of thing that a central bank should be engaged in. Similarly, it was wholly inappropriate for the CBR to own commercial banks abroad as it did in Paris, London, Vienna and Frankfurt. Although they did not make money, these banks were useful to the CBR for carrying out transactions abroad without the transparency that going through major international banks would involve. They also presented opportunities for patronage.

The closer attention that we were forced to pay to the operations of the CBR as a result of the FIMACO affair revealed in a microcosm the complexity of the transition from the old centrally planned economy to a market economy. Here was an institution that, in the monetary policy area that most concerned us, appeared to be making the transition successfully. Apart from the 1992–1994 period and, more excusably, the first few months after the 1998 crisis, it had generally pursued a sensible policy. Its staff were quick to learn the role of a central bank in a market economy and were keen to develop modern methods of monetary control. But at the same time the CBR continued with some Soviet practices that were out of place. The leadership understood this but was unwilling to give up any power.

The first installment of the new loan was paid out to Russia after it was approved in July 1999. That was the last sum that Russia received from the IMF. Although macroeconomic policy was satisfactory in subsequent months, the next instalment was delayed because the CBR had not made as much progress in improving transparency as it had promised.

Meanwhile perceptions towards Russia in G7 countries were changing. In response to this, their governments were becoming increasingly cool about IMF lending to Russia. The shift in attitudes began after the crisis in 1998. Banks and other foreign investors who had lost money became bearish on Russia and no longer had the same interest in seeing active IMF involvement. Public opinion cooled towards Russia as its economic policies were seen to have failed.

Stories began to circulate, first in Russia and then abroad, that the money lent by the IMF had been stolen. The most detailed version of this allegation was publicized by a communist member of the Duma, Viktor Ilyukhin. He alleged in March 1999 that the $4.8 billion disbursed by the IMF in July 1998 had ended up in foreign bank accounts controlled by senior government figures, including Yeltsin's daughter, Chernomyrdin, Kiriyenko and Chubais. To support the story, he produced authentic looking documents showing transfers between various bank accounts in western countries. We were able to establish through contacts with the central banks in the countries concerned that the documents were forgeries. Indeed, some of the banks Ilyukhin cited did not even exist. Moreover, the detailed examination that PricewaterhouseCoopers carried out for the CBR at our insistence showed that the IMF loan was indeed used to support the ruble exchange rate in the weeks before the crisis. It was sold for rubles in fully legitimate transactions to banks who wanted to get out of them. But dirt sticks, even when it is wholly unjustified. The myth that the IMF loans were stolen lingered on for many years, including among otherwise intelligent and well-informed commentators.

Another prominent story that became muddled in people's minds with the stolen IMF money story appeared in the *New York Times* in August 1999. It alleged that billions of dollars, including IMF money, had been channeled through the Bank of New York during the previous year in a major money laundering operation by Russian organized crime. The FBI investigated the case but failed to bring any charges except minor ones involving a completely different operation in a different part of the Bank of New York. The author of the *New York Times* article eventually retracted his claims about money laundering well over a year later. He suggested that he had been set up by an unreliable source.

In addition to these two stories, which were both false, many true and untrue stories about Russian criminality appeared in the western press. Commentators described Russia as a kleptocracy in which the ruling classes helped themselves to public funds and assets. Some people blamed the particular path that economic reforms had taken. A view that was becoming mainstream in the West by 1999 was that the economic reforms were "the products of greed and power politics compounded by incompetence and ignorance," a view attributed to Peter Reddaway and Dmitri Glinski by Robert Cottrell in his review of their major book published in 2001. The IMF was often pilloried alongside naïve or venal Russian reformers and foreign governments, usually that of the United States.

There was not much chance that we could stem the tide of hostile commentary. We corrected obvious inaccuracies but could not easily counter many of the wilder accusations and misunderstandings, not least because those making them dismissed any explanations coming from the IMF. Anyway, corrections often went unremarked as shown by the persistence of the belief that our loans were stolen. G7 governments, which were also accused of nurturing the Russian kleptocracy, generally kept their heads down. This was more difficult for the United States government than for the Europeans and others because of the greater openness of the US and the fact that Congressional opponents of the President's policies were eager to use the Russian situation to attack Clinton.

A convenient battlefield was the confirmation hearing in September 1999 for Lawrence Summers whom Clinton had nominated as Treasury Secretary to succeed Robert Rubin. Summers had previously been Deputy Secretary and had led the US's economic and financial policies towards Russia. When pressed on Russia by the Senate committee, he said that the US was going to insist that the CBR adopt additional safeguards before the IMF could resume lending. The US then persuaded other G7 countries to back the same position. As a result, the IMF was obliged to go back to the Russians and explain that they now had to fulfill additional G7 conditions before we could disburse another loan installment. The Russians were, of course, angry but they could hardly say that they were surprised because their view had always been that our loans were mainly determined by political considerations in G7 countries, especially the US.

Our discussions with the CBR about new measures for transparency were reaching a conclusion by November 1999. But meanwhile a new problem had arisen which prevented our going ahead with another loan installment. In August, Russia sent armed forces into Chechnya to bring the outlaw regime there to an end. The reports of human rights abuses and brutality that emerged enraged public opinion in the west, more in Europe than in the US. Western governments felt that it would be wrong for the IMF to provide the government with money that could be used to finance the Chechen campaign. Camdessus, who was always careful to avoid any situation in which the IMF could be said to be financing armed conflict, decided that the next loan installment should not go ahead because some of the measures to improve CBR transparency had not been implemented in full. In the absence of the Chechen conflict, I believe that the IMF would have overlooked these imperfections in implementation. But, coming on top of changed perceptions of Russia following the 1998 crisis and stories of corruption, the Chechen war pushed the IMF to make a much more literal assessment of Russia's compliance with agreed policies than it had before the crisis.

The shadow of the disagreements of the last few months of 1999 hung over our relations with Russia in the opening months of 2000. Political changes in Russia also slowed down discussions that might have led to a new loan installment. Yeltsin surprised everyone by resigning prematurely on 31 December 1999. According to the constitution, Vladimir Putin, who had been prime minister since August, became acting president and an election for a new president had to be held within three months. Putin was the favorite candidate and won in the first round. After becoming president in May 2000, he appointed Mikhail Kasyanov, who had been finance minister since the middle of 1999, as prime minister. Aleksei Kudrin took over as finance minister. There was little enthusiasm during the hiatus for reaching a new agreement with the IMF. Even after the new government was formed, it took time for it to be fully effective.

The development that dealt the death blow to the prospect of any new IMF lending was the dramatic improvement in the economy. GDP, which had declined in every year since 1989, except for a small rise in 1997, grew by 5 percent in 1999 and 8 percent in 2000. The main reason for this turn round was the switch towards purchases of domestically produced goods after the 1998 devaluation made imports much more expensive. On top of that, the prices of oil and other commodities that Russia exported rose sharply: the price of Urals oil more than tripled between February 1999 and November 2000. This led to more investment in the economy and a surplus in the budget. Russia no longer needed to borrow from us to finance the budget.

Though there were one or two senior officials who favored a new IMF loan, the Russian leadership as a whole was clear by early 2001 that there should be no more borrowing from the IMF. No longer should Russia's economic policy be negotiated with foreigners. Russia could regain the freedom to set its own policies and put behind it the humiliation of borrowing from the IMF.

As lending had come to an end, the character of our relationship with Russia changed. From 2001 our dialogue with the government and CBR focused less on trying to agree to the details of macroeconomic policy and more on open-ended discussions about policy options. In the jargon of the IMF, we shifted from program mode to surveillance mode. (The set of economic policies that forms the basis of a loan from the IMF is called an economic program. Surveillance is one of the IMF's most important activities. It involves monitoring economic developments in individual economies, and interactions between economies, and advising governments and central banks on policies to improve economic performance.) In its relations with the IMF, Russia was becoming a normal country. Of course, it still owed us money from the earlier loans, but it was repaying these on schedule. In January 2005, when its external financial position was strong, it repaid all its outstanding debt to the IMF even though some of it was not due until 2008.

The shift enabled us to reduce the number of staff we had working on Russia, both those based in Washington and those in our Moscow office. There were fewer missions. Any influence we now had over economic policy had to be exerted through persuasion alone as we could no longer use the leverage of a potential loan. While private discussions with the government and CBR continued to be the main vehicle for giving advice, we also contributed more than before to the public debate in Russia about economic policy. For example, Anne Krueger, who succeeded Fischer as First Deputy Managing Director in 2001, spoke about reforms in Russia at a conference in Moscow in March 2002. I spoke at a conference in Moscow in April 2003. Poul Thomsen, who succeeded Martin Gilman as head of our office in Moscow in 2001, spoke on many occasions in Moscow and wrote articles in the local press. He and I jointly published an article in *Vedemosti*, a daily business newspaper in Russia, in April 2002.

The substance of our discussions also changed in response to changes in the problems facing Russia. On the monetary side, the challenge was to continue to bring down inflation in the face of the monetary effects of the inflow of foreign exchange from the strong balance of payments, both current and capital account. The solution we advocated was for the CBR to purchase less foreign exchange and allow the ruble to appreciate more. But the CBR wanted to limit the appreciation to protect the profitability of exporters and the value in rubles of the population's foreign currency savings. As a result, inflation hardly dipped below 10 percent during the 2000s. On the fiscal side, the emphasis shifted from how to raise more revenues to how to contain expenditure pressures. One solution was the establishment of the oil stabilization fund in 2004 in which money could be saved when the oil price was high. We supported the fund and argued during most of the 2000s that more should be saved this way to help sterilize the inflow of foreign exchange.

Despite some disagreements, we were broadly supportive of Russia's macroeconomic policies from 1999 on. The CBR and finance ministry grasped the opportunity afforded by the crisis and its immediate aftermath, especially the enforced fiscal correction, together with the favorable external position from 1999 onwards, to pursue cautious and predictable policies. We were more concerned about the slow progress in completing the reforms in the structural area.

The Putin era started well in this respect. Putin himself seemed to favor more market-oriented reforms. While still prime minister, he set up a commission in late 1999 headed by German Gref, a law professor from St. Petersburg, to produce an economic reform plan with both long-term and short-term action elements. Unlike many earlier economic plans and programs, this one did eventually have a positive impact. Gref, who became minister for economic development and trade in May 2000, consulted widely and produced a program which was adopted as the government's economic reform program in July. Many of the reforms in the program were implemented over the next two years or so, especially in the areas of legal reform, new labor and land codes, deregulation and pensions. Before these, in the summer of 2000, the Duma passed a major package of tax reform measures, most of which had been held over from 1998.

An important aspect of the Gref program was that it was essentially drawn up by Russians with some suggestions from international organizations and other foreigners. Programs in the 1990s, such as the one the IMF supported in 1996, were mostly the other way round. Clearly, the likelihood of successful implementation was greater when the program was home-grown and took account of as many domestic concerns as possible.

Another feature was that the government introduced reform measures sequentially rather than altogether. Putin had told Martin Gilman and me back in November 1999 during his first meeting with the IMF that broad-based reforms across a range of issues had failed in the past because they united all potential opponents. His approach would be to take one issue at a time. In general, he made a positive impression on us on that occasion, appearing to understand the need for more reforms and being ready to push them through. One comment has stuck in my mind. In response to my observation that Gazprom was too independent and behaved in ways that damaged the economy, Putin agreed and said that he would tackle Gazprom in due course, but he would wait until conditions were favorable. I naively thought that he was thinking what I was thinking, namely that the government would make Gazprom pay the taxes and dividends that were due and prevent it exploiting its monopoly power to the detriment of the economy as a whole. But Martin Gilman said afterwards that he thought that Putin intended to take Gazprom back under state control and use it to pursue government objectives. He turned out to be right.

The momentum of economic reforms that built up in 2000 and 2001 slowed down in 2002 and 2003. One reason was that the next areas for reform, such as natural monopolies and trade related issues, were politically more controversial. Politicians were already looking ahead to the Duma elections in December 2003 and the presidential elections the following year.

At the same time Putin's emphasis on restoring the authority of the state and the presidency led to an extension of state ownership and intervention in the economy and strengthened resistance to market-oriented reforms. These tendencies continued into Putin's second term as president which began in 2004, and beyond. The crony capitalism that Camdessus complained about in 1998, far from dying out as reforms continued, became a more dominant part of the system. Prosecutions were brought against those who, like Khodorkovsky, challenged the authority of the state or the presidency, while others who might have been equally guilty of a similar tax offence or other charge were left alone because they cooperated with the Kremlin. Private companies, especially in the natural resources sector, were renationalized or shaken down. Small and medium sized enterprises found it difficult to grow, or, if they did grow, to resist exploitative pressures from larger enterprises or the government. In the last few years (2000–2003) of my work in Russia, we increasingly warned that investment, diversification away from natural resources, and growth were being adversely affected by vested interests, corruption and excessive government intervention. We recommended reforms in public administration (including the civil service), the judiciary, corporate governance (including accounting), the banking system and natural monopolies. Apart from banking, none of these were areas in which the IMF had special expertise. Our advice was therefore only of a rather general nature.

THE LIMITS OF IMF INFLUENCE IN RUSSIA

It is convenient to summarize our story about Russia by considering the influence that the IMF had there. In brief, our influence—for good or for bad—was much less than most people believed. The macroeconomic policies that were actually implemented departed significantly from the plans that we had originally agreed with the government. Had the agreed policies been implemented, macroeconomic stabilization would have come earlier, growth would have resumed a few years before it did, and the 1998 crisis would have been avoided.

The main reason for the poor implementation was that the government, at least until 1998, was weak and divided. The reform minded leaders who designed the policies and agreed them with us were not able to prevent powerful groups in the economy, and their supporters within government and, until 1995, the CBR, from undermining them. Neither Yeltsin nor Chernomyrdin, the prime minister during the five crucial years 1993–1998 and signatory to the agreements with the IMF, was able or willing to ensure that the policies were implemented.

We might have had more influence on the implementation of policies if our threat to cut off lending in the event of poor implementation had been more credible. But, although there were dissenting voices within the IMF, our official view at the time was that long interruptions in IMF lending would undermine the position of reformers within the government and risk turning Russia away altogether from attempting macroeconomic stabilization and other reforms. The G7 countries and especially the United States seemed to share this view although they also had an interest in pushing the IMF to lend more to Russia to reduce the pressure on them to do so. Whatever their motives, their frequent pressure on the IMF to stay engaged with Russia, and to speed up disbursements after interruptions, made it more difficult for us to take a firm stand when agreed policies were not implemented. Certainly, the Russians believed that IMF decisions about lending were determined mainly by the governments of the G7 and they focused their lobbying efforts accordingly.

One consequence of our limited influence was that we had to focus it on macroeconomic policy issues. Although we were concerned about the slow progress of structural reforms, which were of great importance in transforming Russia into a market economy, we could not do much about it. We may, however, have helped to keep such reforms on the agenda, especially in 1996 when the government's medium-term reform program was incorporated in its agreement with the IMF. We also gave detailed technical assistance about structural reforms in the CBR and finance ministry in technical areas such as methods of monetary management, tax administration and setting up a Treasury.

Although limited, our influence was, I believe, positive. It is important to be clear that we were not responsible for the basic strategy of pursuing liberal economic reforms to establish a market economy as rapidly as possible. This was the choice of the leadership of the country. While we fully supported it for reasons explained in chapter 3, the reforms would have gone ahead had the IMF not been involved at all, contrary to what many people believed. Vladimir Mau, a close associate of Gaidar's, summarized the relative roles of the government and the IMF when he wrote: "A good part of the 'IMF conditions' were developed in Moscow, not Washington. Russian politicians are the ones who initiated many of these conditions."

The intellectual leadership of the reforms was provided by a changing group of young Russian economists and officials led by Chubais and Gaidar who understood the essentials of market economics. Yeltsin knew instinctively that Russia had to go in this direction but tried to strike a balance between the reformers and the powerful opponents of market reforms in the state enterprises, the regional governments, the federal government bureaucracy and the Duma. The latter group contained people with similar backgrounds to Yeltsin's and used this, together with personal friendships, to persuade him to oppose the reforms they disliked. As we have seen, the outcome of Yeltsin's vacillation between two views of economic policy was frequent changes in government personnel and a disconnect between good reforms on paper and poor implementation in practice. Yeltsin was better at managing big events than the details of policies and their implementation. Yet it was in the latter arena that the battles between reformers and their opponents took place. As well as a limited interest in the hard grind of policy implementation, Yeltsin withdrew from active government work from time to time, perhaps because of depression. Some writers have dubbed this "political arrhythmia." He also had poor health in his later years. These limitations to his effectiveness prevented him from giving full support to the reformers in government.

Our influence operated primarily through our advice about the design and operation of specific aspects of macroeconomic policy. For example, we helped with the setting of targets for the growth of monetary aggregates and government borrowing consistent with objectives for inflation. We assisted with the design of policies to support the introduction of the exchange rate corridor in 1995. We discussed with our Russian counterparts the likely increase in revenues from various tax measures that were taken during the

1990s. Through the ongoing dialogue about policy and operational issues that took place between IMF economists and TA experts and Russian officials in the government and CBR, over the years there was a significant transfer of knowledge. Although the Russians could have obtained the necessary understanding in other ways, in practice the IMF was an important vehicle for conveying knowledge about macroeconomic policy design and operation. In the 2000s and 2010s, the government and CBR responded successfully to shocks coming from fluctuations in oil prices, the global financial crisis of 2008 and political events (including sanctions), demonstrating a mastery of the principles and practices of macroeconomic stabilization policies in a market economy.

Given the poor record of macroeconomic stabilization during the ad hoc stabilization (1992–1994) and flawed stabilization (1995–1998) periods, the IMF obviously cannot claim much credit for the outcome of policies. As between the gradualist and radical strategies contrasted in chapter 3, Russia followed the gradualist one, not the rapid adjustment that we favored. However, in an indirect way our engagement may have contributed significantly to economic reforms, and not only those in the macroeconomic area, through strengthening the role of reformers in government. Chubais, Gaidar and others faced enormous opposition from within and outside the government. One argument they used to get their way was that their policies would attract money from the IMF whereas those of their opponents would not. Camdessus's relationship with Chernomyrdin also helped the credibility of the reformers. Yeltsin himself, who was buffeted by alternative advice, must have been somewhat reassured by the fact that international opinion, as represented by the IMF among others, believed that the best way to create the market economy he desired was that advocated by the Russian reformers.

The money that the IMF lent between 1992 and 1999 gave us access and leverage. (The total amount of IMF lending to Russia was $22 billion, converted to US dollars at the exchange rates at the time. The maximum outstanding amount was $19 billion just after the large loan in July 1998.) After 2000 when the prospect of new loans receded, the Russians were not obliged to listen to us with as much attention although they still discussed economic policy with us.

But the money did more than give us a voice in policy making. It allowed Russia to run a larger budget deficit consistent with their targets for inflation. We had hoped that they would use the extra room for maneuver this gave them to cushion living standards from the hit they were taking during the difficult transition years. But in practice it was used to buy support from powerful interest groups, especially the major enterprises, which were able to avoid paying their full tax liabilities. This was not our wish, nor was it the government's stated intention. It was, however, the consequence of the weakness of the government. With hindsight, I can say that we should have been less willing to continue lending when the policies that had been agreed with us were not being implemented, so as to put pressure on the government to tackle their fiscal problems more vigorously, as they did after the 1998 crisis.

Although our overall influence was positive, we made some specific mistakes. We pushed for the abolition of the oil export duty in March 1996 and in the same year we advocated the liberalization of the Treasury bill market. Had we not done so and had the government itself not gone ahead with these measures, the 1998 crisis might have been less severe. We also missed the opportunity in late 1997 or early 1998 to advise the government and CBR to abandon the exchange rate peg, although our advice might well have been ignored.

My conclusion that the IMF's influence in Russia was significant but not enormous, and positive, contradicts a widespread view that we had a major and generally malign impact on Russia in the 1990s. The tendency I noted for the western media as early as 1992 to imply that the IMF had much more influence in Russia than we knew to be the case continued up to 1998. It is easy to understand this. Our interactions with Russia could be dramatized in stories about cliff-hanging negotiations in which large sums of IMF money were at stake. By contrast, the actual messy nature of policy making and implementation in Russia was more difficult for reporters to research and write about in an interesting way.

The exaggeration of the IMF's role in the western media was matched in the Russian media. Here other motives were at play. The opponents of the government's economic policies liked to portray the government as the tool of western agents, among whom they placed the IMF. This was in line with the long tradition in Russia, one that remained strong among communists and nationalists, of suspecting foreigners of trying to undermine Russia. As occurs in many countries where the IMF lends, the government itself sometimes found it convenient to blame the IMF for unpopular policies that it knew it had to pursue with or without the IMF. We must also take some of the blame for the exaggeration of our role because we allowed the perception that we were very influential to persist. The perception might have contributed to our actual influence; and to have challenged it might have reduced our influence in Russia, a country where strength is respected.

The exaggeration of the IMF's role by the media was understandable. Less excusable was the same message coming from analysts who knew the complexity of the situation in Russia. Joseph Stiglitz, for example, said in his widely read book, *Globalisation and Its Discontents,* that the "IMF strategy did not work: GDP in post-1989 Russia fell, year after year." In other words, the IMF told the Russians to do the wrong thing, they followed our advice, and the outcome was a disaster. Every part of this is incorrect: our advice was not wrong (I explained why in chapter 3), the Russians did not implement it (the main thrust of this chapter), and therefore the poor performance of the economy was not the result of following our advice. A simpler and even less accurate version of the case against the IMF was that the economic situation in Russia was bad, the IMF was mainly responsible for the economic policies being pursued, and therefore the IMF was to blame for the mess.

However, there were many people who have said that the IMF's influence was positive. Among them were foreign observers who were generally sympathetic to the reforms that the government was trying to introduce. For example, Anders Åslund has said that the IMF largely acted correctly although he criticized us for not pushing for the abolition of the ruble area in 1992. Compared with foreign writers, Russian writers have generally attributed a much smaller role to the IMF, if they have mentioned us at all. They have focused on domestic actors in politics and the economy, leaving little room for foreigners.

The government and CBR generally appreciated the IMF's work despite many disagreements about particular policy issues. It was particularly gratifying to me to hear Russian officials from President Putin down tell Horst Köhler in October 2001 during his first visit to Moscow as Managing Director of the IMF that Russia had benefited from its relationship with the IMF. Köhler was Managing Director from 2000 to 2004. He had previously been President of the EBRD from 1998 to 2000 and had the misfortune to begin his term there as the crisis in Russia was breaking. I visited him in his first few weeks at the EBRD when he was aggrieved because the EBRD had just lost a lot of money in the crisis. He thought that the IMF was partly to blame and was therefore surprised by the positive view of the IMF he encountered in Moscow in 2001.

As we have seen, the Board of the IMF had many doubts about the wisdom of the continuation of lending by the IMF when agreed policies were not being implemented. Despite this, there was no formal opposition in the Board to any specific decisions, partly because the G7 countries indicated that they supported the decisions and controlled almost 50 percent of the votes. The non-G7 advanced countries and countries that borrowed from the IMF were most critical of IMF policy towards Russia. One of the more thoughtful directors, Onno de Beaufort Wijnholds of the Netherlands, wrote many years later in a book about the IMF's role in financial crises that "the Russian debacle was one of the IMF's biggest failures." When I privately queried this judgement, he admitted that he could have put it less negatively.

RUSSIA—THE COUNTRY AND PEOPLE

It would be wrong to end this discussion of my work in Russia without saying something about the country and its people. Russia is a great country, whether judged by its size–the biggest in the world in land area–or the achievements of its people, in science, literature, music and the arts. It was a privilege to be able to work there and learn a little about it.

Regrettably, my interactions with the country and people were limited. Although I visited 39 times between 1991 and 2003, all the visits were short, the longest being only 10 days. All but two of the visits were to Moscow alone, the other two being to St. Petersburg. Apart from the hunting trips and a few half day outings to Golden Ring towns (Sergiev Posad, Suzdal and Vladimir), ancient places from the twelfth to the eighteenth centuries north-east of Moscow, I went nowhere else. Thus, I have seen only an infinitesimal corner of the vast country. Moreover, as is said about the capital cities in many countries, Moscow is not Russia.

An even bigger limitation is that I do not speak Russian. My language skills are anyway minimal. On top of that, I could not find the time to study Russian seriously, despite the IMF's good language training programs. When it came to business communications, I was supported by many fine interpreters, as well as by a few of my staff who spoke Russian, and some Russian counterparts who spoke English. Outside business and the usual contacts in hotels and restaurants, I had virtually no conversations of substance with Russians. Nevertheless, I learned much from casual exchanges with work colleagues, especially those, both Russian and foreign, based in our Moscow office, and Russian counterparts. I supplemented this with reading everything in English I could about current affairs in Russia.

Moscow changed considerably during the twelve years I was going there. In the early days, the shops were almost all Russian and had limited stock. By the end of my time, many international companies had opened shops, including expensive boutiques such as Prada, Louis Vuitton and Gucci, where the rich new Russians shopped. The huge GUM department store on Red Square across from the Kremlin, which was very run down at the end of the Soviet period, was closed for some years before being completely restored and reopened with many fine shops and eating places. The mayor during most of the 1990s, Yuri Luzhkov, encouraged new developments in the city. Among them was the massive Cathedral of Christ the Savior which was built on the site of, and with a similar design to, the nineteenth century cathedral of the same name that was taken down in 1931. By the 2000s, there were many high, modern buildings all over central Moscow, financed by the private sector. Churches, which had been used for other purposes, were cleaned up, their onion domes regilded and, in most cases, reopened as churches. Other old buildings were restored. Once in 1991, Jean Foglizzo and I were driving to a meeting through an old part of the city. Looking at the run-down blocks in the Russian neoclassical style, he predicted that one day, after the economy recovered and there was money available to restore them, these would be beautiful buildings. He was right, and I was happy that I was able to witness the renewal of the city.

The character of the Russian people, like that of other peoples, has been shaped by their geography and history. The philosopher Berdyaev wrote that "The landscape of the Russian soul corresponds with the landscape of Russia, the same boundlessness, formlessness, reaching out into infinity." Coupled with the long, dark winters, the vast territory contributed to the tendency to focus on the inner life of the spirit and on family and friends. Russians' love of literature is another aspect of the retreat from the world outside.

History has not been kind to the average Russian. Wars, famine and predatory governments have imposed heavy burdens. They have also bred a resilience that has enabled Russians to endure hardships. On the other hand, they have allowed governments to believe they can get away with imposing more burdens on their long-suffering people. The dishonesty of governments and officialdom, from Potemkin villages to the propaganda of the communists, encouraged cynicism but also creative (sometimes conspiratorial) thinking as people searched for the underlying truth. Russians have subtle minds and a fine sense of humor which has helped them survive difficult historical times.

The Soviet Union, for all its faults, had a good education system, not least in the sciences. Many examinations had a large oral component and students were trained to present their arguments orally. I admired the ability of our counterparts to think quickly and logically, and to express their thoughts well. Camdessus liked to remind us that Russians were chess players and thought several moves ahead. Most of the people we dealt with were certainly at least as sharp as equivalent people in the West or anywhere else.

Russians have a direct way of speaking to each other, as well as to strangers, not unlike Americans. They often started formal meetings with strong attacks on the IMF's position. In private contacts they may be reserved at first, even discounting the wariness in dealing with foreigners passed down from Soviet times. But underneath they are warm-hearted, generous, and loyal to their friends. In my work, there were not many opportunities to go beyond the first stage. But when I did, it was most rewarding at the human level.

Working on Russia for twelve years during a most unusual and difficult transformation was professionally very exciting. Beyond that, it led me to find out more about Russian art, literature, music and history. For example, I found time in my busy schedules for visits to the Tretyakov Gallery in Moscow and the State Russian Museum in St. Petersburg. And since retiring,

I have worked on piano pieces by Russian composers, including Scriabin and Tchaikovsky, in my amateurish way. But above all, it brought me into personal contact with many wonderful and talented Russians.

1. Michel Camdessus' meeting with Mikhail Gorbachev, October 1991.
Jean Foglizzo (IMF resident representative in Moscow) and John Odling-
Smee are next to Camdessus. Ernest Obminsky (Soviet Union Foreign
Affairs Ministry) and Viktor Gerashchenko (chairman of the State Bank of
the Soviet Union) are next to Gorbachev. *Courtesy of the author.*

2. Michel Camdessus' meeting with Boris Yeltsin, March 1995. With
Camdessus, from left: Yusuke Horiguchi (IMF mission chief to Russia),
John Odling-Smee, Thomas Wolf (IMF resident representative in Moscow).
With Yeltsin, from left: Tatiana Paramonova (acting Chairperson, Central
Bank of Russia), Andrei Kozyrev (Minister of Foreign Affairs, Russia), Viktor
Chernomyrdin (Prime Minister, Russia), interpreter. *Courtesy of the author.*

3. Alfresco dinner after hunting, Russia, February 1996. From left: Sergei Dubinin (Chairman, Central Bank of Russia), Michel Camdessus (IMF Managing Director), Viktor Chernomyrdin (Prime Minister, Russia), John Odling-Smee. *Courtesy of the author.*

4. Michel Camdessus with newly appointed Russian ministers, April 1997: Boris Nemtsov (Deputy Prime Minister, left), Anatoli Chubais (First Deputy Prime Minister, right), John Odling-Smee. *Courtesy of the author.*

5. With Vladimir Putin, Prime Minister of Russia, November 1999.
Courtesy of Alamy.

6. With Leonid Kuchma, President of Ukraine, November 1998.
Courtesy of Alamy.

7. With Levon Ter-Petrosyan, President of Armenia, 1994. The ambassador of Armenia to the United States is in the middle. *Courtesy of the author.*

8. Dinner in Armenia with Prime Minister Vazgen Sargsyan, June 1999. My wife, Carmela Veneroso, is at the left, next to Sargsyan. Among the others are Armen Darbinyan (Minister of Trade and Industry, previously Prime Minister), at the end of the table, right, and George Anayiotos (IMF resident representative in Armenia), to right of Darbinyan. *Courtesy of the author.*

9. With Georgian counterparts, December 1999. From left: Vladimir Papava (Minister of Economy), Deputy State Minister (name not known), Temur Basilia (Economic Adviser to the President), John Odling-Smee, Christopher Lane (IMF), David Onoprishvili (Minister of Finance). *Courtesy of the author.*

10. With a Kantsi, traditional Georgian drinking horn, July 1994. *Courtesy of the author.*

11. Visit to Osh, Kyrgyzstan, October 2002, with Tapio Saavalainen (IMF mission chief to Kyrgyzstan), without jacket, Ulan Sarbanov (Chairman of the National Bank of the Kyrgyz Republic), front right, other Kyrgyz officials and our interpreter, Bakhyt Kenjeev, back left. *Courtesy of the author.*

12. Conference on the tenth anniversary of the Kyrgyz som, Bishkek, May 2003. From left: Ulan Sarbanov (Chairman of the National Bank), Djoomart Otorbaev (Deputy Prime Minister), John Odling-Smee. *Courtesy of the author.*

13. With Emomali Rakhmonov, President of Tajikistan, about 2000. From left: Tajik official, Murodali Alimardonov (Chairman of the National Bank), Rakhmonov, Safarali Najmuddinov (Minister of Finance), Matlub Davlatov (Presidential Administration), Henri Lorie (partly hidden, IMF resident representative in Tajikistan), Bakhyt Kenjeev (IMF interpreter), John Odling-Smee, Tapio Saavalainen (IMF mission chief to Tajikistan). *Courtesy of the author.*

14. Relaxing at the weekend in Tajikistan, April 2002. From left: President Emomali Rakhmonov, my wife Carmela Veneroso, Arkady Tchaikovsky (IMF interpreter), John Odling-Smee in Tajik costume, Robert Christiansen (IMF mission chief to Tajikistan). *Courtesy of the author.*

Chapter 5

Ukraine: Someday We Will

Every day on the way to my office in the IMF, I passed the monument erected in 1964 to Taras Shevchenko, the Ukrainian poet and artist who died in 1861. He was and is a hero of the Ukrainian nationalist movement. An extract from one of his poems is carved on the stone plinth:

WHEN WILL UKRAINE
HAVE ITS WASHINGTON
WITH FAIR AND JUST LAWS?
SOMEDAY WE WILL

(From *The Holy Fool* [1857], translated from the Ukrainian.) Shevchenko was referring to independence from the Russian empire.

As year followed year, I wondered when Ukraine would enact laws and implement policies that would enable it to stabilize the macroeconomic situation and create a market economy. It seemed to be taking longer than in most other transition countries. But, like Shevchenko, I too had faith that Ukraine would get there eventually: "someday we will."

Ukraine was the second largest country that emerged from the Soviet Union. Its population of 52 million when the Union dissolved accounted for about 18 percent of the total (Russia was 51 percent). Its economy was diversified, with important agricultural, coal mining, metals and engineering sectors. Before the dissolution, it traded with all parts of the former Soviet Union. After the dissolution, it acquired geopolitical importance because of its size and geographical and cultural position between Russia and the rest of Europe. So long as it retained its independence, Russia would not be able to recreate a version of the Russian empire. If it returned to some sort of union with Russia, the rest of Europe would feel less secure. Both Russia and the West therefore had a major stake in its future. The significant minorities of Ukrainian origin in some countries in the West, especially Canada and the

United States, increased the political pressure in those countries to do what they could to maintain Ukraine's independence.

We recognized the importance of Ukraine and devoted considerable resources to our work there. Our missions were led by experienced mission chiefs. The mission teams were larger than those for other countries except Russia. We posted two people to the office in Kyiv (using the Ukrainian spelling rather than the Russian Kiev) whereas in other places, except Russia, there was only one. I made 20 visits to Kyiv compared with 5–7 to the other countries, again except Russia (and Turkmenistan). My colleagues in the technical assistance departments also provided a large amount of advice to the central bank and finance ministry.

Unfortunately, for much of the 1990s the government was unwilling or unable to implement serious stabilization and reform measures. There were periods when it looked as though reforms were taking off, but they were short-lived. The "meandering path of reforms," the phrase used by Oleh Havrylyshyn in his retrospective look at Ukraine in 2014, was mainly set by Ukraine's presidents. The first president, Leonid Kravchuk, placed a low priority on economic reforms, and little was achieved. Leonid Kuchma, who succeeded Kravchuk in 1994, began a serious reform program. But it encountered difficulties within a few years and ran out of steam. The next major opportunity for reforms came in 2005 after the election of Viktor Yushchenko as president following the Orange Revolution in late 2004.

The seeds of the poor reform performance were sown in the first period from 1992 to 1994. Kravchuk and the leaders of the country during his presidency had been in power during the Soviet period and had little interest in economic reform. They and the leaders in the enterprise sector had a vested interest in the continuation of the partially reformed economy that emerged from the Soviet Union. They could become the new capitalists, as explained in chapter 3. They also feared the short-term impact on living standards of radical reforms. The Ministers of Economy, Volodymyr Lanovyi in 1992 and Viktor Pynzenyk after that, were reform-minded economists. But Lanovyi resigned after his economic reform program was rejected by the government and Pynzenyk was unable to make much progress.

The main achievement of the Kravchuk period was to create a sense of Ukrainian statehood, including an army, relations with foreign countries, and a national flag. Kravchuk and his supporters and apologists argued that nation building had to have priority over economic reform. But there is no reason why the two objectives could not have been pursued at the same time, as they were successfully in the Baltic States.

Ukraine decided early on to introduce its own currency but was clearly not able to manage it in the early months of 1992. When Russia reduced the supply of ruble notes, Ukraine was one of the countries that tried to get round it by issuing its own coupons which were initially interchangeable with rubles. Despite our advice to restrict the supply of coupons and reach agreement with Russia on monetary and credit emission, Ukraine went its own way. It issued credit on an excessive scale, mainly in a misguided attempt to keep the old economy going. In doing so, it exported inflationary pressures to the rest of the ruble area, to the concern of the other countries, especially Russia. Eventually, in November 1992, Ukraine issued its own currency, the karbovanets. (It was intended to be only a temporary currency and was replaced in 1996 by the hryvnia.) But monetary and fiscal policies were very loose, and inflation soared to over 10,000 percent in 1993. My colorful collection of very large denomination karbovanets notes, which seemed to be printed on regular paper and must have been easy to counterfeit, decorated our house for a while.

In the difficult conditions of 1992–1994, the advice of our teams fell on deaf ears. Our experienced mission chief, Peter Hole, who had led the mission to Poland when it started its successful reform program with IMF support, was frequently frustrated. I was therefore somewhat alarmed when he opened a phone call to me from Kyiv by saying that he had just hit the roof. It turned out that the lift he had taken up to his hotel room had malfunctioned and had indeed hit a barrier at the top of the lift shaft. Fortunately, no one was hurt.

Things began to change in the National Bank of Ukraine (the central bank) after the appointment of Viktor Yushchenko as governor in 1993. However, we had little influence on economic policies in those early years, although our advice was seeping through to lower level officials who were keen to learn about economic policy making in a market economy.

Kravchuk lost the presidential election in July 1994 and was succeeded by Leonid Kuchma, who had been prime minister in 1992–1993. Kuchma was an engineer and had previously been head of the world's largest missile factory in Dnipropetrovsk (renamed Dnipro in 2016). Having failed to make much progress with economic reforms when he was prime minister, and seeing the continued deterioration in the economy, he decided to make a major push for economic reforms as president. Encouraged by Oleh Havrylyshyn who represented Ukraine on the IMF Board at that time, he invited Camdessus to Kyiv. Camdessus, who liked to respond quickly, arrived in Kyiv only a week or so after Kuchma's inauguration. There followed an intense period of negotiations leading up to agreement on economic policies and a first loan from the IMF in October 1994. Meanwhile Kuchma had made an important speech in the parliament outlining a program of radical economic reforms. It looked as though Ukraine was at last embarked on serious reforms.

There was good progress towards macroeconomic stabilization, with inflation coming down from its very high level in 1993 and the budget deficit moving to low single digits as a percentage of GDP. Prices were freed, export quotas and licenses abolished, the exchange rate unified and privatization begun. By 1996, there was sufficient stability to permit the successful introduction of the permanent currency, the hryvnia. However, the economy was still dominated by large state-owned enterprises, and it was not easy for new, more dynamic businesses to thrive. Measured output continued to decline, although perhaps not average living standards which were sustained by the growing unmeasured economy.

Political pressure built up for a change of course. Some of it came from the strong left-inclined group in parliament which wanted a state-controlled economy with more subsidies to maintain economic activity and support living standards. Some on the left blamed the IMF for the policies. I was once meeting Pynzenyk in his office when we were interrupted by a loud demonstration outside. On looking out of the window we saw, among many banners, one that said "Down with Pynzenyk and the IMF." Our attempts to explain to parliamentarians why the government's reforms were the right thing to do were not successful. Even Fischer, always mild mannered and reasonable, was unable to make much of an impression on Natalia Vitrenko, the leader of the most extreme left party, when she unleashed a barrage of ill-informed criticisms of the IMF at him.

Pressure for a change of course also came from the powerful vested interests in the economy. They wanted the partially reformed economy that Ukraine inherited from the Soviet Union, and Kravchuk kept going, to continue. They knew how to make money in such a world. A successful transition to a market economy would remove many of the opportunities for them to buy at controlled prices and sell at world prices, to extract monopoly profits, to strip assets from state enterprises and to engage in all the other activities that the partially reformed economy made possible.

Kuchma had the character and perhaps even the political skills to stand up to these pressures, especially after the new constitution, which strengthened the presidency, was adopted in 1996. But the tragedy for Ukraine was that he himself was not a committed believer in radical market reforms. He was a pragmatic realist who promoted a radical strategy when he felt that it was the best way to get out of the economic and financial mess in 1994. But otherwise, he believed in more government intervention to achieve specific ends than was compatible with the move to a fully functioning market economy. He was not too different in this from the other enterprise managers of his generation. By 1996, his reformist tendencies were beginning to run out of steam.

Our response was to work with the Ukrainian authorities, the World Bank and others on a program of structural and institutional reforms. The aim was to agree on a program that we could support with a large EFF loan, with the World Bank providing a Structural Adjustment Loan. Unlike in Russia or the Baltic States, there were few counterparts on the Ukrainian side with any background in market economics. In addition, our counterparts were not important figures in the government and were reluctant to commit themselves to policies that might not be acceptable to powerful people. We thought that this reflected the continuation of old Soviet practices in which the Finance Ministry had little status and government bureaucrats could be overruled by party functionaries. But the reality was that the powers behind the scenes were the vested interests that resisted market reforms which would cut into their profits. They operated at a higher level than that of our counterparts, who were therefore caught between wanting to agree with us on reforms while not knowing whether they would get support from their seniors, especially the prime minister and president.

We tried to strengthen our counterparts' understanding of, and commitment to, a program of structural reforms by inviting them to a seminar in Washington in July 1996. Four workshops on macroeconomic policy, wages and social safety net, private sector development and trade and sectoral issues discussed policies on the basis of presentations by IMF and World Bank staff. The Ukrainian participants were led by Roman Shpek, who had led the team that agreed the first program with us in 1994, and included deputy ministers of finance and economy, among others. They were not very active in the discussions but followed the presentations carefully while perhaps wondering privately whether the powers that be at home would contemplate many of the reforms being recommended. The presentations were published in 1997 by the IMF in a book with the optimistic title *Ukraine: Accelerating the Transition to Market*.

Shpek was not the right man to lead the reforms. Trained as an engineer, he had worked in the forestry industry before entering the government in 1992. Pynzenyk, on the other hand, understood market economics and, as deputy prime minister for economic reforms from 1995, was in a position where he could lead the reforms. In 1996 he mobilized a group of reform minded economists and produced a program with detailed structural, social and fiscal reforms. But Kuchma did not support him, nor did the prime minister, Pavlo Lazarenko, or the parliament. The reform program died and Pynzenyk resigned in disgust in April 1997. This episode revealed the difference between Ukraine and Russia. Kuchma was no Yeltsin. He did not have Yeltsin's intuitive belief in genuine market reforms, nor his willingness to battle for them for at least some of the time. And Pynzenyk did not have the combination of Gaidar's intellectual leadership and Chubais' political and administrative skills that made the Gaidar/Chubais team so influential in Russia.

Not only was Kuchma not a strong supporter of reforms, except in the year or two after his election in 1994, but the prime ministers, who were in a position to push reforms, were part of the vested interests that resisted reforms, with one exception. They were also in their jobs for very short periods. There were ten prime ministers in the twelve years from independence in 1991 to 2003, not counting short-lived acting prime ministers. Some, such as Yukhym Zvyagilsky (1993–1994), became rich through corruption and rent seeking. Some, notably, Lazarenko (1996–1997) were criminal; later he was convicted in the US for money laundering, wire fraud and transporting stolen goods, and sentenced to nine years in prison. Others, including Valeriy Pustovoitenko (1997–1999), wanted to preserve the Soviet style bureaucracy that stifled private sector activity. Only Viktor Yushchenko (1999–2001) was reform minded, but he was voted out by parliament under the influence of vested interests which did not like his reforms.

The years from 1995 to 1998 were frustrating for our teams working on Ukraine, and their leaders, first Adalbert Knöbl and then Mohammad Shadman-Valavi. While monetary and fiscal policies were broadly consistent with macroeconomic stabilization and the hryvnia was stable, many of the structural reforms we had agreed with the authorities were not implemented. In the absence of major reforms, output continued to decline. At a conference in Kyiv in June 1998, I pointed out in a section of my talk entitled *What has gone wrong in Ukraine?* that Ukraine and Turkmenistan were the only two countries in the CIS where output had continued to decline in 1997. Even Russia had started to grow, a comparison that was particularly hurtful to Ukrainians.

Over a cup of coffee in a break at the conference, I was the witness to a wager between Andrei Illarionov and Marek Dabrowsky. Illarionov, a Russian economist who had been an advisor to Chernomyrdin and was later to advise Putin when the latter was president of Russia, was more optimistic about Ukraine's economic prospects than Russia's. Dabrowsky, a Polish economist who had worked with Balcerowicz on reforms in Poland and was an adviser to the Ukrainian government, was more optimistic about Russia than Ukraine. Illarionov bet that Ukraine would be doing better than Russia economically in five years' time; Dabrowsky that Russia would be doing better. Each of them was unwilling to back the country where he worked, perhaps because he knew the problems there better than he knew those in the other country. As it turned out, output grew quite rapidly in both countries over the following five years. I do not know who won the bet.

Our attempt to make up for the absence of a Ukrainian program of reforms by incorporating structural reform measures in the economic programs the government agreed with us was not a great success. Although the government and National Bank agreed with the programs, and Kuchma also indicated his support, in practice many of the measures were not implemented. Or they were implemented on paper (for example, a law was passed in parliament), but the implementation in practice was postponed or thwarted by administrative interventions. In the language of international organizations, there was insufficient ownership of the programs by the authorities. The reality was that the vested interests that stood to lose from market reforms made sure that the reforms did not work. The government went along with the charade because it wanted the imprimatur of IMF support, not least to enable it to borrow from private lenders, and it also benefited from the first tranche of our money, which we disbursed before the program went off track. We went along with it mainly because the macroeconomic targets in the programs were usually implemented correctly, sometimes after a delay and perhaps an adjustment, and this was our main concern. In addition, some of the structural reforms were implemented, and an increasing number of government officials were coming to understand what reforms were needed to create a market economy.

The development of government debt markets and the relative stability of the hryvnia after 1996 encouraged foreign investors to increase their lending to the government. But this was short-lived because the Asian financial crisis in 1997 caused investors to worry about their exposure to Ukraine, as well as Russia. Money flowed out and Ukraine had to reduce its foreign exchange reserves to maintain the exchange rate. An agreement between Ukraine and the IMF on a large EFF loan in 1998 was delayed by parliamentary opposition and the need to obtain the agreement of three international banks that they would not withdraw their funds in response to a loan from the IMF. By the time these problems were overcome, and the IMF Board was scheduled to meet to approve the loan, the Russian default in August had created a financial crisis in Ukraine. Investors were withdrawing funds quickly and the three large lenders were reluctant to roll over their existing loans. Shadman-Valavi went to Kyiv immediately, and Camdessus met Kuchma in Foros, where he also conferred with Chernomyrdin, as described in chapter 4. Camdessus subsequently had phone conversations with Kuchma who asked President Chirac to intervene with Camdessus. The outcome was that the Board met in early September and approved the loan to Ukraine after the authorities agreed to devalue the hryvnia and widen the band within which it could fluctuate. Some progress was made in restructuring private sector debts, but a comprehensive restructuring did not take place until 2000.

The program that the Board approved included structural reforms in many areas: tax and customs administration, treasury operations, public employment, pension system, external trade, energy and agricultural sectors, banking sector, and privatization. There were 88 measures and 150 sub-measures in the program. While not many of them had to be implemented for Ukraine to qualify for the next disbursement of our loan, they all had to be monitored, which proved to be difficult for our staff, especially as many of them were in policy areas with which we were not familiar. The ex-post review of the program that the IMF conducted in 2005 said that it was a "leading example of excessive structural activism." As we have seen, the IMF's policy changed in 2001 and conditionality was streamlined so that it applied only to areas related to macroeconomic stability. I was not convinced that that this was the right way to go in Ukraine because the long list of structural reform measures provided the authorities with a road map for reforms. We did, however, shorten the list of measures, even before the change in IMF policy.

One particular measure that was heavily criticized by those, inside as well as outside the IMF, who thought that we were micromanaging too much, was a reduction in the export tax on sunflower seeds. In August 1999, Ukraine imposed a 23 percent tax on exports of sunflower seeds, which was contrary to their commitment to us not to impose any new restrictions on exports. Ukraine was one of the world's largest producers and exporters of sunflower seeds. The tax was introduced to benefit the Ukrainian oilseed crushing industry, by reducing the price it had to pay for sunflower seeds, at the expense of producers of sunflower seed who received less from export sales than before the tax. It reduced allocative efficiency in the economy and redistributed income from the sunflower seed producers to the politically more powerful owners of the vegetable oil factories. But it could not be said to be related to macroeconomic stability. We pressed for the tax to be reduced, if not eliminated, but it was not until 2001 that it was reduced to 17 percent. After the change in our structural conditionality policy that year, we no longer asked for a further reduction. However, one of the conditions attached later to Ukraine's accession to the WTO was the gradual phasing out of the tax.

In my meetings with Kuchma in 1999 and 2000, he rolled his eyes when I raised the issue of sunflower seeds. Like many in Ukraine, he could not understand why we were making such a fuss about them. By then, my credibility with him might have been tarnished by a chance remark I made during a friendly chat beside the Black Sea. In July 1999 I was in Kyiv and Kuchma was on vacation in the president's summer residence in Foros. Our counterparts in Kyiv were very keen on taking me and Shadman-Valavi to see him there, for reasons that became clear. We left Kyiv early in the morning in a government plane and landed at a military airfield in Crimea where we were received by representatives of the Crimean regional government. Our party included the deputy prime minister for economic affairs, Sergiy Tihipko; the finance minister, Ihor Mitiukov; the head of the National Bank, Viktor Yushchenko, and a number of others. After refreshments and some business–Mitiukov was cornered by the Crimean finance minister (an elegant lady) who sought some favors from the central budget–our motorcade took us to Foros. Road signs on the way pointed to Balaclava, Inkerman and Sevastopol, names I remembered from the history of the Crimean War. The Foros residence was on a cliff looking south over the Black Sea. During a break in our meeting,

Kuchma took us down to the beach. Once there, most of the Ukrainians who came from Kyiv quickly opened their briefcases, pulled out their swimming trunks, changed and plunged into the water. I had wondered why they had all brought such large briefcases for such a short meeting. Shadman-Valavi and I were left to make conversation with Kuchma and Yushchenko who did not go bathing. Displaying my knowledge of Ukrainian history, I told Kuchma that I passed Taras Shevchenko every day on my way to work in Washington. But I made the mistake of adding that I rode on a bicycle. He looked at me with a puzzled expression, and I feared that he was recalibrating his assessment of my status in the IMF. Our relationship remained cordial during subsequent years, but I wondered whether my credibility had taken a hit.

I rarely had time for tourism on working visits, but Yushchenko insisted that Shadman-Valavi and I should see the Church of the Resurrection of Christ while in Foros. It was further up the mountainside, perched dramatically on a ledge 400 meters above the Black Sea. Commissioned in the 1880s by the landowner, a Moscow tea merchant, to commemorate the survival of Alexander III in a train crash, it was built in a mixture of baroque, Russian revival and Byzantine revival styles and had been recently restored. I would have loved to have been able to explore many other parts of Ukraine. Odessa, for example, where I once landed at the airport only to be whisked away in a motorcade to Chisinau in Moldova without going near the city. However, I did manage to see the fine St Sophia's Cathedral, Lavra monastery and a few other places in Kyiv. It was also very pleasant in the spring and summer just to walk in the park near our hotel, passing the parliament and Mariyinsky Palace and looking down through the woods to the Dnieper River below and across to the modern buildings on the other side of the river. I have a particularly strong memory of the scent of the blossom on the many horse chestnut trees in the streets on the hill down to the city center from our hotel.

Only once did I go outside the center of Kyiv. Mitiukov had been ill and was recovering in a sanatorium on the edge of the city. The medical system still had many Soviet features, including an emphasis on long recuperation periods after an illness. Mitiukov had not been very ill, perhaps influenza or something similar, but he had been away from the office for some time, although continuing to work. When we went to see him in the sanatorium, he was walking around and seemed quite fit. I too would want to extend my stay there if I was sick, as its peaceful location in a sylvan setting and helpful staff created a most restful environment.

There was a rupture in our relations with Ukraine in 2000 as a result of the earlier misreporting to us of its international reserves by the National Bank. It had consistently exaggerated the amount of free reserves, partly by not telling us that some of the reserves were otherwise committed and partly by counting some of the reserves twice by "round tripping" (lending them back to domestic banks which then redeposited them abroad). After the *Financial Times* broke the story in early 2000, the IMF insisted on an external audit, the results of which were published later in the year. The incident led to delays in disbursements because of our insistence on stricter adherence to agreed targets. There was also a cooling of relations between our team and their Ukrainian counterparts.

One of the most important counterparts at a senior level was Yushchenko. He was one of the very few people who consistently supported market reforms. As head of the National Bank when the misreporting occurred, he was almost certainly complicit in it. He became prime minister in December 1999, and we were hopeful that he would be able to accelerate economic reforms. The misreporting incident set back our relationship with him. We continued to work closely with him, although without the same degree of mutual trust.

On our side, any promotion for Shadman-Valavi, who as mission chief in 1998 had some inkling that there was misreporting, was put on hold. I too was formally reprimanded by IMF management in a letter from Fischer. The Board observed that, even though the 1998 crisis demanded quick action, there might have been too much willingness by the staff to overlook problems when trying to put together a program for Ukraine. This was an occupational hazard, which I have already noted in the case of Russia.

However, unlike with Russia, we were not pressed by the G7 to continue lending in conditions that did not warrant it. They were very concerned that Ukraine should create a successful market economy, as this would help ensure its continued independence. But they did not insist that we should cut corners. The US, which watched Ukraine closely, was well aware of the problems we were encountering in trying to help Ukraine reform and generally supported our positions.

The financial crisis in 1998 altered the macroeconomic situation markedly, as it also did in Russia. The devaluation of the hryvnia raised foreign demand for Ukraine's manufactured exports, especially steel, other metals and chemicals. As there was plenty of unused capacity in these industries, output grew rapidly. There were some structural reforms that produced positive results. The energy sector was one area. Yulia Tymoshenko, who was deputy prime minister for fuel and energy in Yushchenko's government in 2000, made enterprises pay cash for electricity and increased sanctions for non-payment. I met her during that period and was most impressed by her reform intentions and her determination to get her way. I fully recognized the description of her in *The Economist* at the time: "If she does not get her way with feminine charm, she will do so with a steely gaze." The growth of output, 50 percent from 2000 to 2004, coupled with the near absence of private sector finance for the budget, brought the fiscal situation under control. The balance of payments current account was strong and there was no need for financial assistance from us. But, despite the structural reforms, the investment climate was very poor, and investment remained low. The prospects for longer term growth once the unused capacity was utilized were not good. Given this, and the fragile state of economic and financial institutions, we continued to have a close policy dialogue with the authorities.

The prospects for serious economic reforms brightened in 2005 after Yushchenko won the rerun of the presidential election in December 2004, following the Orange Revolution. With Tymoshenko as prime minister, a good start was made with some trade and fiscal liberalization measures and the closure of tax loopholes. But the team of Yushchenko and Tymoshenko was not sufficiently united or strong to overcome the opposition of the vested interests and others who supported Viktor Yanukovich, the loser in the presidential election. Tymoshenko was a difficult personality, and Yushchenko, who was jealous of her greater popularity and charisma, failed to develop a constructive working relationship with her. Progress in liberalization and creating the institutions of a market economy was therefore quite disappointing during the five years of Yushchenko's presidency.

Viktor Yushchenko was a central figure in our dealings with Ukraine during my time. He was a consistent supporter of economic reforms from when he was appointed Governor of the National Bank in 1993. Although we would sometimes disagree on details of monetary or economic policy, he regarded us as allies in his drive for reforms. He was willing to fight for what he believed in, something we saw early on when he successfully resisted parliament's criticisms of his tightening of monetary policy in 1993 and 1994. His courage was even more apparent and public when he was the leading figure in the Orange Revolution in 2004, having recovered only months before from an attempted assassination by dioxin poisoning.

He was also a friendly and hospitable host on social occasions. He once invited me to his house where his wife fed us and he asked me to plant a tree in his garden. My wife will always remember him at the beginning of her only visit to Kyiv when he greeted her at the airport with a kiss, a big bunch of roses and a box of chocolates. Normal behavior, perhaps, but he did it with great flair and charm. And he was very handsome at that time, which was before the disfiguring effect of the dioxin. He was religious and enjoyed the arts. He himself loved to paint. When he was Governor, the National Bank made financial contributions to church and arts organizations. Once after a morning meeting, he announced that we were going to have lunch with some senior clerics of the Ukrainian Orthodox Church and whisked me and our excellent interpreter, Olga Chmola, across town for an interesting conversation over the meal.

But he had weaknesses as a leader. He was not always open about what he was doing. He could talk at length at meetings without getting to the point. We were left taking on trust that he would do the right thing. The misreporting episode when he was at the National Bank revealed that he could not always be trusted. His habit of keeping his cards close to his chest hampered his collaboration with colleagues in the government and parliament when he was prime minister and president. It was not, of course, easy for him to govern with a parliament that often had a majority opposed to his policies. But a more skillful and open politician would have more often found compromises that allowed his policies to be enacted. His inability to find a way to work with Tymoshenko, even though they agreed on most aspects of economic reform, was his biggest failure, although it was not all his fault. Nevertheless, despite his weaknesses, he was undoubtedly a force for good when it came to market reforms in Ukraine.

I have mixed feelings about my time working in Ukraine. On the one hand, I liked the people and wanted them to succeed in building an independent state with an open market economy. On the other hand, the many setbacks in the implementation of market reforms were quite frustrating. There was a lack of strategic vision at the highest levels about the course Ukraine should take. There was no Yeltsin, Gaidar or Chubais. Partly as a consequence, there was a lack of consensus in the government and parliament. Sometimes it seemed as though Ukrainians preferred to spend their time arguing about what should be done, rather than coming together to agree on a course of action. (In a private conversation with Camdessus and me, Chernomyrdin expressed what I took to be a common Russian view. He said that Ukrainians would always do the opposite of what you recommended, even when it was the worst option from their point of view.)

Ukraine had got off to a bad start. Vested interests that benefited from a semi-reformed economic system dug in during the early 1990s and were subsequently very difficult to dislodge. Their focus on rent-seeking and asset stripping rather than investing for growth delayed the recovery and pushed many people into the shadow economy. (One example that affected our teams was the absence of the international hotel companies because the local hotel owners had persuaded the Kyiv city authorities to prevent the international companies from opening, in order to keep up the price of hotel accommodation.) The inability of government to insist on hard budget constraints led to a non-payments culture. Corruption was an ever-present problem. The rapid growth of the early 2000s and the cumulative impact of a few structural and institutional reforms brought Ukraine a little closer to a properly functioning market economy. But there was still some way to go.

In February 2003, during one of my last visits to Kyiv, I tried to invoke the spirit of Taras Shevchenko and "Someday we will." I concluded a talk at the Kyiv-Mohyla Academy of the National University with the sentences:

> The good macroeconomic performance of recent years has increased confidence and contributed to a better functioning of the market economy, for example through increased monetization and reduced barter. This provides the basis for pushing ahead with the next wave of structural reforms. If this can be done successfully, and monetary and fiscal policies maintain macroeconomic stability, Ukraine can look forward to many more years of good macroeconomic performance.

The conditional "if" in the final sentence protected me from appearing unrealistically optimistic. However, I really do believe that Ukraine will create a real market economy one day, and certainly in a much shorter time than the 134 years from Shevchenko's "Someday we will" until the emergence of independent Ukraine in 1991.

Chapter 6

The Baltic States

Estonia, Latvia and Lithuania are referred to collectively as the Baltic States or just the Baltics. They were part of the Russian Empire before World War I, after which they were independent countries until they were annexed by the Soviet Union following the Molotov-Ribbentrop pact of 1939. Germany occupied them from 1941 until 1944–1945 when the Red Army took them back. They remained part of the Soviet Union until they became independent in 1991. Many countries, including the US and the UK, considered them to be under Soviet occupation throughout.

With this history, it was not surprising that they were in the forefront of Soviet republics that wanted to break away from the Union. Dramatic protests, such as the Baltic Chain in August 1989 in which 2 million people (out of a combined population of 8 million) held hands in a human chain which stretched over 675 kilometers across the three small countries, drew the attention of the world to their situation. Proponents of independence won elections to the Supreme Soviets of the three republics in early 1990, and the pressure for independence grew, especially in Lithuania. After talks failed, Soviet paratroops and tanks appeared in the streets of Vilnius, including outside the parliament, in January 1991. Citizens poured into Vilnius to show their support for the parliamentarians who were inside. There was shooting and about 13 civilians were killed. Under considerable pressure from abroad, and even within the Soviet Union, Gorbachev distanced himself from the events. From then on it was clear that the Baltics would leave the Soviet Union, which in fact agreed to their independence soon after the August 1991 coup in Moscow.

They are all small, with populations in 1990 of 1.6 million (Estonia), 2.7 million (Latvia) and 3.7 million (Lithuania). High rates of emigration and low birth rates subsequently reduced these numbers, by 20–30 percent by 2020. Estonia and Latvia have large ethnic Russian minorities, between a quarter and a third of the total, mainly as a result of migration from Russia during the Soviet period. Despite their proximity and similar histories, they are proudly separate from each other. This stems partly from cultural and linguistic differences. Estonian is a Finno-Ugric language. Latvian and Lithuanian are Baltic languages and are somewhat different from each other. It was sometimes said during the independence movements of the 1980s that Estonia provided the brains, Latvia the business and organizational skills, and Lithuania the passion. But this suggests a greater degree of difference between them than was or is the case.

As we have seen, our first contact with them was immediately after they declared independence, when Erb met some of their representatives in Tallinn and Bangkok in September and October of 1991. Our relationship developed rapidly after that. Teams went from my department in November and roughly every two months in 1992. They were all led by Adalbert (Bert) Knöbl, an experienced economist who had worked on many European countries. He listened carefully to the arguments of the authorities and worked with them to find solutions to their problems. They trusted him and his teams to give impartial advice, and a productive working relationship with the three Baltics was established from the beginning. After working on those countries for a few years, Bert took over as mission chief for Ukraine, a challenging job. He was, however, most interested in the Baltics, and spent the final years of his IMF career as our resident representative in all three countries. Our first resident representatives took up their posts in Tallinn, Riga and Vilnius by the middle of 1992. Our colleagues in the technical assistance departments of the IMF were also very active providing advice about central banking, introducing new currencies, financial sector supervision and regulation, establishing a treasury, tax reform, tax administration and statistics.

The Baltics were especially hard hit by the collapse of the Soviet economy and the breakup of the Soviet Union because, in addition to the difficulties all former Soviet republics faced, they also had to cope with the sharp increase to world levels of the prices of energy and raw materials imported from Russia. The other countries joined the Commonwealth of Independent States (CIS), and Russia chose to keep the prices of exports of energy and raw materials to the CIS below world levels, at least initially. The Baltics refused to join the CIS and as a result faced world prices for goods from Russia. Their terms of trade deteriorated by over 20 percent, implying a huge loss of real incomes from this source alone. Given all the other changes taking place, output fell sharply, prices jumped and living standards fell drastically. This was the situation in 1992 when we started to work with the countries.

A central political concern of the countries was the introduction of national currencies. They saw this as an essential element of their independence, as well as providing them some protection from the inflationary pressures affecting the ruble. They wanted to introduce the new currencies as quickly as possible. We advised them to put in place tight monetary and fiscal policies first, to ensure the stability of the new currencies. Without such policies we would not be able to provide a loan or endorse their policies.

In the case of Estonia, the government agreed to tighten fiscal policy sharply, by 5–6 percentage points of GDP. The details were worked out in June between Knöbl's team and the finance minister in informal sessions on the island of Saaremaa and the measures were implemented soon afterwards. Others from the IMF worked with the Bank of Estonia on practical aspects of the introduction of the currency, the kroon. We were satisfied that Estonia was ready to introduce the kroon in late June, from both practical and macroeconomic policy points of view. It was the first former Soviet country to introduce its own currency. Although we were not able to arrange that the IMF Board approve a loan to Estonia until September, we issued a statement when the kroon was introduced supporting Estonia's economic and monetary policies. In the meantime, the word got out that we had delayed the introduction of the kroon. It was true that our insistence on the fiscal measures delayed it for a few weeks. But it was not true, as was sometimes implied, that we delayed it because we wanted to preserve the ruble area.

Latvia and Lithuania introduced their national currencies later in 1992. The Latvian case was rather hurried because the Latvians wanted to protect themselves from the influx of rubles following the Estonian currency reform. However, it was successful as monetary and fiscal policies were such as to support the currency and the IMF granted a loan in September. The Lithuanian case was rather different, because the government was not as committed to tight monetary and fiscal policies as was the case in the other two countries. The new currency, the talonas, became sole legal tender in October, having circulated alongside the ruble since May. (The talonas was intended to be a temporary currency and was replaced by the litas in June 1993.) The IMF Board approved a loan to Lithuania later in October. But political pressure to extend credits to enterprises beyond what had been agreed with us together with the weakness of the central bank led to excessive money creation, inflation and depreciation of the talonas. The government was in the hands of the Democratic Labor Party, which was social democratic and had emerged from the old Communist Party. It did not favor the tight monetary and fiscal policies that Estonia and Latvia embraced and that we recommended to deal with the high inflation and establish the credibility of the new currency. However, the top leadership was pragmatic and tightened monetary policy in 1993 before replacing the talonas by the litas.

The key Lithuanian leaders were the president, Algirdas Brazauskas; the prime minister, Adolfas Šleževičius; and the chairman of the Bank of Lithuania, Romualdas Visokavičius. Brazauskas was an important figure in the modern history of Lithuania. He was first secretary of the Communist Party of Lithuania in the late 1980s, but he was more a Lithuanian nationalist than a communist. He broke the link with the Communist Party of the Soviet Union, making Lithuania the first Soviet republic to do so, and renamed the party the Democratic Labor Party. He was out of office during the tumultuous events of 1991, but returned as acting President in November 1992 and, after winning the election, President in February 1993. Šleževičius became prime minister after Brazauskas became president in February and initially promised to implement large wage increases. Knöbl was in Vilnius at the time and persuaded the authorities that this would be a disaster for the currency. Thereafter monetary policies were tightened, and the three principals formed the Litas Committee that oversaw the introduction of the litas and the maintenance of tight fiscal and monetary policies. To provide further protection for the litas, Šleževičius proposed a currency board arrangement. The Bank of Lithuania initially opposed it because of the reduced flexibility to operate monetary policy that it entailed, but eventually accepted it. The currency board arrangement took effect in April 1994. The three members of the Litas Committee appreciated the contribution of the IMF to the success of the litas, as two of them (Brazauskas had died in the meantime) reminded us 22 years later when Knöbl and I met them when we were on a private visit to Vilnius.

My first visit to Lithuania was in July 1993, just after the introduction of the litas. Brazauskas was on vacation in Nida, a holiday resort on the spit separating the Baltic Sea from the Curonian Lagoon. After our meetings in Vilnius, Visokavičius took Knöbl and me to see him there. It was a most interesting trip. We drove from east to west across the country to Klaipeda where we took a ferry across the lagoon and then a 50 km drive south along the spit to Nida. Brazauskas was staying at a resort built in Soviet times for senior government officials. After a meeting with him in his lodgings, we all strolled through the lanes of the resort to the communal dining hall. Although we ate in a separate room, as we passed through the main hall Brazauskas exchanged friendly greetings with the other holidaymakers, many of them in their holiday clothes, as he had done with the people we passed in the lanes. He may have been the president, but he had a warm and informal way of communicating with ordinary people (not that senior government people were all that ordinary). The happy atmosphere of the resort seemed to me to reflect one of the positive features of life under communism, namely the camaraderie among workers and their families. The liberation from Soviet rule less than two years before added a major reason to be cheerful.

The next morning, I visited Thomas Mann's summer house. He had it built in the early 1930s when Nida was a favorite holiday spot for Germans, being only a few kilometers north of the border between Lithuania and East Prussia (today Kaliningrad). There was not much to see, but it was a powerful reminder of the connections, sometimes good, sometimes bad, between Germany, Russia and Lithuania. We were in a place where German and

Russian spheres of influence had touched and at times overlapped. It was heartening to know that Lithuania, its people and culture, had survived all the turmoil of the past centuries and was energetically rebuilding itself.

Inflation fell rapidly in all three countries after monetary policy was tightened in 1992 and 1993. However, measured output continued to fall sharply, and the rise in unmeasured output in the informal part of the economy was probably much less than the fall in the measured part. The structural and other changes in the economy, privatization and the creation of market economy laws and institutions, all of which provided the necessary foundation for renewed growth, could not be done overnight. Growth eventually resumed in 1994 and 1995, although it would be many more years before output returned in the early 2000s to its level at the end of the Soviet period. Compared with other former Soviet Union countries, the Baltics experienced a bigger fall in output in the early years because of the bigger impact of the collapse of the Soviet Union and the rise in energy and raw material prices to world levels. But they returned to growth earlier and were among the first countries, ahead of Russia, in which output rose above its level at the end of the Soviet period. The sequence of their recovery was that macroeconomic stabilization came first, and output growth followed. This confirmed our views, explained in chapter 3, about the importance of early stabilization.

It was striking how young some of the key leaders were. Einars Repse was not quite 30 when he became Governor of the Bank of Latvia in 1991. He conducted a tight monetary policy and ensured the success of the lats, the national currency. Siim Kallas was 43 when he became Governor of the Bank of Estonia in 1991. He pushed through the successful introduction of the kroon in 1992 and later became Finance Minister, Prime Minister and a European Commissioner. Ivars Godmanis became prime minister of Latvia in 1990 at the age of 40 and oversaw the economic reforms before losing his position in 1993. Tiit Vähi was 45 when he became acting prime minister of Estonia at the beginning of 1992. He was succeeded in October by Mart Laar who was only 32. Adolfas Šleževičius was 45 when he became prime minister of Lithuania in 1993. These men, and other men and women in government and the central banks, were critical to the success of monetary and economic reforms in the Baltics because they set their countries on the right course from the beginning. It helped that they were young because they were open to new ways of thinking about the economy and economic policy.

All three countries moved ahead with structural reforms which, as was in the nature of such changes, took a number of years to design and implement. Lithuania was initially slower than the other countries to reform, because of political opposition. Partly as a means of containing the political pressures (and perhaps because it did not want to be left behind by its neighbors), Lithuania, alone among the three countries, decided in 1994 to take a medium-term loan (EFF) from the IMF. This committed it to implementing important structural reforms, mainly in banking, privatization, the enterprise sector and legal reforms, as well as maintaining macroeconomic stability. Estonia and Latvia took their last loans from the IMF in 1995 and 1994 respectively, while Lithuania continued to borrow until 1997. After the last disbursements, all three countries continued to agree their economic programs with the IMF under what was called a precautionary arrangement. Although they were entitled to borrow again, they undertook not to do so unless circumstances changed sharply. The precautionary arrangements gave their policies the IMF's seal of approval and added to their credibility with foreign investors.

There were various setbacks in what was generally a continuous forward movement towards market economies and the recovery of living standards. All three countries experienced major banking crises between 1992 and 1996. However, the banking sectors were small in relation to their economies, so that the macroeconomic impact was not large. The crisis in Russia in 1998 hit them harder because they still had considerable economic and financial links to Russia. On the other hand, the strong recovery of Russia in the following years helped them.

In 2004, the Baltics joined the European Union. Their structural reform agenda in the years leading up to membership was increasingly dominated by the legal and institutional changes required by the EU. While macroeconomic policy was generally in line with EU requirements, they were concerned to continue to earn good marks from the IMF so that they would be readily received as members. We therefore kept up a dialogue with them, but it involved fewer resources than when we had worked on the details of economic programs with them. This allowed us to reduce the frequency of our missions. We also assigned a single resident representative to Estonia and Latvia instead of one to each country. Similarly, the resident representative in Lithuania took on the responsibilities of resident representative in Belarus as well. Although the economies and economic policies of Lithuania and Belarus were very different, the arrangement made good sense in geographical terms. Their capitals were closer than those of the three Baltic states were to each other: 182 kilometers from Minsk to Vilnius (under 3 hours by car), compared with 288 kilometers from Riga to Vilnius (3.5 hours) and 309 kilometers from Riga to Tallinn (4 hours). (I made each of these journeys at least once.) Knöbl was the first joint resident representative in Lithuania and Belarus, based in Vilnius. He then moved to Riga to be the joint representative in Latvia and Estonia. His knowledge of the Baltics was second to none among IMF staff, and his relationships with their leaders served both us and them well. We did not replace him after his time in Latvia and Estonia, as our work there could be managed by locally recruited staff. Later, the Lithuania office was also handed over to local staff, while the work on Belarus was handled by a resident representative based in Moscow.

Independence in the Baltics unleashed not only entrepreneurial spirit in the market economy, but also competition between political parties in the political marketplace. There were a number of political parties in each country, and governments were often formed from coalitions between parties rather than comprising just one party. The coalitions were not always stable and changes in government, or a few ministerial changes, were at least as frequent as in Western Europe. However, such changes did not usually lead to significant changes in economic policy. There was broad agreement across the political spectrum on macroeconomic stabilization policies and on the essentials of structural reforms (privatization, liberalization, and the creation of the institutions of a market economy). But many of the details of policies were disputed both within and outside the government.

Many years later, I heard Balcerowicz say at a conference that his second stint as deputy prime minister and minister of finance in Poland in 1997–2000, a period of "normal" politics, was in some ways more difficult than the first in 1989–1991, the period of "extraordinary" politics. In the first period, there was wide acceptance of the need to move rapidly with major stabilization, deregulation and liberalization measures. In the second period, there was more time to debate alternative measures, and political groups were more active in promoting the interests of their supporters. The same was true in the Baltics where the collapse of the Soviet Union and sharp increase in prices left no alternative to rapid initial reforms, whereas there were more policy choices available after stabilization had been achieved. Our role in the latter period was to provide technical advice in areas such as tax policy, tax administration, public expenditure management, monetary policy, banking supervision and financial market development, while helping the authorities maintain macroeconomic stability. My colleagues in the technical assistance departments of the IMF were active in this work, together with my own staff.

The economic transition in the Baltics was much more successful than that in the other former Soviet Union countries, the members of the CIS. Inflation came down faster, output and incomes grew again before they did in the CIS and the essential elements of a market economy were quickly established. The main reason for this was that the Baltics implemented tight monetary and fiscal policies very early on, having already introduced their own currencies. The CIS countries, by contrast, were half-hearted about macroeconomic stabilization. Even in Russia, where Gaidar and his team were committed to such policies, there was not a sufficiently wide consensus in the government and central bank to ensure their consistent implementation.

I myself was surprised in 1992 when Knöbl was reporting that the authorities were quite prepared to introduce tough measures, such as the 5–6 percentage points tightening of fiscal policy in Estonia, in a situation of great economic disarray and hardship. There are several reasons why the Baltics were willing to bear the burden of the inevitable fall in living standards rather than seek to ameliorate it through less restrictive macroeconomic policies. The most important one was that they were highly motivated to escape from the Russia-dominated system. Their strong sense of national identity, experience of repression in the Soviet Union and knowledge that the EU provided a potential haven, gave them the strength and unity to accept the hardships of the difficult transition. In addition, in the economic arena, there was a collective memory of market economies, which did not appear as alien as they did to people in CIS countries that had lived with planned economies for much longer. The leaders and their advisers in the Baltics were ready to listen to outsiders who could tell them how to move to market economies. They therefore welcomed and trusted us and colleagues in other international organizations. They also drew on the assistance and advice of Estonians, Latvians and Lithuanians who lived abroad, mainly in Finland, Scandinavia and North America, many of whom came to live and work in their countries of origin.

I had hoped that the success of the Baltics would act as an example to the CIS countries. It was therefore helpful that they were grouped in my department in the IMF rather than being in European I Department (covering Western Europe and the former communist countries of Eastern Europe), an arrangement that might have been more logical. My staff working on the CIS countries had sufficient knowledge of the experience of the Baltics to be able to explain why they were successful. But my hopes were not realized. The CIS officials were full of reasons why they could not do what the Baltics had done. Some of them were not correct, for example that the Baltics had received much more foreign financial assistance, or that the economic shock from the dissolution of the Soviet Union was less severe in the Baltics. The one reason that had some firm basis was that the Baltics had a historical memory of having a market economy whereas the CIS countries had none. But even this could not explain why the Baltics were willing to endure considerable hardship whereas the CIS countries mostly opted to reduce short term pain, for example by issuing credits to keep non-viable enterprises alive. One factor was the absence in most CIS countries of economists with the analytical ability of a Gaidar in Russia, a Pynsenyk in Ukraine or a handful of others elsewhere who could understand why rapid reforms were so critical in the early years. Our attempts to convince the leaders of CIS countries of this were, unfortunately, not persuasive enough. Anyway, by the time the success of the Baltics was apparent to everyone, it was too late for most CIS countries to copy them because by then they had entered a partial reform trap.

In their retrospective look at the IMF's work in the Baltics in the 1990s, Bert Knöbl and Richard Haas included the views of some of our counterparts who were generally pleased with our work and our interactions with them. Our counterparts valued our advice, especially in the early years when they had little expertise of their own. They found us to be flexible and ready to take account of their needs. While we could be insistent at times, they did not complain of excessive coercion. In addition to strategic policy advice, they greatly valued the detailed advice we provided about the analysis and management of economic policies. Our teams provided technical notes to and answered questions from their counterparts in the central banks and government ministries which were generally found to be useful.

Even allowing for the fact that the people Knöbl and Haas consulted were known to be well disposed towards the IMF, the picture they presented of the IMF's work was remarkably positive. Of course, the underlying reason for this was that the authorities in the Baltics wanted to follow the policies that we also thought were best for them. We were therefore trusted partners, with an element of a teacher/student relationship. It was not a case of a powerful foreign organization imposing policies on them. Much credit must go to the leaders of the Baltics for taking ownership of the policies and guiding their countries through the difficult transition. A little credit should also go to IMF staff in my mission teams, the technical assistance staff and the resident representatives for earning the trust of their counterparts and providing valuable professional advice and assistance.

I always enjoyed my visits to the Baltics. There were not usually many difficult issues that I had to discuss with my counterparts because our teams had sorted problems out as they arose. Our meetings were amicable, with few moments of tension. It was a pleasure to see the old parts of Tallinn, Riga and Vilnius looking cleaner and renewed on each visit, with more and more goods in the shops. The architecture and the rising prosperity (and the Latin alphabet) created a feeling of Europe. As usual, there was little time for tourism. However, my wife and I did explore the center of Riga where I was happy to pass by the childhood home of Isaiah Berlin whose work I admired and whom I had met in Oxford. We also went to the Museum of the Occupation of Latvia, a depressing reminder of the price the Baltics paid during the Soviet period. Outside the capital cities, we went to Rundale Palace in Latvia and Trakai Castle in Lithuania. Rundale Palace, designed by Rastrelli in his late Baroque style, had belonged to the German Duke of Courland before Latvia was absorbed into the Russian Empire. It was impressive, although we could only see a small part of the interior because most of it was closed for renovations. Trakai Castle had been a seat of the Dukes of Lithuania. It dated from the Middle Ages though it had been much reconstructed. Built on an island, the surroundings were quite dramatic, although the old Soviet style cafeteria where we had something to eat was in serious need of modernizing.

By chance, the only visit my wife made to Lithuania coincided with the marriage in St Anne's church in Vilnius of a long-standing American friend of hers to a Lithuanian woman whom he had met while providing technical assistance in Vilnius under the auspices of the American Bar Association. The reception after the marriage was held in the art gallery run by a friend of the bride's where there was an exhibition of modern and quite explicit paintings of nudes. The bride's relatives, who lived in rural parts of the country, were obviously not familiar with paintings like this, which seemed to me to be a statement about how free the country now was after the artistic repression of Soviet times. On the same visit, the Governor of the Bank of Lithuania, Reinoldijus Šarkinas, who held the post for fifteen years and developed the Bank into a successful institution, took us to the country retreat for Bank employees. It was in the forest beside a pretty lake. The visit was restful after a day of meetings, although the mosquitoes that hovered over the lake and bit me as I emerged after a post-sauna dip took away some of the pleasure.

Chapter 7

Other CIS Countries

There were ten Commonwealth of Independent States (CIS) countries in addition to Russia and Ukraine. Two (Belarus and Moldova) were in the western part of the Soviet Union. The others were spread along the southern regions of the Soviet Union: three in the Caucasus region (Armenia, Azerbaijan and Georgia) and five in Central Asia (Kazakhstan, Kyrgyzstan, Tajikistan, Turkmenistan and Uzbekistan). Before I worked on the Soviet Union, I knew very little about their history, ethnic composition, geography or economies. I quickly learned as much as I could.

I already knew that Byelorussia, which changed its name to Belarus at independence, had a seat in the United Nations General Assembly in its own right, as did the Soviet Union and Ukraine. This curious arrangement was the result of a deal with the US to give the Soviet Union three votes instead of one. It had been absorbed into Russia in the eighteenth century following the division (one of many) of Poland. I now learned that the other countries were all annexed by Russia or the Soviet Union, in some cases after military action, in the nineteenth and twentieth centuries.

The Caucasian countries came first. Part of Georgia sought protection from Russia against Persia in the 1780s and was formally incorporated into the Russian Empire in 1801. Victory in wars with Persia led to the annexation of most of the rest of Armenia, Azerbaijan and Georgia in the next three decades. At the same time, Russia was fighting to subdue uprisings in the mountainous areas of southern Russia to the north of Georgia and Azerbaijan. Imam Shamil, a renowned leader from Dagestan, held out against Russia for many years, assisted by Hadji Murad who had defected from the Russian side. (Tolstoy's novella, *Hadji Murad*, is worth reading for its insight into the attitudes towards Russia of people in the Caucasus at that time.) Shamil's forces were eventually overpowered by Russia and he surrendered in 1859. This led to the consolidation of Russian rule over the whole of the Caucasus region. One of the last areas to be absorbed into Russia was Chechnya. The independence-minded Chechens were to cause Russia more trouble at the end of the twentieth century.

Russia's expansion into Central Asia mostly took place in the second half of the nineteenth century. However, it had already established nominal control in the eighteenth century over the Kazakh tribes in the western and northern parts of Kazakhstan, which were grouped into the so-called Junior Horde in the west and the Middle Horde in the north. The remaining Kazakh tribes in the south, grouped into the Elder Horde, were eventually subjugated around the middle of the nineteenth century. In the second half of the century, Russia gradually took over the areas that now comprise Uzbekistan, Tajikistan, Turkmenistan and Kyrgyzstan. It met some resistance from the Khanates (kingdoms) of Khiva and Kokand and the Emirate of Bokhara where it established protectorates before annexing them entirely.

The British became increasingly concerned about possible Russian designs on India. The Wakhan Corridor, a narrow strip of land, 13–65 kilometers wide and 350 kms long was established in Afghanistan in 1893 to create a buffer zone between Russia (now Tajikistan) and India (now Pakistan). The Anglo-Russian Convention of 1907 agreed to spheres of influence and ended the rivalry between Russia and Britain in Central Asia.

The territories that later became the countries of the CIS were all part of the Russian Empire by the end of the ninteenth century. After World War I and the civil war they became part of the Soviet Union, except for the Bessarabia region of Moldova. The republics of the Soviet Union that became independent countries when the Soviet Union broke up were created in the 1920s and 1930s as administrative units but also as national homes for the main ethnic groups. As the ethnic groups were already somewhat mixed up, most republics had minorities belonging to nationalities other than the main ones. There may have been a deliberate attempt by the Soviet Union to foster instability in the republics by including minority nationalities in each republic. The Soviet Union was one of the world's most ethnically diverse countries, with more than 100 distinct national ethnicities. As such it was a major, land-based, multiethnic empire.

The region which is now Moldova was in the Russian Empire for two different periods in the nineteenth century, the first lasting from 1812 until 1856. From 1856 to 1878, Bessarabia, which is that part of Moldova to the west of the Dniester River, was incorporated in the principality of Moldavia, a vassal state of the Ottoman Empire and later a region of Romania. In 1878, Bessarabia was absorbed again into the Russian Empire. In 1918, it left Russia and joined Romania, only for the Soviet Union to annex it in 1940. Merged again with that part of Moldova which lies to the east of the Dniester, it formed the Moldavian republic of the Soviet Union. In 1991, it became independent Moldova.

Armed conflict broke out in a few countries in the years just before and after the dissolution of the Soviet Union. The main one that involved fighting between two countries was the conflict between Armenia and Azerbaijan over Nagorno-Karabakh, an area within Azerbaijan inhabited mainly by ethnic Armenians. The war, which began during Soviet times, continued until the ceasefire in May 1994, by which time Armenia controlled not only Nagorno-Karabakh, but about 20 percent of the territory of the rest of Azerbaijan. Sporadic skirmishes occurred over the next few decades, until 2020 when Azerbaijan recaptured both Nagorno-Karabakh and the other regions occupied by Armenia.

Separatist movements in Georgia and Moldova led to wars. After ceasefires in the Abkhazia region of Georgia in December 1993 and the region of Moldova east of the Dniester, called Transnistria, in July 1992, the separatist territories (Abkhazia and Transnistria) became effectively self-governed. However, few countries recognized them as independent states. The civil war in Tajikistan lasted for five years until 1997.

Ethnic tensions were present in all four cases, notably in Nagorno-Karabakh, although political and regional (and, in Tajikistan, religious) factors were also important. In each case, Russia played a role as a supplier of weapons, and sometimes provided military support and acted as a peace-keeper. The sides it favored (Armenia, the separatists in Georgia and Moldova and the Tajik government) all came out on top.

Russians accounted for about half of the Soviet Union population in the 1980s, but a higher proportion of the leadership. This was not only because of the centralized nature of the communist system, which was run from Moscow. It was also that Russians occupied top positions in the governments of the republics. The first secretary of the republican communist party, who was effectively the head of government, was usually a national of the republic, but his deputy, who often wielded more power in practice, was a Russian appointed by Moscow. After independence, the top Russians were replaced by nationals in most republics. One of the few who was still in a key position after we came on the scene was Valery Otchertsov. He had been deputy to Saparmurat Niyazov, President of Turkmenistan, from 1989 to 1991, when the latter was chairman of the Supreme Soviet and head of the government. After independence he became deputy prime minister and minister of economy and finance. In 1996 he left Turkmenistan to become deputy head of Itera, a private gas trading company.

The ten countries we are looking at in this chapter contained just over one quarter of the population of the Soviet Union when it broke up in 1991. Most of them were small, with populations of between three and five million. Azerbaijan (seven million), Belarus (ten million), Kazakhstan (seventeen million) and Uzbekistan (twenty million) were larger. When they joined the

IMF, the working language in all countries was Russian. Only a few of our counterparts spoke English so we worked with interpreters. Emine Gurgen, when she was our mission chief in Azerbaijan and Turkmenistan, found that she was able to conduct some meetings without interpreters because the Azeri and Turkmen languages are close to Turkish, her mother tongue. Over time, some of the countries increasingly used the languages of their main ethnic groups, although rarely in official meetings with us.

All of the countries are landlocked, except Georgia which has a coast on the Black Sea. The international transportation routes were initially almost all through Russia. As a result, transportation costs were high. At the end of the Soviet Union, output and incomes per capita were lower than the Soviet average in all countries except Belarus, being less than three-quarters of the average in Central Asia (except Kazakhstan) and Azerbaijan. Social indicators, such as infant mortality rates, housing conditions, educational levels and provision of health care were also lowest in Central Asia (except Kazakhstan) and Azerbaijan. Azerbaijan, Kazakhstan and Turkmenistan were exporters of oil and gas. Most of the others were importers of oil and gas.

The dissolution of the Soviet Union brought out into the open the fact that some of the countries had chronic current account deficits, with Russia being the main counterpart with the surplus. The system of automatic clearance through Gosbank accounts had previously concealed this reality. Two developments made the situation even more difficult. First, the financial transfers from the budget of the Soviet Union to lower income regions had ceased. Second, Russia and Turkmenistan raised the prices of oil and gas to world levels over the first few years after the end of the Union, something that we supported because it contributed in time to a better use of energy. We realized that the importing countries, especially those that had also lost the Soviet transfers, would have to endure major reductions in living standards to make ends meet. The pain could, in principle, be eased but not avoided altogether, by borrowing abroad, which we could help with.

The work we did with the countries is described in general terms in chapter 2. Three major factors accounted for how quickly after a country joined the IMF we were able to reach agreement on its economic policies. First was whether it had issued its own currency. As long as a country remained in the ruble area, monetary policy was outside its control, and we could not consider it for a Stand-By Arrangement (SBA). It could, however, qualify for a loan under the Systemic Transformation Facility (STF) which was introduced in April 1993. The economic program for a SBA was more demanding than that for a STF and took longer to agree. The second factor was whether the country was engaged in civil conflicts which used up resources and reduced its control over the economy of the whole country. The third and most important factor was the willingness of the authorities to implement the macroeconomic and structural reforms that we recommended.

Kyrgyzstan was the first of the ten countries to introduce its own currency, the som. It launched it in May 1993, when its neighbors, Kazakhstan, Tajikistan and Uzbekistan, were still hoping to stay in the ruble area. This enabled us to give it a SBA in 1993. The other countries did not qualify for a SBA until 1994 or later, although they all, except Tajikistan and Turkmenistan, borrowed from the IMF under the STF. My colleagues who provided technical assistance in the monetary area played a very important role in advising Kyrgyzstan on the introduction and subsequent management of its currency. They were to do the same in all the other countries when they in turn launched their national currencies. One of my colleagues who worked on these issues, Warren Coats, later wrote about his experiences in *Building Market Economy Monetary Systems*.

The civil conflicts in Armenia, Azerbaijan, Georgia and Tajikistan delayed our work there and their ability to borrow from the IMF. (The conflict in Moldova was much less serious. It was over in 1992 and did not impinge much on our work.) The IMF generally does not lend to countries when there is a risk that its money could finance military action, or be perceived to be doing so. We therefore did not lend until the fighting had finished, except in Tajikistan where it was dying down when we made our first loan. In the meantime, it was heart-wrenching to see the hardships that the civilian populations were undergoing, and to know that a loan from us, together with other foreign finance that our loan would trigger, could ameliorate the situation somewhat. Levon Barkhoudarian, the finance minister of Armenia, moved us with his stories of shortages, power cuts and the desperation of the residents of Yerevan, the capital, who cut down trees in a city park to get wood for heating and cooking. After the fighting was over and we were able to lend, the economic consequences of the conflicts were apparent in the need to spend money on basic human needs, reconstruction and, in Azerbaijan and Georgia, housing for refugees from conflict areas.

While the ruble area issue and the civil conflicts were resolved within a few years, the willingness of the authorities to implement the macroeconomic and structural reforms that we recommended was always at the heart of our work. None of the ten countries wanted to follow the example of the Baltics and implement radical reforms immediately after independence. Nor were there influential leaders in government, such as Gaidar and Chubais in Russia, to push for far-reaching reforms. In most countries there were a handful of reform-minded officials who were open to our recommendations. But the course that a country took was largely determined by the views of the President and his immediate circle.

As mentioned in chapter 3, the leaders of Belarus, Turkmenistan and Uzbekistan opted for minimal reforms because they wanted to maintain as much of the old system as they could. At first, it looked as though they were ready to reform. Both Belarus and Uzbekistan agreed on economic programs with us and borrowed under the STF and SBA in 1993–1995 and 1995–1996 respectively. However, it gradually became clear that they were not willing to give up the levers that existed in Soviet times for controlling the economy.

Elsewhere, there was a willingness in principle to undertake the basic elements of market reforms, especially macroeconomic stabilization, liberalization and privatization, albeit with more of a role for government, with associated corruption and cronyism, than was conducive to a rapid transformation. We worked hard with the latter group of seven countries to help them implement market reforms. The first phase of reforms focused heavily on macroeconomic stabilization and the control of inflation. We provided loans in the form of STFs and SBAs to support it. As in Russia and Ukraine, the next phase involved a wider range of structural reforms in addition to continued macroeconomic stabilization. We supported this with medium-term loans under either the Extended Fund Facility (EFF) or, for lower income countries, the Enhanced Structural Adjustment Facility (ESAF). Most countries began to borrow under either the EFF or ESAF in 1996 although Kyrgyzstan was earlier (1994) and Tajikistan was later (1998).

The shift from the emphasis on macroeconomic stabilization to concerns about slow structural reforms was our response to the failure of the economies to grow after inflation had been brought down, as noted in chapter 3. Most of the seven moderate reforming countries made a little progress with market and institutional reforms in the mid-1990s and growth began in some of them. Unfortunately, the Russia crisis in 1998 reduced growth in the whole region and undermined political support for reforms.

The disappointing growth performance had serious consequences for the external debt burden of most of the countries. Since they became independent, we had been part of an international effort to mobilize money in the form of grants and loans to cushion the blow of the transition. We joined other international financial institutions, especially the World Bank, the EBRD, and the ADB, and friendly countries, mostly in North America and Europe, in contributing financial support. At the time we believed that the countries would have the capacity to repay the loans when their economies started to grow again. But we were too optimistic about the likely recovery in output and incomes. Nearly all countries experienced declining output up to 1995, and a few for a year or more after that as well. We had projected that the economies would turn round earlier than they did. As a result, the debt burden of borrowing countries was higher in relation to their economies than we had expected. The situation worsened sharply after 1998 when the countries devalued their currencies in order to maintain approximate parity with the ruble, which Russia had devalued by a large amount. With most external borrowing denominated in dollars or other major currencies, the debt burden took a big step up.

The IMF, as the main international organization responsible for advising countries on the sustainability of external indebtedness, had to accept some of the blame for allowing debts to rise so much. Our excuse was that the transition to market economies was an unprecedented event, and we did not fully anticipate the length and depth of the decline in output and living standards before economies started to grow again. Had we done so, we might have advised countries to borrow less and take more of a hit to living standards in the short term to avoid excessive indebtedness in the longer term.

Six low income countries, where GDP in 2000 was at most two thirds of its level in 1990, were especially hard hit by the collapse of the Soviet Union and its economic system and the crisis in Russia in 1998: Armenia, Azerbaijan, Georgia, Kyrgyzstan, Moldova, and Tajikistan. Together with the World Bank, the EBRD and the ADB, we launched what we called the CIS-7 Initiative in 2002. (Uzbekistan was also included to make seven countries.) The idea was for our institutions to make special efforts to help these countries, and for them to work harder to introduce reforms that would improve their economic performance. One concrete element of this on our side was to raise more money, including debt relief where needed, from our own sources and from friendly countries.

It is difficult to say how successful the Initiative was, as we do not know what would have happened without it. The economies of all the CIS-7 countries grew rapidly during the 2000s until the global financial crisis of 2008. However, much of this was due to strong growth in Russia and other trading partners. The CIS-7 benefited from both increased exports and a rise in emigrants' remittances, as many of their citizens had left home to improve their economic situation in Russia, Kazakhstan and elsewhere. While welcome, the increased dependence on remittances was, of course, a symptom of the failure of their economies to provide employment opportunities.

More generally, as explained in chapter 3, vested interests, cronyism and corruption continued to weaken efforts to implement genuine market oriented reforms in all the CIS countries, not only the CIS-7. The political institutions protected rather than challenged such activities. The Presidents of Azerbaijan, Belarus, Kazakhstan, Tajikistan, Turkmenistan and Uzbekistan were close to absolute rulers. In the other countries, Armenia, Georgia, Kyrgyzstan, and Moldova, there were authoritarian tendencies alongside weak democratic institutions. In all cases, cronyism and corruption went all the way up to the President, or at least to members of his family, and involved many senior people in government. This was not conducive to the creation of an efficient market economy in which the private sector could expect to be rewarded fairly for taking risks and expanding production.

While growth was hampered by vested interests, cronyism and corruption, all countries were fairly successful at bringing inflation down and stabilizing the macroeconomic situation. This was done primarily through monetary policy. The central banks must take much of the credit for this. In most countries, the leaders of the central banks were younger than those in government and were not steeped in the Soviet way of doing things. They were keen to learn how to run a central bank. They sought advice from IMF central banking experts and elsewhere and sent their junior staff abroad to get relevant training, including at the Joint Vienna Institute. In our attempts to persuade the government to move faster on market reforms, we often had the central bank on our side, implicitly if not explicitly.

While I personally made more visits to Russia and Ukraine than to the other countries, I was no less involved in our work on the latter than on Russia and Ukraine. They needed our assistance, whether it was policy advice, technical assistance or financial assistance. As explained in chapter 2, they generally trusted us and were receptive to our advice. In view of the complex transition they were going through, we bore a heavy responsibility to do the best for them. Of course, it was also exciting to be involved at such a historically important time.

I came to know all the countries well, with the exception of Turkmenistan with which I was less engaged because of our cooler relationship with them. They all had different characteristics and problems which made each one interesting. Having described our work in the countries collectively, I will now add a few memories and reflections on them individually.

BELARUS

At the beginning of the transition, Belarus looked as though it would be among the first to introduce market reforms. Stanislav Bogdankevich, the head of the central bank, had a good understanding of what was needed. Stanislav Shushkevich, the President, was a scientist with liberal democratic leanings, and the government officials we met were practical and seemed willing to move to a market economy. The IMF provided considerable technical assistance. But there was opposition to reforms in the strong state enterprise sector and elsewhere, and progress was slow. We were hopeful that the election in 1994 of Alexander Lukashenko as President would speed up the reforms. He was young and energetic, and anxious to improve conditions in the country.

Camdessus made his first and only visit to Belarus soon after Lukashenko's election to encourage him to work closely with us. One of my memories of his visit was the tour we were given of the small area in the center of the capital, Minsk, that had been completely rebuilt after WWII to be how it was before the war. Minsk was flattened in the war, and largely rebuilt in a concrete brutalist style. The reconstruction of the traditional style of buildings in a small area was a reminder of a different world. It was not only the buildings that suffered in the war. The human casualties were enormous. About 10 percent of the prewar population of Belarus did not survive the war.

Our hopes for the economy were dashed when Lukashenko turned out to be a Soviet style autocrat who wanted to control the economy, the politics and much else in the country himself. I never managed to engage him in a serious discussion about economic reform. He would appear to listen and then lecture me at length in a loud voice (and almost crush my hand in his strong handshake at the end).

Lukashenko set the policy, and government and National Bank officials had to follow it even if, as we suspected, they were not all in favor of it. The official I spent more time with than anyone else was Pyotr Prokopovich. Trained as an engineer, he was an economic adviser to Lukashenko in the early years of his presidency and then became Governor of the National Bank from 1998 to 2011. He was awarded the title of Hero of Belarus in 2006, an honor which only a handful of people were granted. We had many discussions in which I tried to persuade him that genuine market reforms would benefit Belarus, and he made the case for a very gradual transition.

On one occasion he argued that the government was seeking to create a social market economy as had been advocated by Ludwig Erhard when he was German Minister of Economic Affairs from 1949 to 1963. Erhard was regarded as the architect of West Germany's post-war economic miracle. Prokopovich claimed that a slow transition which avoided some of the short term fall in living standards that came with a rapid transition was the way to create a social market economy. I replied that gradual reforms merely prolonged the period of low incomes, created vested interests and made it more difficult to build a successful German-style economy. I assumed at the time that Prokopovich appealed to Erhard's model as a debating point, not because he really believed it. However, I heard people in other CIS countries refer to it and wondered whether there might be a treatise in Russian advocating the model as a real alternative to the kind of reform strategy we were advocating. If there was, I never managed to track it down.

However, I did not give up hope for the country. Meetings with government officials and members of the upper house of parliament convinced me that there was a significant constituency for genuine market reforms, an understanding of what was involved and the administrative skills to design the necessary policies. As I used to say to our excellent office manager in Minsk, Julia Lyskova, once Lukashenko and his cronies left, things could move quickly in the right direction. Alas, I found myself saying this for decades, not just a few years, because Lukashenko refused to stand down.

MOLDOVA

Whereas politics in Belarus were frozen, in Moldova they were fluid. Political parties came and went. During my twelve years, there were six prime ministers, who were the effective heads of government, from five parties. The big political divide was between parties which wanted closer relations with Europe and those which favored relations with Russia. The former attracted the Romanian speaking majority and the latter the Russian speaking minority, but there were many crossovers. All parties professed to want to move to a market economy, but in practice they were preoccupied with ensuring that their supporters got a fair share of the spoils of office. Corruption and cronyism were rife, and economic growth suffered as a result. Moldova was one of the poorest countries in Europe and large numbers of young people emigrated in pursuit of higher incomes in Europe and Russia.

Monetary policy was in the safe hands of Leonid Talmaci, the governor of the National Bank from 1991 to 2009. He pursued a strict policy which brought inflation under control earlier than in most of the other countries. The economic policy makers in the government were less effective because of the unsettled political situation and vested interests. One of the few people we thought could improve the economy was Ion Sturza, an entrepreneur with practical ideas. He was Minister of Economy and Reforms in 1998 and Prime Minister in 1999. But politics did not suit him and he did not stay long enough to change things. An interesting feature of the finance ministry was that a number of senior positions (heads of department and deputy ministers) were held by women. In 2002, Zinaida Greceanîi became the first female Finance Minister after having worked her way up in the ministry. She did well and in 2008 became Prime Minister in the communist government.

My first few visits to the capital, Chişinău, were in the summer when the trees and flowers in the parks were looking good and the walnuts on the trees that lined many of the roads outside the city were filling out. On one visit, we were taken to the Cricova winery, one of the better wine producers in a country of good wines. The cellars were inside a limestone hill from which the stone had been taken out to build Chişinău. In addition to the current operations of the winery, the cellars contained a wine museum. One room contained the wines that the Red Army "liberated" from Berlin at the end of World War II. We were told that they came from the private collection of

Goering, who himself had taken them from Paris during the German occupation. We gazed at the dust-covered bottles of fine Bordeaux wines from the
1930s and wondered how they would taste now.

A few years later my wife came with me and we took advantage of a free
weekend to drive across the border to see the painted monasteries in the
Bucovina region of Romania, a UNESCO site since 1993. Both the inside and
outside walls are covered with paintings of scenes from the bible, Jesus' life
and the lives of the saints. They date from the fifteenth and sixteenth centuries
and are in the Byzantine style. They were intended to bring the stories alive
for illiterate people. It is remarkable how the colors have remained so bright
despite the exposure to wind, rain and sun. They are in small villages in the
wooded foothills of the Carpathian Mountains, a situation which adds to their
charm. Seeing those monasteries was one of the most exhilarating cultural
experiences of my years working in the region of the former Soviet Union.

Unfortunately, our return to Chişinău was marred by a delay at the border
where we discovered that my wife had a single entry visa for Moldova and
could not enter a second time. (I had a multiple entry visa.) Frantic efforts by
our mission chief and resident representative in Chişinău and the intervention
of the Foreign Affairs Ministry eventually allowed us to enter.

Turning to the Caucasus countries, the early years were dominated by the
wars: in Georgia, the separatist war with Abkhazia, and in Armenia and
Azerbaijan, the war over Nagorno-Karabakh. On top of the shortages of food,
energy and other important items that all countries in the region experienced
during the early years of the transition, these countries also had shortages due
to the wars. There was also political instability during this period in Georgia
and Azerbaijan. It was only in 1994 that governments were in place that could
give serious attention to economic issues.

ARMENIA

Armenia was particularly badly hit. It was more dependent on trade with the
other former Soviet Union countries than most of them, so the disruption of
that trade was particularly damaging. As a result of the Nagorno-Karabakh
war, Turkey severed relations with Armenia and closed the border between
them, raising still further the cost of international trade. On my first visit to
the capital, Yerevan, in 1994, the fuel shortage was brought home to me when
the lights went out and the water stopped flowing, leaving me in the dark in
the shower covered in soap. A unique feature of my hotel during that visit was
the presence of floor ladies. In Soviet times, floor ladies sat in a public space
on each floor to help the guests but also, it was assumed, to spy on them and

report their movements to the authorities. In other hotels I stayed in around the region, the institution of floor ladies was abolished soon after the end of the Soviet Union. It was therefore surprising to see them in Yerevan in 1994. They had disappeared by the time of my next visit in 1997.

The Central Bank of Armenia was well run, first by Bagrat Asatryan and, from 1998, by Tigran Sargsyan (who served later as Prime Minister from 2008 to 2014). Hrant Bagratyan pushed for a radical reform program when he was Minister of Economy in 1991–1993 and then Prime Minister in 1993–1996. He had known Gaidar since the 1980s and wanted Armenia to implement similar reforms to those advocated by Gaidar in Russia. But there were powerful vested interests in the economy and the need to focus on the provision of necessities to the population further reduced his room for maneuver. He was blamed for the hardships of the early years of independence and did not hold a government position after 1996. Armen Darbinyan was also reform minded but could not achieve much in his short period in office from 1997 to 2000 as, successively, Minister of Finance, Prime Minister and Minister of Trade and Industry.

Many among the big diaspora of Armenians around the world were successful in business and wanted to invest in Armenia. The money they brought in helped the balance of payments, and also raised the growth rate. But there was a lack of transparency in some of the deals, and corruption and cronyism were common features. At a meeting I attended in Yerevan between government officials and potential Armenian investors from overseas, there was no interest in the program of reforms that I argued would be best for the country.

The Armenian church is one of five Eastern Oriental Orthodox churches. It plays an important role in Armenian communities around the world, which contain nearly nine million Armenian Apostolic Orthodox Christians, according to the church's website. (The population of Armenia is about three million.) I met the head, the Catholicos of All Armenians, on one of my visits. He was friendly, but berated the IMF for advocating economic policies that impoverished the people. This is, of course, a common criticism of the IMF in many countries. I regret that I was unable to convince him that the transition from a planned economy could not be painless, especially when it coincided with the breakup of the Soviet Union, a war and the Turkish blockade, but that moving as quickly as possible to a market economy would minimize the pain.

The mother cathedral of the church at Etchmiadzin dates from the fourth century although most of it was built later. On standing inside it, I could not help thinking of the trials and tribulations of Armenians through the ages, as their country was overrun by different invaders, its boundaries shifted and its people scattered throughout the world and sometimes persecuted.

The Nagorno-Karabakh problem loomed large in Armenian politics. Armenians from that region were overrepresented at the top of the government. Robert Kocharyan, who was President of Armenia from 1998 to 2008 (the second President, the first being Levon Ter-Petrosyan), had previously been prime minister and then President of Nagorno-Karabakh. Economic policy was not a major concern of his and he usually endorsed whatever had been agreed between the economic ministers and the IMF.

Vazgen Sargsyan (not closely related to Tigran Sargsyan) was an important commander of Armenian forces during the Nagorno-Karabakh war and was Minister of Defense of Armenia from 1995 to June 1999 when he became Prime Minister. My wife and I visited Armenia shortly after his appointment and he was a charming and friendly host at the dinner he gave for us. In the coming months he supported the tightening of economic policies that we advocated to cope with the difficult adjustment called for by the Russia crisis the previous year. Disaster struck in October when five gunmen burst into the National Assembly building and opened fire with Kalashnikovs. They killed Sargsyan, the Speaker of the National Assembly and six other people, and injured many more. The mastermind behind the attack was never identified, although there were many theories, conspiracy and otherwise, about who ordered it and with what motive.

Although much of Armenia is mountainous, the capital, Yerevan, is on a flat plain. However, to remind you of the mountains, it looks out at Mount Ararat some 65 kilometers away, just on the other side of the border with Turkey. A dormant volcano, its snow-capped cone rises to over 5000 meters. It is a national symbol of Armenia and is considered sacred by Armenians. The highest mountain in Armenia itself is Mount Aragats, at 4090 meters. On a weekend in June 1999, my wife and I were taken by Darbinyan to a small lake high up on Mount Aragats where we had a picnic. The main dish was a festive soup made by boiling sheep parts for many hours then serving it with much garlic and broken pieces of lavash. The scenery as we drove up the mountain was stunning. On the way, we passed the Byurakan Observatory, a center of astronomy in Soviet times and now part of the Armenian Academy of Science.

Another natural attraction in Armenia is Lake Sevan, a large lake 74 kilometers long by 32 kilometers wide. In July 2001, Tom Wolf, who was mission chief for Armenia, and I had a meeting with President Kocharyan sitting on the terrace of the presidential villa overlooking the lake. It was difficult to focus on the topics under discussion when the view of the lake and the mountains coming down to the lake on the east side were so distracting.

AZERBAIJAN

Azerbaijan lies to the east of Lake Sevan, with the border being only 10 or so kilometers from the lake at the nearest point. Since the war over Nagorno-Karabakh, the border had been closed. The only time I went to both Armenia and Azerbaijan on the same trip, in September 1994, I travelled between them via Moscow. The more usual route to Azerbaijan from Europe or the United States was through Istanbul as there were close relations between Turkey and Azerbaijan and frequent flights.

There was considerable political instability in the first few years of independence in Azerbaijan. There were two presidents and four prime ministers between independence in 1991 and October 1993. That month, Heydar Aliyev became president, which he remained until 2003. Seventy years old when he became president, he had already had a successful career in Azerbaijan and Moscow during Soviet times. He was head of the KGB in Azerbaijan in the 1960s and first secretary of the Communist Party and effective leader of Azerbaijan in the 1970s and early 1980s. He then went to Moscow as first deputy prime minister of the Soviet Union and member of the Politburo. He returned to Azerbaijan in 1990 and became head of Nakhchivan, an autonomous republic of Azerbaijan and his home region. After independence, he formed a new political party and in due course became president.

Aliyev was a strong autocratic leader and skillful politician. Under him, Azerbaijan was generally stable, with little room for political opposition or freedom of expression. He generally supported market economy reforms, with government intervention when he saw fit. In practice, he had a say in all the important parts of the economy. The clans that supported him and related vested interests had to accommodate themselves to him. His economic adviser, Vahid Akhundov, an economist with some knowledge of market economics, would explain to us how they were progressing with reforms, but could be evasive when we asked about inappropriate government interventions or failures to deal with corruption in, for example, the tax authority.

Aliyev was one of the most impressive of all the presidents I met. His qualities were on full display in the meeting I had with him in 2000. As was common, I spoke first and raised six or seven issues of concern to us. He listened attentively without taking notes. After half an hour or so, he responded to my points, one by one in the order in which I had presented them. He gave substantive, reasoned answers, speaking calmly and with some charm. That evening, we were surprised to hear that the whole meeting had been broadcast unedited on local television. We wondered about his motive. Was he showing his people that he could better the IMF? Or that he was fully on top of economic issues (which he was)? Or just that he remained in charge of everything, part of his cult of the personality? He was only a few weeks short of his 77th birthday at the time.

Azerbaijan managed to achieve macroeconomic stability by the middle of the 1990s after the turbulent early years of the decade. But output did not grow until the second half of the decade, and then it took off, propelled by rising oil production. The National Bank of Azerbaijan under Elman Rustamov played an important part in bringing about stability. Rustamov became Governor in 1995 after a spell as Deputy Governor and remained in the position for well over two decades. The Finance Minister for part of the 1990s, Fikrat Yusifov, managed to keep the budget under control. Once I asked him how he resisted pressures to spend more money. He opened the top drawer of his desk, took out a hand gun and pointed it at an imaginary supplicant for funds. He greatly alarmed Peter Keller, our mission chief to Azerbaijan, when he jokingly held the gun to my temple during an official dinner. I liked him for his willingness to fight for good fiscal policies, even though his theatricality could be startling.

The special macroeconomic issue in Azerbaijan was how to handle the big flows of money associated with major foreign investments in the oil sector, and later the revenues from increased oil exports. Much of the initial investment was spent on importing equipment so that the overall balance of payments was not much affected. Once oil exports rose rapidly, there was a risk of Dutch disease associated with an appreciating exchange rate. (Dutch disease is the term used by economists to describe a situation in which the exploitation and export of natural resources in a country causes the exchange rate to appreciate and consequently makes other sectors of the economy less competitive internationally. The name comes from the experience of the Netherlands in the 1960 and 1970s after the growth of exports of natural gas.) We advised the government to set up a fund to take the oil revenues and invest them abroad. This would reduce the pressures for the exchange rate to appreciate and allow future generations to benefit from the oil, even after it had run out. The government created the State Oil Fund for this purpose. John Wakeman-Linn, our mission chief, and his colleagues produced a book, *Managing Oil Wealth: the Case of Azerbaijan*, incorporating our wisdom on the subject.

My last visit to the capital, Baku, in 2003 occurred after Aliyev had resigned due to ill health and shortly before he died. He had arranged for his son, Ilham Aliyev, to succeed him. This was the first case of a family dynasty being created in a former Soviet Union country. Ilham Aliyev continued the authoritarian regime his father had created. My meeting with him was perfunctory because he was not yet knowledgeable about economic issues.

Baku is built round a curved bay looking south over the Caspian Sea. There is no outlet from the Caspian. The level of water in it therefore depends on rainfall, evaporation and the inflow from rivers, especially the Volga, which provides 80 percent of the total inflow. Over the eighteen years up to 1995, it rose by ten meters and after that there were smaller fluctuations in both directions. On my early visits, the water was over the top of the promenade that runs along the sea shore. Later the promenade was raised to keep the water away. It was pleasant to walk near the sea, and also in the Old City with its Maidan Tower dating from the eleventh–twelfth centuries and its caravanserai, an old inn for travelers. There is an area of grand buildings from the end of the nineteenth century when the oil fields were first developed. That period was when Baku was a cosmopolitan city with Muslims, Christians and Jews; and Russians, Azeris, Turks, Georgians, Armenians and many others. Its international character was wonderfully captured in *Ali and Nino*, a novel from the 1930s that Basil Zavoico, our resident representative in Baku, kindly gave me on my final visit. The Soviet period and the oil revolution of recent decades brought many modern buildings rising up the hillside from the sea. One was the National Bank headquarters opened in 1998. Covered in gold colored glass, it acquired the nickname of the Golden Tooth.

GEORGIA

The civil unrest and separatist movement in Georgia in the first year or two after independence prevented the government from giving serious attention to macroeconomic problems. The work of our missions was more limited than we wished, and was sometimes even directly affected by the unrest. One morning, a mission led by Donal Donovan heard shelling and tank fire from their hotel. It seemed to have stopped by lunchtime and Donal's counterpart, the deputy prime minister, called to say "coup over, finished, beaten the rascals." He proposed that they meet in the afternoon to continue their discussions and arranged an armed escort. Donal and his team bravely accepted. They were met by a disheveled deputy prime minister who showed them fresh bullet holes. However, substantive progress was unlikely in that unstable situation so the team called for their charter plane and flew out that evening.

Inflation in Georgia, as a result of the initial liberalization and then the disruption caused by war, was higher than in any other former Soviet Union country. In 1994 it was over 15,000 percent, year on year. GDP fell by 77 percent between 1990 and 1994, the biggest fall in all the former Soviet Union countries. There was no effective macroeconomic policy in the early years.

After Eduard Shevardnadze effectively assumed the leadership in 1992, it took him some time to turn his attention to economic issues. A crucial turning point came in 1994 when he accepted the argument of Mohammad

Shadman-Valavi, our mission chief, that the bread subsidy had to go. The price of bread increased by over 250 times, with only the poor and the elderly being partly protected by the social safety net.

Our main interlocutor in the government was Temur Basilia, Shevardnadze's economic advisor and a deputy prime minister. He, the ministers of finance and the governors of the National Bank of Georgia worked to persuade others in government of the importance of stabilization policies and market reforms. But corruption was severe and the vested interests were against them. The reversal of the huge output falls in the early 1990s was slow in coming

Shevardnadze was the dominant figure in Georgia from when he returned to the country in 1992 until he resigned as President in 2003. He had been the first secretary of the Communist Party in Georgia from 1972 until 1985 when he introduced some minor economic reforms. Output growth was quite good but his anti-corruption efforts were unsuccessful. As Foreign Minister of the Soviet Union from 1985 to 1990, he played a major part, along with Gorbachev, in reducing Cold War tensions and withdrawing the Soviet Union from Eastern Europe. His main concern as de facto head of Georgia from 1992 and President from 1995 was to unify the country and secure its independence. He oriented it towards the West as a counterbalance to Russia which was giving some support to the separatist movements in Abkhazia and South Ossetia.

Shevardnadze was a clever politician and used his personal charm effectively. In my meetings with him, he spoke with apparent candor about his concern for the many groups whose standard of living was very low, not least the refugees from Abkhazia and elsewhere who were housed in overcrowded accommodation with little income. He wanted Georgia to have a successful market economy but, like other former communist leaders, thought of economic policy as the organization of production rather than the creation of conditions in which the private sector could thrive.

My most interesting meeting with him was my last one. It took place on the afternoon of Friday 21 November 2003, three weeks after a disputed parliamentary election which led to major demonstrations in the capital, Tbilisi, and other cities. Freedom Square in Tbilisi, called Lenin Square during Soviet times, was packed with opponents of the government who alleged that their parties had won the election, with some support from exit polls. The music coming from speakers in the square was very loud outside the nearby building housing the president's office. Inside it was quiet. I was surprised when Shevardnadze came into the room alone, apart from his interpreter, as usually members of his economic team accompanied him. (I was with Jonathan Dunn, our resident representative.) Even more surprising was his demeanor. He was calm and apparently oblivious to the clamor outside, which included calls for his resignation. I had expected him to make at least a reference to the unsettled political situation. Instead he talked candidly about the economic situation, including the problem of corruption, and how he wanted to create a properly functioning market economy with honest institutions. He focused almost exclusively on the economy which had not always been the case in my previous meetings with him. He came across as a good man who wanted to improve his country, but who knew that his achievements had fallen short of his aspirations.

I had dinner afterwards with Basilia and Irakli Managadze, the Governor of the National Bank of Georgia. They were, of course, eager to hear about my meeting with Shevardnadze. When I explained how calm he had been and his willingness to discuss the economy despite the political agitation outside, they offered two possible interpretations. One was that he had decided to resign and was in a reflective mood. The other was that he had prepared the security forces to see off the demonstrators so that he and the government could stay in power. The next day or two were to reveal which was closer to the truth.

Tension was building up on the streets even as we were having dinner. Busloads of supporters and opponents of the government were pouring into town. The following morning I walked out from my hotel on Rustaveli Avenue, the main street in Tbilisi, and saw both groups of demonstrators. One party had camped on Freedom Square and the other was spread over Rustaveli Avenue and neighboring streets. As I did not recognize their flags and could not understand the Georgian words of the songs that were blaring out, I could not tell which party was which. All the people looked the same: mostly young men wearing leather jackets. Buses had been parked across Rustaveli Avenue to stop traffic and separate the camps. Together with many other people, including women who were going shopping, I had to climb over the fenders of the buses to get to Freedom Square. There was a slight carnival atmosphere, but I also had the feeling that anything could happen. A few hours later it did.

I had to go to the airport at midday for a flight to Armenia. As soon as I reached my hotel in Yerevan, I switched on the television and saw the key moment of the Rose Revolution when demonstrators led by Mikheil Saakashvili and holding roses burst into Parliament while Shevardnadze was opening the new session. I saw Shevardnadze being taken out of a door at the back of the chamber by his bodyguards. The following day, he resigned and a couple of months later Saakashvili won the election to succeed him as president. It seems likely that Shevardnadze was psychologically prepared for resignation when I saw him the day before the rout in parliament, although he did try to rally the security forces to his side after escaping from the building.

Saakashvili and his government started a program of radical economic and institutional reforms that moved Georgia from the category of slow reformers to a much higher position. Notably, they made a successful attack on corruption. The economy performed much better as a result. However, he had an authoritarian streak in his character which led to his eventual downfall and exile from Georgia. Having experienced his pugnacious personality when I met him briefly at a reception when he was Minister of Justice during the Shevardnadze years, I was not too surprised that he became increasingly authoritarian after he became president.

Any account of Georgia has to mention the extraordinary hospitality extended to visitors. There is a saying in Georgia that "a guest is a gift from God." This applies even to business visitors, including the IMF. Our teams were treated to long meals, punctuated by many toasts, and with much food and wine. The quality was good. I liked the Georgian cuisine the best of all the ones in the region, and Georgian wine, which had a good reputation before the Soviet anti-alcohol campaign in the 1980s destroyed some of the vineyards and production facilities, was gradually regaining its former status. The problem was the quantity. Our missions, who needed time in the evenings to work in their hotel rooms as the days were taken up with meetings, were exhausted. My most testing experience was drinking from a kantsi, a traditional Georgian drinking horn usually made from a goat or ram's horn. At a dinner, I was given a kantsi into which almost a whole bottle of white wine had been poured. Thinking that no one could see that I had only drunk some of the wine, I put it down. But my Georgian hosts, who were skilled at judging how much had been drunk from the angle at which the horn was held, insisted that I had to empty it. So I did. Perhaps my performance was slightly impaired the following day. But it was not possible to resist playing a full part in traditional Georgian feasts when our hosts were so friendly and hospitable.

When my wife came with me in November 1997, Nodar Javakhishvili, the Governor of the National Bank, took us on an interesting excursion to the Kakheti wine-producing region where we saw the ancient technique of storing wine in clay vessels buried in the ground. There was also, of course, an extended break for a large lunch at which my wife helped me out by drinking some of my vodka. On the same visit, I arrived in a meeting room and took off my winter coat before sitting down. The host whispered that it might be better to keep my coat on because there was very little heating in the room. Like many countries in the former Soviet area, it took many years for Georgia to recover from the energy shortages that followed the breakup of the Soviet Union and the subsequent problems of obtaining and paying for energy imports, mainly from Russia and Turkmenistan. Our missions often had to work and live in unheated rooms in the early days.

The five Central Asian countries that emerged from the collapse of the Soviet Union are very different from each other. Geographically, Kyrgyzstan and

Tajikistan contain high mountain ranges, as do parts of Kazakhstan. However, most of Kazakhstan, which is the largest of them with an area as big as Western Europe, consists of a vast steppe (grassland). There are large desert areas in Turkmenistan and Uzbekistan. All the countries are landlocked, with Uzbekistan being double landlocked (having borders only with countries that are themselves landlocked). Linguistically, the Kazakhs, Kyrgyz, Turkmen and Uzbeks speak Turkic languages, being descended from the tribes which moved into Central Asia from Mongolia. The Tajiks speak Dari, a Persian language. During Soviet times, there were Russians in all countries, especially Kazakhstan (38 percent of the 1989 population) and Kyrgyzstan (21 percent); Russians accounted for fewer than 10 percent in the other countries in 1989.

Economically, Kazakhstan and Turkmenistan are major oil and gas exporters. Uzbekistan produces oil and gas but exports very little. Other minerals are mined in many places, especially Kazakhstan, and gold in Kyrgyzstan and Uzbekistan. Historically, the Kazakhs and Kyrgyz were nomads who moved with their herds of horses over big distances, both seasonally and for longer periods. The Uzbeks settled in the valley of the Syr Darya and developed agriculture. With such different histories, cultures and ways of life, it is not surprising that there were tensions between the countries. Since independence these have been aggravated by disputes over energy supplies and water resources that did not arise under Soviet rule.

KAZAKHSTAN

The economic transition in Kazakhstan and the IMF's role in it were much influenced by the importance of the mining sector and the dominant role of President Nazarbayev. Kazakhstan was a significant exporter of oil, gas and other natural resources during Soviet times and the prospects for increasing such exports in the future were bright. Nazarbayev wanted to attract foreign investment to help develop the mining sector. More generally, he saw the need to modernize the economy and move to a market economy that was integrated with the world economy. With one important exception, which I come to later, he gave important positions in the central bank and the economic parts of the government to young people who wanted to push ahead with market reforms.

While Nazarbayev generally favored market reforms, he wanted to retain overall control of the polity and economic policy. Thus he moved ministers and other senior policy makers every few years to prevent them from building up a power base of their own and to ensure their loyalty to him. He tolerated a certain amount of corruption, not only among government officials but also within his own family and inner circle. The couple of attempts I made to explain to him the costs in terms of slower growth of the poor governance (IMF-speak for corruption) in the country were met with a frosty response.

Kazakhstan was not one of the first countries in the region to borrow from the IMF because it was slow to clarify its monetary arrangements. Its economy was closely tied to the Russian economy because of the cross border trade between enterprises that were placed fairly close to each other during Soviet times but on opposite sides of the border between the two Soviet republics. The Kazakhs therefore hoped that the ruble area could be made to work, although they were not willing to subject Kazakhstan to a monetary policy run by Russia alone. It was only after Russia insisted on total control of ruble area monetary policy that Kazakhstan decided that it had to introduce its own currency, the tenge, which it did in late 1993.

After that, we were able to lend to Kazakhstan. We had little difficulty reaching agreement on economic policies, helped by the fact that the strong export sector and foreign investment flows to develop it further created a favorable balance of payments. Inflation came down and the economy grew for the first time in 1996. As in other countries in the region, we moved from short-term lending to longer-term lending under the EFF in 1996, in support of an economic program designed to promote structural reforms as well as macroeconomic stabilization. But unlike the others, Kazakhstan chose not to draw on the available funds as it did not need them, except in 1998 when the crisis in Russia hit Kazakhstan's exports and capital inflows. Even though they did not need the money in other years, the Kazakhs welcomed the seal of good approval of its economic policies provided by an agreement with the IMF.

Our interlocutors in the government and National Bank of Kazakhstan were mostly young and quick to understand the essentials of macroeconomic policy in a market economy. There was, however, one older man who played an important role in the early years. Daulet Sembayev was born in 1935 and started his career as an engineer. For the last 25 years of the Soviet Union, he worked in the secretariats of the Planning Committee and the Council of Ministers of the Kazakhstan republican government. In early 1992, after the disintegration of the Soviet Union, he was appointed first deputy prime minister with responsibility for economic policy. He later became Governor of the National Bank. With his knowledge of the workings of government, his good relations with Nazarbayev and his talent for encouraging younger people and drawing on their expertise, he was a most effective manager of the transition to a market economy. I took the opportunity of the dinner he gave for me in Almaty in 1993 to compliment him on his leadership of economic reform teams consisting of considerably younger people.

As the guest of honor at that dinner, I had the privilege of cutting pieces off the steaming sheep's head that was placed in front of me and serving them to the others at the table. I was well briefed by Ishan Kapur, our mission chief, that, according to local customs, I had to make a wish for each person I served. For our excellent interpreter, Marina Marton, I therefore wished that the sheep's lips I gave her would sustain her interpretation at a high standard. I wished that Sembayev, to whom I gave the ears, would listen to the advice of the IMF. Fortunately, they both took my rather cheeky remarks with a good spirit.

Kazakhs were traditionally great meat eaters, with the common meat being horse rather than sheep. Our hotel delicately described one dish as "Meat à la Kazakh" so as not to put off guests who did not like the idea of eating horsemeat. In fact it was quite a good dish. I was lucky not to be invited to go hunting. Camdessus was taken on a pheasant hunt when he visited, and Donal Donovan, the mission chief who followed Kapur, joined with his hosts in eating the raw liver of a deer that was shot when they took him hunting.

The capital of Kazakhstan was Almaty (the Russian version of the name, Alma-Ata, was used during Soviet times) until 1998 when Akmola became the capital. Until 1961, Akmola was called by its old Russian name, Akmolinsk. From 1961 to 1992, it was called Tselinograd, meaning City of the Virgin Lands, as it was at the heart of Khrushchev's virgin lands campaign. In 1992 its name reverted to Akmola, a version of Akmolinsk. When it became the capital in 1998, it was renamed Astana, meaning Capital City. One of the official reasons for the move of the capital was that Almaty was exposed to risks of earthquakes. But the main reason was to place the capital closer to the geographical center of the country instead of in the south-east corner.

After the breakup of the Soviet Union, there was speculation that further disintegration might occur, especially in Russia. In the case of Kazakhstan, the risk was that the population around the western and northern border areas might look more to Moscow than to Almaty, especially as there was a large minority, perhaps even a majority, of ethnic Russians living in those areas. (In 1989, Russians accounted for 40 percent of the population of Kazakhstan as a whole.) By moving the capital to the center of the country, people in the border areas would feel more connected to Kazakhstan. Also, the capital would be further away from China, the growing influence of which has been a worry for Kazakhstan.

There was a frenzy of construction in Astana which eventually became an ultramodern city with some striking architecture. But in the first few years, government officials who moved from Almaty had to make do with offices and apartments in utilitarian Soviet buildings. This, together with their separation from friends and families in Almaty and from its cultural life, did not endear them to Astana. In addition, the climate was worse. The summers were hotter than in Almaty, the winters were colder and strong winds often rushed in from the steppe surrounding the city. Astana displaced Ottawa from its position as the second coldest capital city in the world (Ulan Bator was the first). On my only winter visit, the daytime temperature in February 2001 was -25°C.

The first new buildings to go up were on either side of the central avenue. This gave rise to the nickname for Astana of Five Minute Hollywood. Driving down the avenue, everything was glitzy as in a Hollywood set, but there was nothing behind it and you reached the end in five minutes. Despite the early problems, Astana grew to become a major city with a population of nearly 2 million and a full range of modern services. In 2019 it was renamed Nur-Sultan after Nursultan Nazarbayev on his retirement from the presidency.

KYRGYZSTAN

As Nazarbayev was central to the course that Kazakhstan took after independence, so Askar Akaev was the major influence on developments in Kyrgyzstan, Kazakhstan's neighbor. Akaev was president of Kyrgyzstan from 1990 to 2005. His background was very different from that of Nazarbayev who rose during Soviet times through the ranks of the Communist Party as a bureaucrat. By contrast, Akaev was a research physicist who worked in Leningrad before returning to Bishkek where he became president of the Academy of Sciences. He was elected president of the Kyrgyz Republic of the Soviet Union in 1990 as a compromise candidate when two men more experienced in government were unable to secure a majority of votes in the Supreme Soviet. After independence, he became president of Kyrgyzstan and set the country on a course towards democracy and a market economy. At least initially, he promoted democratic institutions, such as a free press, fair elections and political parties. He was popular among Western governments which viewed Kyrgyzstan as a beacon of democracy in Central Asia.

In economics, Kyrgyzstan under Akaev chose a radical reform path, with rapid privatization, liberalization and stabilization. Although initially fearful of leaving the ruble area, the Kyrgyz realized earlier than some of the other countries that they would be better off with their own currency. Kyrgyzstan was therefore the first CIS country to introduce its national currency in May 1993. This enabled us to lend to them under the SBA, and we were subsequently closely involved in advising on macroeconomic policy and providing financial support for the years that followed. In 1994, Kyrgyzstan began to borrow from the IMF under the ESAF, the first of five CIS countries to do so. It was also the first of all CIS countries to join the World Trade Organization.

The National Bank under its first three Governors, Kemelbek Nanaev, Marat Sultanov and Ulan Sarbanov, managed monetary policy effectively from 1993 onwards. While the government had good intentions with respect to macroeconomic stabilization, it faced greater difficulties in conducting fiscal policy. The collapse of the economy at the end of Soviet times and in the early years of independence reduced the tax base sharply. The problem was compounded by the loss of subsidies from the Soviet budget. The government responded by cutting expenditures and by borrowing abroad, which it was able to do because official lenders were very supportive of Kyrgyzstan. As was the case throughout the region, the recovery of economic output took longer than expected, and the external indebtedness grew rapidly, as noted earlier.

Although inflation did not come down to single figures until nearly the end of the decade, the economy started to grow in 1996. We expected growth to be more rapid than it turned out to be because Kyrgyzstan had made more progress than nearly all other CIS countries in introducing the laws and other formal arrangements for a market economy. As time went on, however, it became apparent that there was a big gap between these and what went on in practice. In the early 2000s, we named this the "Implementation Gap" and urged the government to focus on the reforms needed to ensure effective implementation of market enabling measures. In practice, this was an enormous task. The government, at regional and local levels as much as (perhaps even more than) at the national level, had not shed old Soviet attitudes and practices of wanting to intervene in the decisions of private businesses. This stifled enterprise, discouraged investment and encouraged soft budget constraints and corruption. Inefficiencies in enterprises and arrears in payments of taxation, interenterprise debts and even wages were tolerated by political leaders whose priority was to maintain jobs and the appearance of economic activity.

Akaev's commitment to democracy and rapid market reforms was admirable, but not enough to overcome the problems of poor implementation. Although he had the right ideas, he did not have enough political skills and contacts and connections in all parts of the country to be able to overhaul the governance arrangements at every level and hold vested interests and corruption at bay. He was an intellectual rather than a doer who could effect deep changes in governance and society.

He revealed his intellectual bent in his book, *The Transition Economy Through the Eyes of a Physicist* (written in Russian and published in English in 2000). Most of the book was a conventional presentation of the progress in the economic transition in Kyrgyzstan compared with other CIS countries. It also contained a defense of Kyrgyzstan's choice of a rapid reform strategy. Akaev's unique contribution was his mathematical model of the transition economy which drew on probability distributions developed by Erlang in the early twentieth century to explain the arrival of phone calls at a telephone exchange. Akaev built models of the growth of private enterprises in

Kyrgyzstan using Erlang's distributions. I did not find the models useful as a guide to developments in Kyrgyzstan, nor, I suspect, did anyone else. It is even possible that Akaev himself did not believe in them. Although there is no mention in the book of any collaborators, it is likely that the models, and the descriptions of developments in Kyrgyzstan, were prepared by others, with Akaev claiming authorship.

When the book was being written, he told me jokingly that there would be a chapter on the IMF which would be called "Kyrgyzstan's most helpful, but difficult, friend." There was no such chapter, but a couple of sentences in the book conveyed the same message. "We may responsibly say that those [the IMF's] conditions did not impede the successful implementation of reforms. On the contrary, the conditions set have been helpful, as they disciplined us and encouraged us to look for reasonable and efficient solutions for the rational use of loans."

After I retired from the IMF, I had the opportunity to have private conversations with Akaev who had asked me to be a freelance advisor. With financial support from the UK's overseas aid program, I visited Kyrgyzstan twice in 2004 to catch up with developments and talk to Akaev, with whom I also left written reports. (I made no visits after that because Akaev lost his position as president in March 2005.) His intelligence, intellectual honesty, charm and courtesy always made meetings with him good experiences. In addition to specific economic issues, such as impending Paris Club meetings, tax issues, the budget and banking, the heart of our conversations was the poor climate for business and resultant low levels of investment and slow growth. He was fully aware of the problems of poor governance, vested interests and corruption that contributed to the Implementation Gap and the poor business climate. In his book, which was written a few years earlier, he had stressed that the reform of state governance was the most important factor for advancing social and economic transformation. He agreed with the need to reduce both low and high level corruption and the size of government, and to reform the civil service and the judiciary. But the reality was that he was not strong enough to overcome the vested interests and fundamentally change the way the system worked. Moreover, he was seriously compromised by the correct public perception that he allowed members of his family to become rich through dubious practices (something I did not mention in our conversations).

Growing popular resentment about the failure of living standards for the vast majority to improve at the same time as Akaev's family and some others became very rich erupted in the so-called Tulip Revolution in March 2005 which led to his flight from the country and permanent exile. I have not found it easy to balance in my mind my admiration for Akaev's democratic leadership and commitment to reforms in the early stages of independence with my disappointment that he failed to prevent vested interests, including those in his own family, from stifling the reforms and undermining enterprise and growth in the later stages. Comparing Kyrgyzstan with comparable CIS countries, its early lead in economic reforms did not result in a sustained superior economic performance. In the political sphere, perhaps it has remained a more open society than comparable CIS countries. But even there, the various unconstitutional changes of government, starting with Akaev's dismissal, were not obviously better than, say, the stable but authoritarian regime of Nazarbayev in Kazakhstan.

Macroeconomists assess the economic situation in a country by looking at statistics of output, incomes, prices and other indicators, and talking to people who also keep an eye on the economy as a whole. However, it is always useful to supplement the big picture with small examples of markets, individual enterprises and the experiences of individuals. I had one or two opportunities for such bottom-up views in Kyrgyzstan.

In 2002 or 2003, I went with Tapio Saavalainen, our mission chief, and Bolot Abildaev, the Finance Minister, to Dordoi Market on the outskirts of Bishkek. This was a huge, mostly wholesale market in which imported goods from many countries, mainly China and, in smaller amounts, Turkey, were sold to traders who distributed them in Kyrgyzstan and also Uzbekistan, Kazakhstan and Russia. Although it had been operating since the collapse of the Soviet Union, it still had an impermanent feel to it. The goods were kept in shipping containers piled two high, the lower one for displaying them and the upper one for storage. Most of the ground was unpaved and must have been muddy in wet weather. While most of the traders were Kyrgyz, there were also Kazakhs, Uzbeks, Uighurs and Han Chinese, with Russian being the main lingua franca. For an economist, it was a fine example of how the liberalization of foreign trade and prices can lead very quickly to more trade and greater efficiencies.

There was a similar but smaller market in Kara-Suu, near Osh in the southern part of Kyrgyzstan. Because of its mountainous terrain, the population of Kyrgyzstan was concentrated in the northern areas centered on Bishkek, and the Fergana Valley in the south of the country, with overland travel between the two being slow and circuitous. The market in Kara-Suu functioned mainly as a distribution center for goods destined for Tajikistan and Uzbekistan, as well as southern Kyrgyzstan. I asked to go there, not so much to see the market itself, but rather to see the damaged bridge across the river which separated Kara-Suu in Kyrgyzstan from the town in Uzbekistan with the same name. Uzbekistan tried to prevent imports of low cost goods, especially from China, to protect its own industries. When it was unable to stop smugglers who bought cheap goods in Kara-Suu market to sell in Uzbekistan, it resorted to the crude method of blowing up the bridge. While economists are familiar with the imposition of barriers to trade, it was a rare experience to see a barrier in the form of a bridge that was impassable because half of it had fallen into the river.

In the early 2000s, Tapio Saavalainen and I met a couple of times with a pensioners' association in the capital, Bishkek. It was led by Lydia Fomova who was an ethnic Russian, as were most of the group. She spoke forcefully and convincingly of the poverty of pensioners and how it affected their lives and health. They had suffered a sharp decline in living standards after the collapse of the Soviet Union and the emergence of independent Kyrgyzstan, with little, if any, improvement in subsequent years. She said that the government had not honored the implicit promise that it would look after pensioners who had given so much during their working lives. Our attempts to persuade her and her associates that the hardships were temporary until the market economy took root and flourished were unsuccessful. They had had too many years of hearing that the future would be brighter to believe it any more. (I did not have the courage to point out that the loss of transfers from the Soviet Union would have a permanent effect on government expenditures in Kyrgyzstan.) Nor did they hold out much hope for a positive response from the government if they were to propose, as I suggested, that more of its limited budget should be devoted to pensions.

I admired and respected Fomova for her persistence and fortitude, even as her health was visibly deteriorating. My meetings with her and her associates were a salutary reminder that there were many losers from the transition. Years later I recalled the expressions of frustration, resentment and helplessness among the group when I read some of the stories in Svetlana Alexievich's book. While their misery did not cause me to change our economic advice to the government, perhaps it gave me more energy to press the government to improve the prospects for growth, and to collect more taxes so that the budget could expand.

Compared with other Central Asian countries, Kyrgyzstan during the Akaev years, which were also my years, was a more open society. Whether because of this, or perhaps the innate friendliness of the Kyrgyz people, personal interactions with our counterparts and other people we met were easy and relaxed. My visits there were pleasant also because of the natural beauty of the mountains. Bishkek is on the southern edge of the steppe, with the snow-covered Tian Shan mountains rising behind it. More spectacular was the view from the northern shore of Lake Issyk-Kul to a still higher range of the Tian Shan on the southern side. The lake, the tenth largest in the world by volume (although not by surface area), was the site of a secret torpedo testing operation during Soviet times, as well as a tourist industry along the northern shore. The main hotel, the Aurora, was an unbeautiful concrete block shaped like the Russian naval vessel, the Aurora, a shot from which signaled the start of the October revolution in Petrograd. There were some pleasant sandy beaches, with reminders of the economic cost of the transition in the rusting deck chairs and sun umbrellas when my wife and I were there in May 2003.

TAJIKISTAN

Tajikistan faced some of the same difficulties as Kyrgyzstan when it emerged from the Soviet Union as an independent country. It was landlocked with long and complicated transport connections. Mountains covered 93 percent of the country. It had the lowest per capita income of all the former Soviet Union states and it had lost the subsidies from the Soviet budget. On top of all this, a major civil war broke out in 1992.

The war was initially a political and religious one, with an opposition alliance of Islamic groups and liberal democrats seeking to replace the government that was descended from the communist rulers of Soviet times. It became more of a regional clash, with the opposition garnering support from the Garm and Gorno-Badakhshan regions in the east and south-east, and the government side being backed by groups in the Khujand region in the north and the Kulyab region in the south. It ended with a ceasefire and peace agreement in 1997. The government side won, helped by military and other support from Russia. Under the peace agreement, power was to be shared between the two sides, but in practice few opposition representatives were given significant positions in the government. Out of a population at independence of just over 5 million, between 10 percent and 20 percent were internally displaced by the war and many tens of thousands were killed.

The civil war delayed our work in Tajikistan. It did not become a member until 1993, and it did not introduce its own currency until 1995. Although we sent missions, the security situation and the weak institutions delayed our reaching agreements about an economic program and extending loans. The first person we sent as a resident representative, Jennaro Simpson, decided not to stay there after a disturbing event at the airport. He went to catch a plane, but flights were few and hopeful passengers many. When the terminal doors were opened, there was a mad rush for the plane. It was controlled only by soldiers standing at the top of the steps to the plane and firing over the heads of the approaching horde.

Later, a mission led by Peter Keller had to drive every day past a tank which was guarding the compound where they were staying in a government guest house. The tank was there primarily to protect the president and other senior officials whose houses were in the same compound. But the IMF mission appreciated its presence, not least when their al fresco dinner was interrupted as rocket fired grenades hit nearby buildings. Peter and Tapio Saavalainen, who was mission chief later, met some of the combatants when their missions were taken into the mountains for relaxation at weekends. There was plenty of weaponry around, and mission members were invited to try some of them out. Even after the ceasefire, there were occasional outbreaks of fighting. When I went in May 1998, my plane was held up for many hours in Moscow because of an outbreak of shooting at Dushanbe airport, as I learned after I arrived there. The passengers had been told some false story in Moscow about technical problems with the plane.

The capacity of the government and central bank to design and implement market reforms was weaker in Tajikistan than in the other former Soviet Union countries, reflecting its lower incomes and levels of education. My colleagues in the technical assistance departments of the IMF provided considerable help with introducing the national currency, modernizing the National Bank, tax reform and administration, budgeting, statistics and other issues. My own staff worked with the Tajiks on economic policies. The agreed programs allowed us to lend to Tajikistan, starting in 1996. In most years after that there was some slippage from the programs because of pressures to spend more from the budget or extend more credits in the economy, especially to the cotton sector. Our lending was interrupted from time to time. Each time we renegotiated the monetary and fiscal targets and later resumed lending. Inflation came down more slowly than originally planned, not reaching single figures until 2004. Output fell sharply at the beginning of the transition, especially during the civil war. Subsequently it recovered well from a low base, with growth turning positive in 1997 and exceeding that in most other CIS countries in the early 2000s. The measures of structural reforms compiled by EBRD in the early 2000s placed Tajikistan in the bottom half of CIS countries, although above average in price and trade liberalization.

As in other Central Asian countries, the president determined the main direction of economic policies. President Emomali Rakhmonov, who derussified his name to Rahmon in 2007, was elected chairman of the Supreme Soviet of Tajikistan in 1992 and, after the adoption of a new constitution, president in 1994. Subsequent changes in the constitution enabled him to remain president for well over 25 years. He was chairman of the state farm in his home region when he was elected to the Supreme Soviet in 1990, aged 38. As a young man, who had not worked in the central bureaucracy of Soviet Tajikistan, he accepted the need for market reforms. He also welcomed advice (and money) from the IMF and told the government and National Bank to work with us.

He was a strong leader with an authoritarian streak which had enabled him to lead the government, including the warlords on his own side, through the civil war. I witnessed the more extreme version of his leadership style on only one occasion. In a meeting with him and the main members of his economic team, I criticized something that had happened (or not happened—I do not remember the details). He responded with a theatrical spectacle, demanding that the Governor of the National Bank, the finance minister and the economy minister stand up while he berated them. I felt bad that my remarks had placed our counterparts in the president's line of fire, although they were obviously used to it and my relationship with them did not suffer.

Inevitably, there were times when Rakhmonov had objectives that conflicted with the economic program we had agreed to with the government. His team had to do their best to accommodate them, which they were not always able to do within the parameters of the program. But in general, Rakhmonov was supportive of the programs. In this he was different from Presidents Lukashenko of Belarus and Karimov of Uzbekistan. They were also strong, autocratic leaders, but their views about economic policy differed so much from ours that we were rarely able to agree on economic programs for their countries.

As time went on, it became apparent that corruption and cronyism, with the President's family and friends being prominent among the cronies, were impeding the growth of small and medium sized enterprises and hence output and employment growth. Large numbers of Tajiks were leaving the country to work abroad. Their remittances were essential to the wellbeing of their families, but they were also a symptom of the failure of the economy to provide jobs and incomes at home. Although we were concerned about corruption, cronyism and vested interests in many countries, not only Tajikistan, our focus on macroeconomic stability limited our influence in this area, as explained in chapter 3.

However, after I retired from the IMF I was able to raise these issues directly with Rakhmonov with whom I worked as a freelance economic advisor, operating in much the same way as I was doing with President Akaev in Kyrgyzstan. In three visits in 2004 and 2005, I discussed many issues with him, but emphasized the need to reform the civil service and public administration, deregulate the economy and tackle what I called the "anti-market exercise of power by vested interests." I made clear that this included high level corruption as well as extortion, rigged privatizations and suppression of competition. He appeared to agree with me, and issued instructions that my recommendations should be pursued. Government officials did indeed work diligently on specific measures. But few of them were implemented and, even when they were, various vested interests found ways to prevent them having the full intended effect.

The counterpart with whom we had the closest relationship was Murodali Alimardonov (Alimardon from 2007). He was governor of the National Bank from 1996 to 2008 after which he was deputy prime minister for the agricultural sector. As governor, he was in charge of Tajikistan's interactions with the IMF and facilitated our work. However, he himself was reticent about engaging in substantive discussions about monetary, or any other, policies. For many years, I attributed this to a lack of confidence in his understanding of the issues. We found this in many of our counterparts in all countries, although it was sometimes partially hidden under superficial braggadocio. As Tajikistan had been the poorest part of the Soviet Union, the Tajiks had long struggled with anxieties about inferiority.

As time went on, we came to realize that Alimardonov was more on top of issues than he let on. He also knew about financial transactions that were not consistent with the monetary programs we had agreed to with him. On more than one occasion, the National Bank reported incorrect information to the IMF thereby enabling us to make the next disbursement of a loan which would not have been justified on the basis of the correct information. Some of the problems arose from financing of the cotton sector which was always given priority even if it conflicted with what the program agreed to with us. In 2008, it was found (and confirmed by an audit in 2009) that large loans were made by the National Bank to a private company that was engaged in financing the cotton sector, and a further sum for developing the cotton industry had disappeared. It is likely that Alimardonov's own agricultural ventures and those of his family members were among the beneficiaries. He was moved from the National Government to a deputy prime minister position, but was not charged with an offence.

As well as overseeing our relations with Tajikistan, Alimardonov was an excellent host. In the absence of international standard hotels in Dushanbe, he arranged for our missions to stay in a guest house in the government compound which included the residences of the President and other senior officials. He even sent the National Bank chef to the guest house every morning to prepare breakfast for us. On the one occasion that my wife visited Tajikistan, he invited us and the IMF mission team to his country estate one Sunday. We drove up the mountain through his huge fruit farm to a lodge outside of which a marquee was being prepared for lunch. After I planted a tree at his request, we were surprised to see President Rakhmonov, who was close to Alimardonov, arrive on horseback. We all drove further up the mountain, where I was treated to a ride over bumpy ground on an all-terrain vehicle. I clung on to the president who was in the driver's seat, while our interpreter, Arkady Tchaikovsky, bravely ran along beside us. We returned to the marquee for lunch in a Lexus SUV driven by the president who skillfully kept the vehicle away from the precipitous edge of the slippery mud road.

When I visited Tajikistan as an advisor after retiring from the IMF, Alimardonov invited me to his home. Once we went even further up the mountain to a new lodge, which he had recently built. The views from the road were spectacular. Another time, I was privileged to be the only non-Tajik at a ceremony in which his one-year-old son had his hair cut for the first time. I was told that this was an old Tajik custom, which reflected the relief that families felt that their son had survived the most dangerous year of his life, from a health point of view. The ceremony was performed by two mullahs who recited the Koran. Only male family and friends were present; the women of the household could be seen in the distance in another building.

It was difficult not to like Alimardonov. He was friendly, charming and generous with his hospitality. We knew, of course, that his houses and commercial farms could not be paid for from his salary, and there were plenty of rumors about corruption and cronyism in the government. In the interests of good working relations, we accepted his explanation that he had financed everything through legitimate bank loans. As in other CIS countries, and discussed in general in chapter 3, we were in no position to question the financial probity of Alimardonov or other counterparts unless clear evidence of wrong doing appeared. It was quite likely that almost everyone we dealt with was receiving money on the side through legitimate or illegitimate channels. Alimardonov's solicitous behavior towards me and our missions may have been intended to disarm us so that we would not ask difficult questions. Whether this was true or not, I still like to remember him as a very agreeable host.

I explained in chapter 3 why human rights issues were outside our terms of reference. Rakmonov's reputation for not respecting human rights by imprisoning political opponents, controlling the media and restricting religious freedom was not in principle our business. It was, however, difficult not to be aware of his hostility to Muslims and Muslim practices, even though he himself was a Muslim. At various times he banned beards, closed madrassahs, restricted access to mosques and criticized the wearing of Islamic clothing, including the hijab for women.

I witnessed his anti-Muslim bias when he took me and my wife for lunch at the Rohat Chaikhanna (tea house) in the middle of Dushanbe. He was visibly upset by a group of bearded men dressed in flowing robes and wearing Muslim caps sitting at a table and made sure that we sat well away from them. Later in private he spoke emotionally about the danger posed to Tajikistan by Islamic movements. He had, of course, faced organized Islamic groups in the civil war, one of which, the Islamic Renaissance Party (IRP), became the main political opposition. From 1996 to 2001, the Taliban was in power in neighboring Afghanistan and gave some support to Islamic groups in Tajikistan. Rakhmonov was right to be concerned about the possibility of an uprising against his rule led by Islamic insurgents, and his security forces kept a close eye on the situation. I have, however, wondered whether his attacks on Muslim institutions and practices, and banning the IRP in 2015, were the best way to proceed.

On one visit to Dushanbe, I met with the leader of the IRP, Sayid Abdulloh Nuri, to find out where the IRP stood on economic reforms. By then, the IRP had become the main opposition party, having been denied by Rakhmonov the power sharing role envisaged in the peace agreement of 1997. Nuri came across as a reasonable and thoughtful man who seemed to support market oriented economic reforms. I concluded that opposition to reforms would not come from the government's formal political opponents. As it turned out, it was the vested interests among the government's own supporters that prevented the full range of structural and institutional reforms needed to create a competitive market economy from being implemented.

Dushanbe was a pleasant city to visit. Most of the offices where we met people were on Rudaki Avenue, which was wide, lined with trees and had a few modest neoclassical buildings in the Russian style. When I visited it, the Museum of National Antiquities could have benefited from a facelift. But the 12 meter long reclining Buddha from the seventh or eighth century AD was striking. The main attraction of Tajikistan for a visitor was, of course, the mountains, the beginnings of which I saw from Alimardonov's property as well as from the air. After I retired from the IMF and was spending weeks at a time in Dushanbe as an advisor, my wife and I considered whether she should join me so that we could explore the country together. We soon abandoned the idea after reading in a guidebook that Tajikistan was "at the cutting edge of adventure tourism." Adventure tourism alone, which seemed to mean mountain climbing combined with undeveloped tourism infrastructure, was beyond us, let alone its cutting edge.

UZBEKISTAN

Islam Karimov was president of Uzbekistan from independence until he died in 2016 aged 78. He had been first secretary of the Uzbekistan Communist Party at the end of the Soviet era and had previously been minister of finance and head of the State Planning Committee. He was unable or unwilling to change his views from state planning to market economy mode. He was the absolute ruler of everything in Uzbekistan, not just the economy. He allowed some price and trade liberalization and privatization, but considerably less than in other CIS countries, except Belarus and Turkmenistan. In 2005, the private sector's share of GDP was only 45 percent, whereas it was 60 percent or more in all other CIS countries except for Belarus (25 percent), Tajikistan (50 percent) and Turkmenistan (25 percent).

Despite the slow progress of reforms, our missions led by Leif Hansen, who was very patient with his Uzbek counterparts, reached agreement in 1995 and 1996 on programs that enabled us to lend small amounts under the STF and SBA. But the government imposed exchange and trade controls during 1996 that were contrary to the program, and we halted disbursements, never to resume them during my time. A few years later, the controls became more extensive. Among other measures, the government closed bazaars and, as noted earlier, blew up the bridge crossing to Kyrgyzstan. While some of the measures were part of a misconceived plan to improve the economy through old-fashioned controls, others were introduced to create new rent-seeking opportunities, or protect existing ones, for the friends and families of the elite, including Karimov's own family.

After it became clear that the government of Uzbekistan was unlikely to move far in the direction of genuine market reforms, our relations became increasingly strained. The Uzbeks wanted to resume borrowing, not so much for the money but because of the boost to its reputation and the improved options for attracting funds from elsewhere, including other international organizations. But they were not prepared to remove some of their non-market interventions, especially exchange rate and trade controls. Instead they lobbied other countries to put pressure on us to change our position.

They began by escalating their case within the IMF, a common tactic of aggrieved governments. Karimov invited Fischer to visit Uzbekistan in May 1997. However, Fischer did not believe Karimov's promise to reform. Even with a visit to Samarkand thrown in, he stuck to the line which our mission had taken. As the Uzbeks were not prepared to liberalize the economy, our mission could not reach an agreement with them. They also tried to persuade the Japanese government to press us to change our position. From the beginning of the transition Japan had indicated in a very mild way that they thought that we should be more willing to support gradual as opposed to radical reforms if countries wished to take that course. They made comparisons with the post-World War II reconstruction in Japan which included a significant role for government intervention in, and control of, the economy. As it happened, the deputy managing director of the IMF who oversaw our work on Uzbekistan was Shigeo Sugisaki. Being Japanese, he provided a convenient route through which Japan's voice could be heard. But this approach also did not work.

Picking up on the Japanese experience and that of other successful Asian economies, the Uzbeks believed that there was an Asian model of economic development that suited them better than what they thought of as the Western model that we advocated. They thought that they would have more of a meeting of minds with the economists in the IMF's Asian Department than with my economists who were in a "Western" department. The Deputy Prime Minister for the Economy, Bakhtior Hamidov, asked Camdessus when they met during the Annual Meetings in Hong Kong in 1997 if he would move responsibility for Uzbekistan to the Asian Department. Camdessus responded forcefully: "Some people say that I can make history. Perhaps I can. But I certainly cannot make geography." We did not hear about this proposal again.

The strained relations at an official level discouraged friendly, informal relations between my economists and their Uzbek counterparts. The situation was not helped by the fear that our counterparts had of getting into trouble if they stepped out of line. My meetings with people like Rustam Azimov, the deputy prime minister for economic affairs in the 2000s (and finance minister before that), and Vyacheslav Golishev, the President's economic advisor, were tense. They stuck to their story, which reflected Karimov's position, and bluntly rejected our suggestions that market reforms would benefit the country. Sometimes they pretended that reforms were in fact going ahead.

The one person who was able to get past the generally frosty contacts was Christoph Rosenberg, our resident representative in Uzbekistan at the end of the 1990s. As he lived in Tashkent, he was able to develop personal friendships which enabled him to have a deeper understanding of the economic and political situation than our missions could obtain. But it was a luxury for us to have a resident representative in a country where we were not lending. We therefore did not replace him when his term was up, much to the annoyance of the Uzbeks who viewed it as another rejection. We did however, keep our office in Tashkent open, staffed by a local employee. And our regular missions continued to discuss an economic program, with partial success when we reached an agreement on a program that we would monitor but without an accompanying loan.

My last visit to Tashkent was in May 2003 when the EBRD was holding its annual meeting there. Arriving a day or two earlier, I met my usual Uzbek counterparts including Karimov. As on other occasions, he pressed me to reopen negotiations on an economic program but was not willing to commit to implementing some of the important reforms that we said should be part of the program. Sensing that he was preparing to announce progress in relations with the IMF at the opening meeting of the EBRD the next day, I got my story out first by telling the press after I met Karimov that there was no agreement between us. The story appeared early the next day in the special newspaper prepared for the people attending the EBRD meeting. I also told Jean Lemierre, the President of the EBRD, and the British officials who would be briefing Clare Short, the UK Minister who was the formal chair of the EBRD annual meeting.

There had been much controversy over the decision to hold the EBRD's annual meeting in Tashkent. Some Western member countries were opposed on the grounds that Uzbekistan's human rights record was inconsistent with the EBRD's mission to promote human rights and democratic institutions as well as market reforms in countries in transition from communism. In deciding to go ahead with the meeting, the EBRD extracted some minor concessions from Uzbekistan. One procedural concession was that the Uzbeks agreed that the opening session would be broadcast live on Uzbek TV.

The opening session turned out to be a remarkable spectacle, not only for Uzbeks but for people everywhere who were interested in Uzbekistan. Karimov sat in the center of the stage flanked by the Presidents of Georgia, Kazakhstan, Kyrgyzstan and Tajikistan, Clare Short and Jean Lemierre. The EBRD thought that they had extracted a promise from the Uzbeks that Karimov would condemn torture in his opening remarks, but he made no reference to it, instead boasting of the democratic and economic renewal of Uzbekistan. Short and Lemierre made strong criticisms of Uzbekistan's economic policies and poor human rights and democracy performance. (Short's staff told me before the meeting that they did not know whether she would use the stronger or the weaker of the critical words they had given her. When Karimov failed to address the issues, she chose to use the stronger ones.) Karimov was shocked. In a dramatic gesture, he took off his headphones while Short and Lemierre were speaking and covered his ears with his hands. His defiance might have impressed some people, but there can be no doubt that the criticism was damaging to his reputation, especially outside the country. (However, one or two of our counterparts from neighboring Central Asian countries whom I spoke to at a reception later that day said that it was not the Central Asian way to criticize someone in public. Even Nazarbayev, who was known to have bad personal relations with Karimov, put his hand on Karimov during the meeting to indicate sympathy.) The immediate domestic repercussion was the firing of the producer and director of Uzbek TV.

As I had expected, Karimov claimed in his speech that he and I had an agreement to reopen discussions on an economic program which the IMF could support. Of course, this was not so, and I had made sure that those who needed to know understood that it was not true. I liked to joke afterwards that I was privileged to be one of only two foreigners whom he mentioned by name in his speech. The other, who was also British, was Rudyard Kipling. Karimov quoted his line that "East is East, and West is West, and never the twain shall meet" to illustrate his point that the Uzbek way of doing things was different from that in the West. Therefore it should not be criticized by people and institutions based in the West who did not understand Uzbekistan.

My wife was with me during the EBRD meetings. The Uzbeks were very hospitable to the spouses of meeting attendees, and took them to see local cultural and artisanal activities in Tashkent. My wife especially enjoyed meeting the Rahimov family who had been making pottery with traditional designs for three generations. She and I planned to add a few days to our visit so that we could visit Samarkand and Bukhara as tourists. Marina Marton, who had been working as an interpreter at the EBRD meeting, was going to come with us. I arranged for a local travel agent to make the travel and hotel arrangements. The government would probably have done it for us, but I wanted to avoid incurring a debt to them in view of our poor relations. However, when the government heard about our plans, they insisted that we should be accompanied by a deputy governor of the central bank and that I should meet the local representatives of the central bank and regional governments in Samarkand and Bukhara. No doubt they were motivated by a wish to show Uzbek hospitality. But I suspect that their main reason was to keep me away from situations where I might learn things about the economy and society that they wanted to keep secret.

In the event we had a pleasant trip, with the architecture of Samarkand and Bukhara, even when clumsily restored, and the associated history, gripping our attention. I felt that I had let Marina down, because she had to translate for me in my meetings with officials instead of enjoying some well-earned time off after the intense work of the EBRD meetings. But she rose to the occasion generously and professionally. The one positive outcome for me from a professional point of view occurred when a senior representative of the regional government in Samarkand with responsibilities for economic policy suggested that he and I, with Marina, take a walk in the open air where we could not be overheard. He told me that the economic situation in the country was much worse than we were being told by the government in Tashkent, that the government's attempts to control the economy were a failure and that the only way forward was to move quickly with genuine market reforms. It was a measure of Karimov's firm grip on the government that we had to go outside Tashkent to hear such things, unsurprising though they were in substance.

Karimov was President until he died in 2016, bringing his years in charge to twenty-six, including the couple of years at the end of the period when Uzbekistan was in the Soviet Union. He was succeeded as President by Shavkat Mirziyoev who had been Prime Minister since 2003. Mirziyoev soon launched a program of economic liberalization which was long overdue.

Uzbekistan took up somewhat more of my time than the general nature of our relations with the country required. Despite their reluctance to reform, the government valued the IMF's seal of good approval and repeatedly tried to restart discussions about an economic program. Important IMF member countries lobbied us on its behalf, thereby raising its profile in the IMF and my workload. I have mentioned Japan. After the US invasion of Afghanistan, the US looked for ways of helping the Uzbeks in return for Uzbek military cooperation, which included allowing the US to use an air base for logistical purposes. The foreign policy and security parts of the US government would have liked to see some IMF support for Uzbekistan, but we were spared much pressure because the Treasury Department, which agreed with the position of the IMF staff and management, usually protected us. Switzerland, which represented Uzbekistan on the Executive Board of the IMF, also kept it on our agenda. Despite all this international interest, Karimov was not prepared to embrace market reforms. It was disappointing to us that our efforts to persuade him and his associates that reforms would benefit the country were unsuccessful.

TURKMENISTAN

There was general agreement among international organizations and most other observers that Belarus, Turkmenistan and Uzbekistan were different from the other former Soviet Union countries in keeping much of the Soviet economic system in place. However, these three were not alike. In particular, Turkmenistan stood out as being not at all interested in changing the system. It scored lower than the other two countries on almost all the indicators of reforms published by the EBRD. By contrast, the other two undertook a few reforms, which we were able to support with loans for a few years.

Two main characteristics of Turkmenistan defined its economic policy and our relations with the country: its large reserves of oil and gas, and the ideas and dictatorial tendencies of the president of Turkmenistan, Saparmurat Niyazov. Turkmenistan was a major natural gas producer and supplier to other former Soviet Union countries. After independence, it raised the price of gas towards world levels. However, many of the customers had serious financial problems even without the price increase and fell into arrears. I explained our efforts to resolve the resulting indebtedness problems in chapter 2. The arrears problem did not, however, prevent Turkmenistan from borrowing from commercial lenders in Europe and the US on the strength of its gas reserves and prospects for future income from them. With an increasingly comfortable external financial position from a combination of revenues from oil and gas sales and capital inflows, there was no formal case for us to lend to Turkmenistan.

Niyazov had been first secretary of the Communist Party and also chairman of the Supreme Soviet of Turkmenistan at the end of the Soviet era. He became president in 1991. He was an absolute ruler, and encouraged the cult of (his) personality. He gave himself the title of Turkmenbashi, meaning head of the Turkmen. After Turkmenistan introduced its own currency in 1993, there was a possibility that we might be able to agree an economic program with them. Our team, headed by Mohammad Shadman-Valavi, came close to an agreement with their counterparts on the first stage of reforms, including macroeconomic stabilization and liberalization measures. But when Niyazov realized that he would lose some control over the economy, he halted the discussions.

Then, and later, our work was hampered by the secrecy that Niyazov insisted upon. For example, a considerable part of the country's foreign exchange earnings went into the Foreign Exchange Reserve Fund (FERF) which was under the direct control of the president. We were not allowed to see the accounts of the FERF and thus had no knowledge about that part of government expenditure which was financed from the FERF. (IMF colleagues who worked on the oil-producing Gulf countries where the royal families directly controlled expenditures separately from the government had to deal with similar problems.) There were other areas where the government provided incomplete or obviously unreliable data. A failure of a member to report economic information to the IMF was a breach of our rules. This was another reason why we could not lend money to Turkmenistan, even if we had been able to agree an economic program with them. It was the only one of all fifteen former Soviet Union countries that did not borrow from us. For some years, we could not even complete the regular review of the economy, known as the Article IV review, because we did not have access to all the relevant information.

Because of our limited work there, I only visited Turkmenistan twice. My main interlocutors stuck closely to the president's position that there would be no significant market reforms, except some price liberalization. The government would continue to own and manage most enterprises; it would not move from being directly in charge of the economy to a role where it provided the conditions in which private enterprises could operate freely. As time went on, Niyazov became increasingly dictatorial. The contrast between my two meetings with him illustrated this. At the first one in 1995, he was accompanied only by his deputy for economic and financial affairs, Valery Otchertsov. Although Niyazov spoke most of the time, Otchertsov was allowed to speak (and also to pour more tea for Niyazov when his cup was empty). On the second occasion, in 1998, Niyazov had his whole economic team round the table. They did not speak unless he called on them, and they had to stand up at their places when Niyazov spoke to them. I was not allowed to bring my interpreter into the meeting. Niyazov told the Minister for Foreign Affairs, Boris Shikhmuradov, that he had to do the interpretation, which was obviously beneath him.

Although our interlocutors stuck to the president's line, we sometimes saw signs that they thought differently and privately favored market reforms. This seemed to be the case with Otchertsov when we had a private conversation with him over a meal at Shadman-Valavi's house in Washington. He was an ethnic Russian and moved to Russia in 1996 on becoming deputy head of Itera, a gas trading company started by another Russian from Turkmenistan, Igor Makarov. Itera managed much of Turkmenistan's gas trade and was also involved in construction there. The governor of the Central Bank from 1993 to 1999, Khudaiberdy Orazov, favored market reforms and also a more democratic political system, as became apparent after he went into exile in 2002 and was a leader of the opposition to Niyazov. Otchertsov's successor as our main counterpart in the government and Niyazov's deputy, Yolly Gurbanmuradov, ran afoul of Niyazov and was sent to prison in 2005 where he died in 2015 without having had any contact with his family. Shikhmuradov was imprisoned in 2003 having been accused of being a leader of the attempted coup against Niyazov in 2002; his whereabouts, or even whether he was still alive, were unknown as late as 2019.

The main features of Niyazov's dictatorship and personality cult are well known: taking the title of Turkmenbashi; the gold statue which rotated so that the sun always shone on him; the huge pictures of him all over Ashgabat; his book *Rukhnama*, a rambling meditation on Turkmen values, which was taught in schools in place of regular education; renaming the months of the year, including one named after him and another after his mother; and his paranoia which lay behind, among other things, his brutal treatment of perceived enemies. I was being prepared for this in 1998 by the TV at the front of my cabin on the Turkmenistan Airlines flight from Istanbul which cycled continuously through images of Niyazov, the Turkmenistan flag and the slogan "We must glorify our motherland." That Niyazov stood at least as high as the country itself was apparent from the slogan on many buildings in the town: Halk, Watan, Turkmenbashi, meaning People, Motherland, Turkmenbashi. I am reminded of him every day when I see his profile in gold on the face of the wrist watch which he gave me. Below his portrait is the pronouncement (in Turkmen) that "The XXIst Century is the Golden Age of Turkmenistan."

I had hoped that, when Niyazov left the scene, the prospects for economic reforms would improve. This happened in Uzbekistan after Karimov died. I continue to hope that Lukashenko's successor in Belarus will move the country in the reform direction. Alas, in Turkmenistan we already know that this will not happen. Niyazov died in 2006 and his successor, Gurbanguly Berdimuhamedov, has followed a similar path. The pictures on the buildings have changed, and Ashgabat has become even more of a gleaming white marble city with grandiose monuments, but the old economic system remains in place.

Chapter 8

A Longer Perspective

Looking back at the years covered in this book and the subsequent decades from the vantage point of the 2020s, four points stand out.

First, the recovery of growth in the economies of the former Soviet Union countries after 1999 continued through the 2000s but declined after the global financial crisis of 2008. In the 2000s, the economies were recovering from the long "transition recession" during which unproductive enterprises had been hit hard by the collapse of the Soviet economy and the external trade links, and by the large changes in relative prices and profitability. As the transition proceeded, many enterprises found new products and markets. New economic activities emerged in response to the changed environment. The devaluations following the Russian crisis stimulated exports. The oil and gas exporting countries, and exporters of other primary products, benefited from the rise in world prices for their products. The close links between the economies of the region spread the improvement in performance from oil and gas exporters to other countries, especially from Russia to Central Asian and Caucasus countries. Booming global credit markets before the global crisis helped to finance additional expansion in those countries, especially the Baltics, that were able to borrow abroad. All countries were making progress towards normal economies, albeit at different speeds.

It was true that the recovery from the massive shock of the collapse of the Soviet Union and the old planning system still had a long way to go. The infrastructure had deteriorated and the maintenance backlog was enormous. Government services, especially health and education, had been deprived of funds for many years, and providers often charged for their services, both openly and under the table. Most of the CIS-7 countries (Armenia, Azerbaijan, Georgia, Kyrgyzstan, Moldova, Tajikistan and Uzbekistan) experienced massive emigration, mainly to Russia and in some cases to Kazakhstan, Turkey and Western Europe, in search of employment. Poverty was widespread and many people were worse off than in Soviet times. Nevertheless, economies were moving in the right direction. When I retired as director of the European

II Department of the IMF in October 2003, I was moderately optimistic about the longer-term economic prospects for most countries.

Alas, the good performance of the 2000s did not last. Growth declined after the global financial crisis of 2008 to a greater extent than in other emerging market middle income countries. The burst of growth as underutilized capacity was brought back into use in response to the changed relative prices, profitability prospects and entrepreneurial efforts petered out. In technical terms, the rapid growth of total factor productivity came to an end, although the slowdown was less in this respect in Central Asia than elsewhere. The low hanging fruit of productivity gains from reallocating resources from unproductive to productive enterprises and activities had been picked. What was now needed was for the growth of the capital stock to make a bigger contribution to output growth, supported by greater efficiency gains throughout the economy. But capital inflows from abroad slowed down after the global crisis, except in the oil producing countries. More importantly, the business climate in most countries was not attractive for either foreign or domestic investors.

Second, CIS countries have generally failed to fully establish market-friendly laws, institutions and practices. The structural and institutional reforms that were central to the transition were introduced too slowly to prevent the build-up of vested interests and cronies which, together with complicit governments, resisted moves to full market economies. As a result, problems of corruption, inefficient (and sometimes predatory) regulation, lack of independence of the judiciary, poor enforcement of competitive market rules and government interference in private business have persisted. Consequently, the business climate was poor, investment was low, and growth was slow. By contrast, the reforms in the Baltics created fully functioning market economies and rapid growth.

The failure to create full market economies in CIS countries reflected political choices. In the case of Belarus, Turkmenistan and Uzbekistan, their leaders did not want a market economy. They could not accept that what happens in the economy is the result of the separate decisions of free economic agents. They wanted to make those decisions themselves. Control was also a factor in Azerbaijan, Kazakhstan and Tajikistan and sometimes elsewhere.

Unlike Belarus, Turkmenistan and Uzbekistan, the remaining nine CIS countries professed to want to move to market economies. But their leaders also had other objectives, such as to ensure that their own supporters, who might be a region, a tribe or just the ruling family and its associates, received more than their share of the economic spoils. As a result, despite there being a considerable amount of private ownership of the economy, problems of vested interests, cronyism, corruption and the absence of independent judicial systems and regulators prevented the full establishment of market-friendly laws, institutions. and practices. The ruling elites were not concerned that their behavior damaged the growth of the economy as a whole. Indeed, they may have not believed that it did. Thus, my observation when working in the UK Treasury years before, that political factors often outweigh economic considerations in the design and implementation of economic policy, was confirmed in strength in CIS countries. Disappointing though this was to me, it was nevertheless fascinating to watch it, and to have been a minor actor on the stage.

The broad international context had a strong impact on countries' attitudes to reforms. The drive in the Baltics to join the European Union, which they did in 2004, enabled them to overcome domestic opposition to the major structural and institutional reforms that EU membership required. There was nothing like that in the CIS countries, although countries with aspirations to join the EU, such as Moldova and Ukraine, made half-hearted attempts at reforms. For historical and cultural reasons, and because it shared similar autocratic regimes to many other CIS countries, Russia was the main external exemplar for them. But Russia was itself ambivalent about creating a fully functioning market economy and its example could not lead other CIS countries to full market economies.

Although it has been disappointing to watch the economic reform process in CIS countries slow down almost to a halt in the late 2000s and 2010s, there have been a few bright spots. Following the election of Mikheil Saakashvili as president in 2004, Georgia embarked on a major program of reforms, most of which survived after he left office in 2013. In Uzbekistan, the death of Karimov in 2016 and his replacement as president by Shavkat Mirziyoyev led to an increase in economic reforms. My hope had always been that younger people, especially those with little memory of Soviet times or with some exposure to, or education in, market economies elsewhere, would be reformers when they moved into leadership positions. But it would not be easy for them as they would have to overcome the opposition of those who benefited from the prevailing system.

Third, the IMF's contribution to macroeconomic policymaking was generally positive. Our recommendation to bring inflation down as quickly as possible after the huge jump in prices following the collapse of the Soviet Union and the liberalization of prices was proved right by the success of the Baltics, which were the only countries to follow this route. The economic problems the countries faced were much bigger than the usual macroeconomic disequilibria of established market economies, but most countries had achieved macroeconomic stability by the late 1990s or early 2000s. They continued to implement macroeconomic policy reasonably successfully in the subsequent years.

Our advice about how to conduct monetary and fiscal policies to bring inflation down to single figures was largely accepted, although implemented at different speeds in different countries. Just as important if not more so, our technical assistance experts and consultants helped countries create modern central banks and finance ministries. The training provided by the IMF at the Joint Vienna Institute and elsewhere also made an important contribution to the understanding of macroeconomic policy issues in the countries. In both policymaking and institution-building areas, IMF staff successfully transferred knowledge to their counterparts through face-to-face meetings between resident IMF staff and visiting missions on the one hand and government and central bank officials on the other hand, backed up by written papers and reports. The leverage that the IMF could exert through the conditionality attached to its loans also helped. But over the years, our educational role was more important.

Our effectiveness was strengthened by the trusting relationship that generally existed between the IMF and its members in the region. Policymakers and their staff were eager to learn from us about macroeconomic policymaking and institutions in a market economy as there was limited knowledge of these issues in most countries. The trusting relationship started when we sent the first missions before the breakup of the Soviet Union. After the Soviet Union broke up, the newly independent countries valued their relations with international organizations and other public and private foreign advisers as they worked to place their independence, including from Russia, on a sound footing.

One might have expected that the relationship would become less intense after countries had built up their own expertise in macroeconomic policy. Many countries around the world have governments and central banks that are just as capable of designing good macroeconomic policies as the IMF teams that advise them. Even in those countries, however, there is a role for the IMF to act as a sounding board for the local economic policymakers and to add to their credibility in their interactions with the top leaders and the public. Russia and the Baltics reached that stage during the first decade of the twenty-first century, and some other countries were close behind. However, almost all the countries have continued to value their relations with the IMF. The good relations and mutual trust of the 1990s have persisted into the subsequent decades.

In advising on policies to achieve macroeconomic stability, we were helped by a natural conservatism among the leaders in the region. Spendthrift populism, as found in other countries at various times, has not been a feature of the former Soviet region. Even President Putin, whose legitimacy depends partly on the living standards of the Russian population, has ensured macroeconomic stability despite major shocks, which included the global financial crisis, the collapse of the oil price and economic sanctions. He has supported the good policies of the CBR and the establishment of the fund for oil revenues which helped to stabilize the exchange rate and the public finances.

My conclusion that the IMF's contribution to macroeconomic policymaking was generally positive might surprise people who remember the 1990s, when economies collapsed, poverty was widespread, law and order broke down, and some people became very rich through dubious means. Many people, both inside and outside the countries, thought that the IMF was responsible for the situation. However, those difficulties are now usually understood, both in the countries themselves and elsewhere, to have been the consequence of the disruption caused by the collapse of the old system and the transition to the new one. The IMF's role was to recommend policies for dealing with the problems of the transition. Most commentators now recognize that we and other international organizations made recommendations that helped to improve rather than worsen the economic situation. In the countries themselves, books and articles about the 1990s rarely mention the IMF, unless it is their specific focus. We have faded into the background, which is where we should be.

Fourth, the IMF's efforts to persuade CIS countries to make the major structural and institutional reforms that were needed to create a market economy were not very successful. Except in central banking and fiscal areas, the IMF did not have special expertise in such reforms. Nevertheless, they were so important, not only for the performance of the economy, but also for the success of the macroeconomic policies we were most concerned with, that we did our best to persuade countries to move faster on structural reforms.

The IMF was not alone in attempting to persuade countries to create properly functioning market economies and providing technical assistance to do so. Among international organizations, the World Bank had a much bigger role, reflecting its wider mandate. The ADB, EBRD and UNDP also offered advice. Many governments, especially those in North America and Europe, provided advice and assistance directed, in most cases, at encouraging reforms that would create market economies and institutions similar to those in their own countries. These efforts contributed to the sought-after results in the Baltic States, which were highly motivated by their desire to join the EU. Most of the CIS countries, however, failed to overcome the domestic resistance to reforms mounted by vested interests and the leaders of autocratic regimes.

This failure illustrates a general proposition: outside bodies or countries cannot bring about changes in a country that does not want them. This is another way of saying that a country must own any economic program advocated by the IMF or any outside body if it is to succeed. International institutions and foreign governments sometimes forget this and try too hard to make countries change their ways when they do not want to do so.

Countries should, of course, choose their own economic systems and governance arrangements. They do not have to follow the model of an open, liberal economy advocated by the IMF. One can ask whether the IMF, other international institutions and foreign governments were correct to continue to emphasize reforms aimed at creating full market economies in countries where the leadership clearly preferred to govern through interventionist measures. The question is most pertinent in countries with autocratic regimes, which was, and still is, the case in most CIS countries.

I believe that the reforms we recommended were the first-best ones that would produce the best economic performance over time. But, when they could not be implemented because of the strength of vested interests, cronies, and corruption which governments tolerated or even encouraged, were there second-best reforms that would have been both better than nothing and acceptable to the government? This is a big question which is beyond the scope of this book. It was no doubt right to emphasize first-best reforms in the early years of the transition when the political situation was fluid and governments had not fixed on particular reform paths. Even later, when vested interests and autocratic regimes became embedded, frequent reminders of first-best reforms helped to keep such options alive, at least on paper and, I hoped, in the minds of younger people who would later become leaders. As time went on, however, more emphasis should have been placed on second-best reforms that could be implemented in countries with strong vested interests and active government interventions.

I shall end on a personal note. My department in the IMF, European II Department, was abolished in October 2003 because its workload had declined as reforms in our countries advanced and the economic situation improved. Seven of the fifteen countries covered by the department were reassigned to the European Department and the other eight to the Middle East and Central Asia Department. Among the remarks I made at the party in the IMF to mark the end of the department were these:

> We have been extraordinarily privileged to be part of such a major transformation of a very important part of the world. We have witnessed dramatic changes and we have had the opportunity to influence some of them. There have, of course, been failures as well as successes in our policy advice and interactions with the authorities but, overall, I am convinced that we have made a major contribution for the good to the transition process. . . . There are still enormous challenges ahead, especially in building institutions for a market economy, improving governance, reducing corruption and creating a better investment climate so that higher rates of growth can be sustained. But the countries are

now more like normal countries, especially in their macroeconomic policies, and there is no longer a strong case for treating them as members of a unique class of transition economies.

These remarks are as relevant now as they were then.

Further Reading

The numbers in parenthesis indicate the chapters to which the references are most relevant.

IMF WORKS

Berengaut, Julian, Augusto Lopez-Claros, Françoise Le Gall, Dennis Jones, Richard Stern, Ann-Margret Westin, Effie Psalida, and Pietro Garibaldi. *The Baltic Countries: From Economic Stabilization to EU Accession.* Washington DC: International Monetary Fund, 1998. (6)

Boughton, James M. *Tearing Down Walls: The International Monetary Fund 1990–1999.* Washington DC: International Monetary Fund, 2012.

Camdessus, Michel. *Economic Transformation in the Fifteen Republics of the Former USSR: A Challenge or an Opportunity for the World?* Address to Georgetown University School of Foreign Service, April 15 1992. Washington DC: International Monetary Fund, April 1992. (3)

Camdessus, Michel. *We Had a Chance: Thirteen Years at the Helm of the IMF.* London: Sage Publications Ltd., 2016.

Christensen, Benedicte Vibe. *The Russian Federation in Transition: External Developments.* Washington DC: International Monetary Fund, 1994. (1, 4)

Citrin, Daniel A., and Ashok K Lahiri, eds. *Policy Experiences and Issues in the Baltics, Russia and Other Countries of the Former Soviet Union.* Washington DC: International Monetary Fund, December 1995. (3)

Coats, Warren. *FSU: Building Market Economy Monetary Systems: My Travels in the Former Soviet Union.* Independently published, 2020. (7)

Cornelius, Peter K., and Patrick Lenain, eds. *Ukraine: Accelerating the Transition to Market.* Washington DC: International Monetary Fund, 1997. (5)

Cottarelli, Carlo, and Peter Doyle. *Disinflation in Transition, 1993–97.* Washington DC: International Monetary Fund, 1999. (3)

Fischer, Stanley. "Exchange Rate Regimes: Is the Bipolar View Correct?" *Journal of Economic Perspectives* 15, no. 2, (2001): 3–24. (3)

Fischer, Stanley, and Ratna Sahay. "The Transition Economies after Ten Years." *IMF Working Paper WP/00/30* (2000). (3)

Gilman, Martin. *No Precedent, No Plan: Inside Russia's 1998 Default.* Cambridge, MA: The MIT Press, 2010. (4)

Havrylyshyn, Oleh, and John Odling-Smee. "Political Economy of Stalled Reforms." *Finance and Development*, September 2000. (3)

Havrylyshyn, Oleh, Thomas Wolf, Julian Berengaut, Marta Castello-Branco, Ron van Rooden, and Valerie Mercer-Blackman. *Growth Experience in Transition Countries, 1990–98.* Washington DC: International Monetary Fund, 1999. (3)

Hernández-Catá, Ernesto. "Russia and the IMF: The Political Economy of Macrostabilisation." *Problems of Post-Communism* 41 (May/June 1995). Reprinted in *Policy Experiences and Issues in the Baltics, Russia and Other Countries of the Former Soviet Union*, edited by Daniel A. Citrin and Ashok K Lahiri. Washington DC: International Monetary Fund, December 1995. (3, 4)

Hobdari, Niko A., John Wakeman-Linn and others. *Managing Oil Wealth: The Case of Azerbaijan.* Washington DC: International Monetary Fund, April 2004. (7)

International Monetary Fund. *Economic Review of the Russian Federation.* Washington DC: International Monetary Fund, 1992. (4)

International Monetary Fund. *The Economy of the Former USSR in 1991.* Washington DC: International Monetary Fund, 1992. (1)

International Monetary Fund. "Ukraine: Ex Post Assessment of Longer Term Program Engagement." Accessed March 29, 2022. https://www.imf.org/en/ Publications/CR/Issues/2016/12/31/Ukraine-2005-Article-IV-Consultation-and-Ex -Post-Assessment-of-Longer-Term-Program-18717. (5)

International Monetary Fund. *World Economic Outlook: Focus on Transition Economies.* Washington DC: International Monetary Fund, September 2000. (3)

International Monetary Fund, International Bank for Reconstruction and Development, Organisation for Economic Cooperation and Development and European Bank for Reconstruction and Development. *The Economy of the USSR: Summary and Recommendations.* Published jointly by the four institutions, 1990. (1)

International Monetary Fund, International Bank for Reconstruction and Development, Organisation for Economic Cooperation and Development and European Bank for Reconstruction and Development. *A Study of the Soviet Economy, Volumes 1–3.* Published jointly by the four institutions, 1991. (1)

Keller, Peter M., and J. Thomas Richardson. "Nominal Anchors in the CIS." *IMF Working Paper WP/03/179* (2003). (3)

Knöbl, Adalbert, and Richard Haas, "IMF and the Baltics: a Decade of Cooperation." *IMF Working Paper WP/03/241* (2003). (6)

Köhler, Horst. "The Continuing Challenge of Transition and Convergence." Address at the East-West Conference 2000 in Vienna in November 2000. In *Completing Transition: The Main Challenges,* edited by Gertrude Tempel-Gugerell, Lindsay Wolfe, and Peter Mooslechner. Berlin: Springer-Verlag, 2002. (3)

Odling-Smee, John. "The IMF's Approach to Economies in Transition." Paper delivered at the sixth conference of the Robert Triffin-Szirak Foundation in Brussels, November 1994. In *Fifty Years After Bretton Woods: The New Challenge of*

East-West Partnership for Economic Progress, edited by Miklós Szabó-Pelsőczi. Avebury, 1996. (3)

Odling-Smee, John. Remarks at the conference on June 11, 2002 dedicated to the 10th anniversary of the reintroduction of the Estonian kroon. In *Alternative Exchange Rate Regimes in the Globalised World*, edited by the Bank of Estonia. Tallinn: Bank of Estonia, 2002. (3)

Odling-Smee, John. "The Next Ten Years of Transition: The Challenges Ahead." Speech at the International Seminar Dedicated to the 110th Anniversary of the Establishment of the State Bank of Armenia and the 10th Anniversary of the Introduction of the National Currency of Armenia, 23 November 2003. Accessed March 29, 2022. www.imf.org/news/articles/2015/09/28/04/53/sp112303. (3)

Odling-Smee, John. "The IMF and Russia in the 1990s." *IMF Staff papers* 53, no.1 (2006): 151–94. (4)

Odling-Smee, John, and Gonzalo Pastor. "The IMF and the Ruble Area," *IMF Working Paper WP/01/101* (2001). Reprinted without some annexes in "Special Symposium: The IMF and the Ruble Zone." *Comparative Economic Studies* 44, no.4 (Winter 2002): 1–84. (2)

Odling-Smee, John, and Thomas Richardson. "Transition and Vested Interests." Paper presented at the East-West Conference 2000 in Vienna in November 2000. In *Completing Transition: The Main Challenges*, edited by Gertrude Tempel-Gugerell, Lindsay Wolfe, and Peter Mooslechner. Berlin: Springer-Verlag, 2002. (3)

Odling-Smee, John, and Ron van Rooden. "Growth in Ukraine—Lessons from Other Transition Countries." Paper presented at a conference in Kyiv in June 1998. In *Ukraine at the Crossroads: Economic Reforms in International Perspective*, edited by Axel Siedenberg and Lutz Hoffmann. Heidelberg: Physica-Verlag, 1999. (5)

Owen, David, and David O. Robinson, eds. *Russia Rebounds.* Washington DC: International Monetary Fund, 2003. (4)

Shiells, Clinton R., and Sarosh Sattar, eds. *The Low Income Countries of the Commonwealth of Independent States: Progress and Challenges in Transition.* Washington DC: International Monetary Fund, April 2004. (2, 7)

Spencer, Grant H. *Common Issues and Interrepublic Relations in the Former USSR.* Washington DC: International Monetary Fund, April 1992. (2, 3)

Wijnholds, Onno de Beaufort. *Fighting Financial Fires: An IMF Insider Account.* Basingstoke and New York: Palgrave Macmillan, 2011. (4)

Wolf, Thomas, Warren Coats, Daniel Citrin and Adrienne Cheasty. *Financial Relations Among Countries of the Former Soviet Union.* Washington DC: International Monetary Fund, February 1994. (2)

Wolf, Thomas, and Emine Gürgen. "Improving Governance and Fighting Corruption in the Baltics and CIS Countries." *IMF Economic Issues 21* (2000). (3)

OTHER WORKS

Alexievich, Svetlana. *Secondhand Time: The Last of the Soviets.* New York: Random House, 2016.

Allison, Graham, and Grigory Yavlinsky. *Window of Opportunity: the Grand Bargain for Democracy in the Soviet Union.* New York: Pantheon Books, 1991. (1)

Åslund, Anders. *Russia's Capitalist Revolution: Why Market Reform Succeeded and Democracy Failed.* Washington DC: Peterson Institute for International Economics, 2007. (1, 2, 3, 4)

Åslund, Anders. *How Ukraine Became a Market Economy and Democracy.* Washington DC: Peterson Institute for International Economics, 2009. (5)

Åslund, Anders, and Simeon Djankov, eds. *The Great Rebirth: Lessons from the Victory of Capitalism over Communism.* Washington DC: Peterson Institute for International Economics, 2014. (3, 4, 5, 6, 7)

Braithwaite, Rodric. *Across the Moscow River: The World Turned Upside Down.* New Haven and London: Yale University Press, 2002. (1)

Cottrell, Robert. "Russia: Was There a Better Way?" *New York Review of Books,* October 4, 2001. Review of *The Tragedy of Russia's Reforms: Market Bolshevism Against Democracy* by Peter Reddaway and Dmitri Glinski. Washington DC: US Institute of Peace Press, 2001. (4)

Dubinin, Sergei. "Macroeconomic Stabilization in Russia: The Lessons of 1992–95 and the Outlook for 1996–97." In Per Jacobsson Foundation, *Economic Transformation: The Tasks Still Ahead.* Per Jacobsson Foundation: Washington DC, 1995. (4)

European Bank for Reconstruction and Development. *Transition Report.* London: European Bank for Reconstruction and Development, annual.

European Bank for Reconstruction and Development. *Transition Report 2013: Stuck in Transition?* London: European Bank for Reconstruction and Development, 2013. (8)

European Bank for Reconstruction and Development. *Transition Report 2017–18: Sustaining Growth.* London: European Bank for Reconstruction and Development, 2017. (8)

Fischer, Stanley, and Alan Gelb. "The Process of Socialist Economic Transformation." *Journal of Economic Perspectives* 5, no.4 (1991): 91–105. (3)

Freeland, Chrystia. *Sale of the Century: Russia's Wild Ride from Communism to Capitalism.* Canada: Doubleday Canada, 2000. (4)

Gaidar, Yegor. *Days of Defeat and Victory.* Seattle and London: University of Washington Press, 1999. Published in Russian in 1996. (1, 2, 3, 4)

Gaidar, Yegor. *Collapse of an Empire: Lessons for Modern Russia.* Washington DC: Brookings Institution Press, 2007. (1)

Goldman, Marshall. *Lost Opportunity: Why Economic Reforms in Russia Have Not Worked.* New York: W.W. Norton & Company, 1994.

Havrylyshyn, Oleh. *Divergent Paths in Post-communist Transformation: Capitalism for All or Capitalism for the Few?* Basingstoke and New York: Palgrave Macmillan, 2006. (3)

Havrylyshyn, Oleh. "Ukraine: Greatest Hopes, Greatest Disappointments." In *The Great Rebirth: Lessons from the Victory of Capitalism over Communism,* edited by Anders Åslund and Simeon Djankov. Washington DC: Peterson Institute for International Economics, 2014. (5)

Havrylyshyn, Oleh. *Present at the Transition: An Inside Look at the Role of History, Politics and Personalities in Post-Communist Countries*. Cambridge: Cambridge University Press, 2020. (3)

Mau, Vladimir. "Russian Economic Reforms as Perceived by Western Critics." In *Russian Crisis and its Effects,* edited by Tuomas Komulainen and Likka Korhonen. Helsinki: Kikimora Publications, 2000. (3, 4)

Primakov, Yevgeny. *Russian Crossroads: Toward the New Millenium*. New Haven and London: Yale University Press, 2004. (4)

Saakashvili, Mikheil, and Kakha Bendukidze. "Georgia: The Most Radical Catch-Up Reforms." In *The Great Rebirth: Lessons from the Victory of Capitalism over Communism*, edited by Anders Åslund and Simeon Djankov. Washington DC: Peterson Institute for International Economics, 2014. (7)

Schecter, Jerrold L. *Russian Negotiating Behavior: Continuity and Tradition*. Washington DC: US Institute of Peace Press, April 1998. (4)

Schimpfössl, Elisabeth. *Rich Russians: From Oligarchs to Bourgeoisie*. New York: Oxford University Press, 2018. (4)

"Special Symposium: The IMF and the Ruble Zone." *Comparative Economic Studies* 44, no.4 (Winter 2002): 1–84. (2)

Stiglitz, Joseph E. *Globalization and Its Discontents*. New York: W.W. Norton & Company Norton, 2002. (3)

Tolstoy, Leo. *Hadji Murad*, translated by Aylmer Maude. New York: The Modern Library, 2003. (7)

World Bank. *World Development Report 1996: From Plan to Market*. Washington DC: The World Bank, 1996. (3)

Index

Page references for figures are italicized.

500 day program, 46

Abalkin, Leonid, 10, 91
Abbado, Claudio, 23
Abildaev, Bolot, 184
Abkhazia, 161, 169, 175
Adams, Charles, 37
ADB. *See* Asian Development Bank
ad hoc stabilization, in Russia, 85–95
Aeroflot, 21–22
Afghanistan: Soviet Union and,
    6; Taliban in, 190; Wakhan
    Corridor in, 160
agriculture in the Soviet Union, 3–4, 5
Ahtisaari, Martti, 93
Aitken, Brian, 95
Akaev, Askar, 181, 182–83
Aleksashenko, Sergei, 74
Alexander, Bill, 114
Alexievich, Svetlana, 68
Alimardonov, Murodali, 188–90
Ali and Nino, 174
Aliyev, Heydar, 172–73
Aliyev, Ilham, 173
Allison, Graham, 10–11
Anglo-Russian Convention, 150
Anjaria, Shail, 101

Armenia, 21, 27, 30, 35, 169–71;
    Azerbaijan and, 161; civil conflict
    in, 49, 163; currency of, 40, 70;
    exchange rate policy of, 60; language
    in, 33; Moldova and, 169
Arrow, Kenneth, 92
Articles of Agreement, 26–27
Asian Development Bank (ADB), 29,
    53, 164, 203
Asian financial crisis, 68, 96, 107, 141
Åslund, Anders, 73, 76
asset stripping: in CIS, 66–67; in
    Russia, 98
Aven, Pyotr, 3–4, 74, 113
Avtovaz, 67, 100
Azerbaijan, 21, 26, 30, 35, 169, 172–74,
    200; Armenia and, 161; balance of
    payments of, 61; civil conflict in,
    49, 163; exchange rate policy of, 60;
    MOU and, 13
Azimov, Rustam, 193

Bacalu, Veronica, 28
Bagratyan, Hrant, 170
balance of payments, 61; of Armenia,
    170; of Azerbaijan, 173; exchange
    rate policy and, 59; of Kazakhstan,

213

About the Author

John Odling-Smee is a retired economist who taught economics at Oxford University, advised the governments of Ghana and the UK on economic policy and headed the department at the International Monetary Fund responsible for relations with the fifteen countries of the former Soviet Union.